If you don't see the object constancy — the object disappear

Mind Works

21st June col- Kalkn

In *Mind Works* Antonino Ferro uses clinical material such as detailed reports of sessions, together with clients' analytic histories, to develop Bion's original findings and illustrate complex concepts in the field of psychoanalytic technique. These concepts include:

- interpretive modalities
- the end of analysis
- psychosomatic pathologies
- narcissism

Mind Works: Technique and Creativity in Psychoanalysis also suggests that dreaming is a fundamental moment in analytic work, and Ferro discusses how dreams can go beyond the present to become a continuous act of the mind in the waking state, allowing internal and external stimuli to be transformed into thoughts and emotions.

Focusing on how the minds of the analyst and the analysand work in psychoanalysis, this book will appeal to psychoanalysts, psychotherapists, and psychiatrists and will be helpful in psychoanalytic and psychotherapeutic work on a day-to-day basis.

Antonino Ferro is a Training and Supervising Analyst in the Italian Psychoanalytic Society and the International Psychoanalytical Association. He has been a visiting professor of psychoanalysis in various institutions and was president of the Milanese Centre of Psychoanalysis.

GW00568318

THE NEW LIBRARY OF PSYCHOANALYSIS
General Editor   Dana Birksted-Breen

The New Library of Psychoanalysis was launched in 1987 in association with the Institute of Psychoanalysis, London. It took over from the International Psychoanalytical Library which published many of the early translations of the works of Freud and the writings of most of the leading British and Continental psychoanalysts.

The purpose of the New Library of Psychoanalysis is to facilitate a greater and more widespread appreciation of psychoanalysis and to provide a forum for increasing mutual understanding between psychoanalysts and those working in other disciplines such as the social sciences, medicine, philosophy, history, linguistics, literature and the arts. It aims to represent different trends both in British psychoanalysis and in psychoanalysis generally. The New Library of Psychoanalysis is well placed to make available to the English-speaking world psychoanalytic writings from other European countries and to increase the interchange of ideas between British and American psychoanalysts.

The Institute, together with the British Psychoanalytical Society, runs a low-fee psychoanalytic clinic, organizes lectures and scientific events concerned with psychoanalysis and publishes the *International Journal of Psychoanalysis*. It also runs the only UK training course in psychoanalysis which leads to membership of the International Psychoanalytical Association – the body which preserves internationally agreed standards of training, of professional entry, and of professional ethics and practice for psychoanalysis as initiated and developed by Sigmund Freud. Distinguished members of the Institute have included Michael Balint, Wilfred Bion, Ronald Fairbairn, Anna Freud, Ernest Jones, Melanie Klein, John Rickman and Donald Winnicott.

Previous General Editors include David Tuckett, Elizabeth Spillius and Susan Budd. Previous and current Members of the Advisory Board include Christopher Bollas, Ronald Britton, Catalina Bronstein, Donald Campbell, Sara Flanders, Stephen Grosz, John Keene, Eglé Laufer, Juliet Mitchell, Michael Parsons, Rosine Jozef Perelberg, David Taylor and Mary Target, and Richard Rusbridger, who is now Assistant Editor.

ALSO IN THIS SERIES

Impasse and Interpretation Herbert Rosenfeld

Psychoanalysis and Discourse Patrick Mahony

The Suppressed Madness of Sane Men Marion Milner

The Riddle of Freud Estelle Roith

Thinking, Feeling, and Being Ignacio Matte-Blanco

The Theatre of the Dream Salomon Resnik

Melanie Klein Today: Volume 1, Mainly Theory Edited by Elizabeth Bott
  Spillius

Melanie Klein Today: Volume 2, Mainly Practice Edited by Elizabeth Bott
  Spillius

Psychic Equilibrium and Psychic Change: Selected Papers of Betty Joseph
  Edited by Michael Feldman and Elizabeth Bott Spillius

About Children and Children-No-Longer: Collected Papers 1942–80 Paula
  Heimann. Edited by Margret Tonnesmann

The Freud–Klein Controversies 1941–45 Edited by Pearl King and
  Riccardo Steiner

Dream, Phantasy and Art Hanna Segal

Psychic Experience and Problems of Technique Harold Stewart

Clinical Lectures on Klein and Bion Edited by Robin Anderson

From Fetus to Child Alessandra Piontelli

*A Psychoanalytic Theory of Infantile Experience: Conceptual and Clinical
  Reflections* E. Gaddini. Edited by Adam Limentani

The Dream Discourse Today Edited and introduced by Sara Flanders

*The Gender Conundrum: Contemporary Psychoanalytic Perspectives on
  Feminity and Masculinity* Edited and introduced by Dana Breen

Psychic Retreats John Steiner

The Taming of Solitude: Separation Anxiety in Psychoanalysis Jean-Michel
  Quinodoz

Unconscious Logic: An Introduction to Matte-Blanco's Bi-logic and its Uses
  Eric Rayner

Understanding Mental Objects Meir Perlow

Life, Sex and Death: Selected Writings of William Gillespie Edited and
  introduced by Michael Sinason

*What Do Psychoanalysts Want?: The Problem of Aims in Psychoanalytic
  Therapy* Joseph Sandler and Anna Ursula Dreher

Michael Balint: Object Relations, Pure and Applied Harold Stewart

Hope: A Shield in the Economy of Borderline States Anna Potamianou

Psychoanalysis, Literature and War: Papers 1972–1995 Hanna Segal
Emotional Vertigo: Between Anxiety and Pleasure Danielle Quinodoz
Early Freud and Late Freud Ilse Grubrich-Simitis
A History of Child Psychoanalysis Claudine and Pierre Geissmann
Belief and Imagination: Explorations in Psychoanalysis Ronald Britton
A Mind of One's Own: A Kleinian View of Self and Object Robert
    A. Caper
Psychoanalytic Understanding of Violence and Suicide Edited by Rosine
    Jozef Perelberg
On Bearing Unbearable States of Mind Ruth Riesenberg-Malcolm
Psychoanalysis on the Move: The Work of Joseph Sandler Edited by Peter
    Fonagy, Arnold M. Cooper and Robert S. Wallerstein
The Dead Mother: The Work of André Green Edited by Gregorio Kohon
The Fabric of Affect in the Psychoanalytic Discourse André Green
The Bi-Personal Field: Experiences of Child Analysis Antonino Ferro
*The Dove that Returns, the Dove that Vanishes: Paradox and Creativity in
    Psychoanalysis* Michael Parsons
*Ordinary People, Extra-ordinary Protections: A Post-Kleinian Approach to
    the Treatment of Primitive Mental States* Judith Mitrani
The Violence of Interpretation: From Pictogram to Statement Piera
    Aulagnier
The Importance of Fathers: A Psychoanalytic Re-Evaluation Judith Trowell
    and Alicia Etchegoyen
Dreams That Turn Over a Page: Paradoxical Dreams in Psychoanalysis
    Jean-Michel Quinodoz
*The Couch and the Silver Screen: Psychoanalytic Reflections on European
    Cinema* Edited and introduced by Andrea Sabbadini
In Pursuit of Psychic Change: The Betty Joseph Workshop Edited by Edith
    Hargreaves and Arturo Varchevker
*The Quiet Revolution in American Psychoanalysis: Selected Papers of Arnold
    M. Cooper* Arnold M. Cooper. Edited and introduced by Elizabeth
    L. Auchincloss
*Seeds of Illness and Seeds of Recovery: The Genesis of Suffering and the Role
    of Psychoanalysis* Antonino Ferro
The Work of Psychic Figurability: Mental States Without Representation
    César Botella and Sára Botella
*Key Ideas for a Contemporary Psychoanalysis: Misrecognition and
    Recognition of the Unconscious* André Green
*The Telescoping of Generations: Listening to the Narcissistic Links Between
    Generations* Haydée Faimberg

Glacial Times: A Journey Through the World of Madness Salomon Resnik
This Art of Psychoanalysis: Dreaming Undreamt Dreams and Interrupted
  Cries Thomas H. Ogden
Psychoanalysis as Therapy and Storytelling Antonino Ferro
Psychoanalysis and Religion in the 21st Century: Competitors or
  Collaborators? Edited by David M. Black
Recovery of the Lost Good Object Eric Brenman
The Many Voices of Psychoanalysis Roger Kennedy
Feeling the Words: Neuropsychoanalytic Understanding of Memory and the
  Unconscious Mauro Mancia
Projected Shadows: Psychoanalytic Reflections on the Representation of Loss
  in European Cinema Edited by Andrea Sabbadini
Encounters with Melanie Klein: Selected Papers of Elizabeth Spillius
  Elizabeth Spillius. Edited by Priscilla Roth and Richard
  Rusbridger
Constructions and the Analytic Field: History, Scenes and Destiny
  Domenico Chianese
Yesterday, Today and Tomorrow Hanna Segal
Psychoanalysis Comparable and Incomparable: The Evolution of a Method to
  Describe and Compare Psychoanalytic Approaches David Tuckett et al.
Time, Space and Phantasy Rosine Jozef Perelberg
Mind Works: Technique and Creativity in Psychoanalysis Antonino Ferro

TITLES IN THE NEW LIBRARY OF PSYCHOANALYSIS
TEACHING SERIES

Reading Freud: A Chronological Exploration of Freud's Writings
Jean-Michel Quinodoz

THE NEW LIBRARY OF PSYCHOANALYSIS

General Editor: Dana Birksted-Breen

Mind Works

Technique and Creativity in Psychoanalysis

Antonino Ferro

Translated by Philip Slotkin

The translation of this book has been partly funded by SEPS
SEGRETARIATO EUROPEO PER LE PUBBLICAZIONI SCIENTIFICHE

SEGRETARIATO EUROPEO PER LE PUBBLICAZIONI SCIENTIFICHE

Via Val d'Aposa 7 – 40123 Bologna – Italy
seps@alma.unibo.it – www.seps.it

Routledge
Taylor & Francis Group
LONDON AND NEW YORK

Title of the original Italian edition: *Tecnica e creatività: Il lavoro psicoanalitico*
© 2006 Raffaello Cortina Editore, Milan

First published 2009
by Routledge
27 Church Road, Hove, East Sussex BN3 2FA

Simultaneously published in the USA and Canada
by Routledge
270 Madison Avenue, New York, NY 10016

Routledge is an imprint of the Taylor & Francis Group, an Informa business

English translation © 2009 Antonino Ferro
Title of original Italian edition: *Tecnica e creatività: Il lavoro psicoanalitico*
© Raffaello Cortina Editore, Milan

Typeset in Bembo by RefineCatch Limited, Bungay, Suffolk
Printed and bound in Great Britain by TJ International Ltd, Padstow, Cornwall
Paperback cover design by Sandra Heath

This publication has been produced with paper manufactured to
strict environmental standards and with pulp derived from
sustainable forests.

British Library Cataloguing in Publication Data
A catalogue record for this book is available from the British Library

Library of Congress Cataloging-in-Publication Data
Ferro, Antonino, 1947–
[Tecnica e creatività. English]
Mind works : technique and creativity in psychoanalysis / Antonino Ferro ;
translated by Philip Slotkin.
p. ; cm. – (New library of psychoanalysis)
Includes bibliographical references and index.
ISBN 978–0–415–42991–7 (hardback) – ISBN 978–0–415–42992–4 (pbk.)
1. Psychoanalysis–Methodology. 2. Creative ability. I. Title. II. Series: New
library of psychoanalysis (Unnumbered)
[DNLM: 1. Psychoanalytic Therapy–methods. 2. Creativeness. 3. Imagery
(Psychotherapy) 4. Mental Disorders–therapy. 5. Professional-Patient Relations.
6. Psychoanalytic Theory. WM 460.6 F395t 2008a]
RC506.F423713 2008
616.89′17—dc22

2008004725

ISBN 978–0–415–42991–7 (hbk)
ISBN 978–0–415–42992–4 (pbk)

To my patients, my supervisees and the participants in my clinical groups, who inspired these thoughts as the ongoing fruit of a joint construction

Contents

1 Screenplays and film sets   1
  The opening up of possible worlds   2
  Supervisions as detective stories   7
  How to speak in order to be understood   14
  Recapitulation   24

2 Digressions on interpretation   39

3 Psychosomatic pathology or metaphor: problems
  of the boundary   73
    Minimum certainties   73
    Maximum (optimistic) aspirations   85

4 Homosexualities: a field ripe for ploughing   107

5 A model of the mind and its clinical implications:
  how to turn back in order to move forward   133

6 Instructions for seafarers and the shipwrecked: signals
  from the analytic field and emotional transformations   151

7 The patient's response to interpretations and events in
  the field   167
    A disease called 'compulsive transference interpretation'   171
    The truth of autobiography and the lies of psychoanalysis   177

Contents

8 Terminations orthodox and unorthodox   181

9 Narcissism and frontier areas   201

   References   217
   Index   221

Every effort has been made to trace the copyright holders and obtain permission to reproduce material from other sources. Any omissions brought to our attention will be remedied in future editions or reprints.

1

Screenplays and film sets

In this chapter I wish to illustrate the high degree of interdependence between the patient's and the analyst's mental functioning and to show how it contributes to defining the field and its movements, as well as situations of turbulence or impasse. The implicit references for this chapter are all my recent contributions on the field – those involving developments of Bion's thought – and certain narratological concepts that cannot but be relevant to a consideration of the models of psychoanalysis (Ferro 2002a, 2005a, 2005b, 2006).

The analyst, in my view, engages in an ongoing *baseline activity of reverie*, which is the way in which his[1] mind constantly receives, metabolizes and transforms everything that reaches it from the patient in the form of verbal, paraverbal and non-verbal stimulation. The same reverie activity operates in the patient in response to any interpretative or non-interpretative stimulus from the analyst. The purpose of analysis is first and foremost to develop this capacity to weave a fabric of images (which remain not directly knowable). These can be accessed indirectly through the 'narrative derivatives' of waking dream thought, as we shall see below. This baseline reverie activity is the cornerstone of our mental life, and our psychic health, illness or suffering is determined by its functional or dysfunctional status.

The same applies to another entity – namely, the ongoing activity of *baseline projective identification*, which is the indispensable engine of any reverie activity. In certain circumstances, reverie manifests itself in explicit and meaningful form – usually, but of course not exclusively, on the visual level.

---

[1] Translator's note: For convenience, the masculine form is used throughout this translation for both sexes.

1

Situations of sensory overload, greatly exceeding the mind's capacity for digestion, transformation and visual representation, call for separate consideration. The following examples are drawn from the infinite range of possibilities:

- Sexual abuse in infancy, where the problem concerns not only sexuality but also unmanageable sensory overload (whether involving pleasure, pain or violence).
- Non-sexual infant abuse, for example, when, with the best of intentions, the staff of hypermedicalized neonatal pathology wards forbid the application of the 'buffer solution' of parental presence but when the parents could, at least in part, perform the functions of digestion and transformation of which the (often premature) baby's mind is not yet capable.
- The enormously wide range of other situations of sensory overload that exceeds the mind's capacity to represent, dream, and hence forget them. These extend from disasters to overintense proto-emotional impact situations and torture.

That said, let us now consider the possible ways in which a whole panoply of defences can be deployed against this kind of sensory violence. These defences range from autism – an extreme measure whereby the mind dismantles itself, as it were committing mental suicide in order to survive – to extreme forms of narcissism and disavowal, splitting, or indeed actual suicide, which is the most extreme form of defence possible against unmetabolizable floods of anxiety or pain. Why does this overload sometimes give rise to so-called psychosomatic illness and not merely to narrations of psychosomatic illness or of illness in general? This is the question that we shall address below.

The opening up of possible worlds

Saverio's woods

Saverio is an eight-year-old boy, whose parents describe him as delicate and vulnerable. His mother tells me that, when she once gave him a little box as a present and asked him what she had put inside it, Saverio, to her surprise, replied: 'The scent of the woods.'

The parents present themselves: the father is depressed and the mother hypomanic.

2

The therapist who brings this case to supervision describes Saverio as of frail build but always on the go, and her experience of him is that she 'cannot find him' and 'never knows where he is', because he is always dashing about from one place to another in the room.

Saverio immediately starts playing the 'chameleon', who fights and overcomes all his enemies; this is precisely his strategy for victory – to make himself invisible, to escape attention and to play repetitive games that leave not the slightest chink for access.

On one occasion he draws the enemies as frightening presences (see below). In a second drawing, they are represented as swords and bombs.

The enemies to be avoided seem to be precisely the emotions aroused by the encounter with the Other – lacerating emotions that would tear him to pieces. So not only emotions themselves but also the encounter generated by them are avoided. These enemies, Saverio says, are far away, in South America or Sweden (in other words, they cannot be reached by classical interpretation). His physical jumping about, and the way he leaps from one scribbled drawing to another, clearly form part of his strategy, as in Woody Allen's film *Zelig*, whose chameleon-like hero is impossible to pin down.

One day, Saverio unexpectedly makes up a story about the 'war of the stoppers', in which a 'yellow stopper' always defeats all the other stoppers, who are stupid, but then they decide to organize so as to unmask the strategy of the 'yellow stopper' and thus find a way of fighting it on more equal terms. He seems to be realizing that, whereas by deploying the chameleon strategy he will always overcome the therapist, she is not merely suffering her defeat passively, but seeking a way of opposing the chameleon or an alternative approach.

Again and again, Saverio now brings comics along to his sessions; he makes drawings, which increasingly take the form of indecipherable scribbles, and so the available time goes by. The chameleon strategy has paralysed the field; the problem of Saverio as an adapted, emotionless child has become the problem of the field. The field has caught Saverio's illness.

This, then, is a possible starting point for change and transformation, which can be mediated by a wide range of strategies. These might extend from the classical approach of demonstrating how Saverio controls the situation to the point of making it impossible for the therapist to think, via the more descriptive approach of showing how he makes time go by without anything being able or needing to happen,

to the more directly relational approach ('you seem to be behaving in the room as if I didn't exist, or as if I was very dangerous') – or, in other words, addressing the terror of the 'chameleon', which always has to use camouflage for fear of being torn apart by the beaks of birds of prey or by the therapist's words. All these options would lead to the development of different possible stories.

Yet there is also another way: the therapist could help to modify the emotional and climatic coordinates of the field in such a way that Saverio would no longer need to play the part of the chameleon.

Thinking along these lines, I immediately associate to Giuseppe Ferrandino's book *Saverio of the North-West*, an account of the thrilling adventures of a small boy who has somehow to survive in a remote Canadian forest and is confronted by difficulties of every kind, including a violent struggle with an eagle, which tears at him but which he is able to overcome, not to mention fights with a terrifying bear emerging from hibernation, as well as appalling weather conditions.

In this way a vista appears before my eyes, and then before the therapist's, of those other woods of Saverio's of which all that had remained 'alive' was the scent preserved in the little box, all the rest having been as it were freeze-dried, or rather split off and banished far, far away – even if it was constantly pressing to return to the field, giving rise to the defences of hesitation that Saverio equally constantly deployed. It was as if Saverio's mother had basically provided her son only with a tiny little box of a mind, which could manifestly 'contain' only the scent of the woods and not all its denizens.

In this way, then, a 'story of the woods' is opening up with Saverio, with the little box containing the scent actually constituting its starting point, but which will gradually grow to fruition thanks to the work done in the therapy room.

A necessary oscillation exists between creativity and technique (C ↔ T). The one is in the service of the other: there are moments when technique predominates, with different possible options, and others in which reverie and fantasy are prevalent, as well as those massively fruitful moments that permit the opening up of new and unforeseen meanings. These, of course, are 'couple-specific', and steer the therapy in a particular direction, rather than in other directions that might be possible with other therapists who would have other reveries and would open up vistas on other possible worlds.

Of course, both therapeutic and ethical considerations require these worlds to be opened up on the basis of the emotional ingredients brought by the patient; they must not be worlds that alter the patient's proto-narremes and do violence to them.

A more technically oriented interpretative choice is safer, but often less fertile. A more creative option is riskier in terms of subjective drift, but may afford access to previously unthinkable spaces. The analyst's subjectivity (Renik 1993) obviously plays a major part – can he be himself and be creative, or does he need to operate like a 'chameleon', with a theory that protects him from the risk of original thinking?

Bion said that 'thinking' was a new function of living matter and was for that reason complex and difficult. The history of psychoanalysis includes some highly creative analysts – for instance, Melanie Klein or Bion himself – who were responsible for 'leaps' in general theory and the theory of technique, whose ideas were contested in their lifetime, and who subsequently became models to be imitated. An artistic analogy might be that of a painter with an idiosyncratic technique and poetic genius who meets with nothing but execration, whereas later the academies are full of works 'in the style of . . .'. On a smaller scale, it is not unusual for this to occur in psychoanalytic societies or, to an even greater extent, psychoanalytic institutes, wherever grey conformity is valued most and any creative originality rings alarm bells. No student (or, I would say, teacher) of psychoanalysis should, in this connection, fail to read Otto Kernberg's (1998) paper on thirty methods of preventing the development of creativity in young analysts.

Failure to listen

A seriously ill patient is asking his therapist questions about his anxieties and panic. Instead of helping him to expand on the subject of the day (anxiety and panic), the therapist defensively resorts to a kind of pedagogic description of the characteristics of panic attacks. The patient responds by describing his rage at his driving instructor, whom he felt like beating up. Then he immediately says that when he sees himself in the mirror, he looks different from when he was small, in particular since his recent motorcycle accident. Then he talks about how he has been abused, and the charges he would like to bring.

At this point, the therapist's mobile rings; the patient tells her it is all right for her to answer it, but she turns it off and puts it on the table. When he asks 'May I see it?' the therapist replies 'No'. He then mentions a woman doctor whom he hates: 'I trusted her, but I don't trust her any more.' Finally, he tells the therapist directly that he would like her to be more human: perhaps they could go and have a drink together. The therapist responds by talking about the setting.

This session is in my view an exemplary demonstration of a constant series of misunderstandings, of breaks in microcommunication and of ongoing attempts by the patient – which are not picked up by the therapist – to kick the ball back into play. The patient broaches a subject: panic. The therapist withdraws. Her defence and non-availability kindle anger towards the 'driving instructor', who is indeed failing to perform his/her task properly (teaching him to negotiate a path through the winding roads of his emotions). The patient then reflects on how he feels different at this point in the session from when he came in ('when I was small'), i.e. after the accident (the lack of receptivity). So he ends up full of rage and anger, and is transformed and unrecognizable. He then immediately tells the therapist how he feels abused by her failure to listen and by the emotions that this has aroused inside him. He then hopes that the therapist will 'answer' the call and make herself available for listening; but once again, her answer is 'No'. The patient then loses hope and trust in the possibility of feeling listened to and makes another attempt, hoping for 'more humanity' and simplicity in the encounter (going for a drink together), but the therapist takes the communication literally and defends herself against the possibility of a more 'human', receptive relationship.

Supervisions as detective stories

A particularly constructive approach to supervisions, which breathes life into the cases brought by supervisees, is to consider the 'cases', whether in individual or group supervisions, as detective stories, thrillers or mysteries, where everything that is presented is seen as evidence, clues or exhibits, all of which are highly significant. This entails, as it were, resetting all one's knowledge of psychopathology to zero and proceeding in the manner of Lieutenant Columbo or Inspector Maigret, seeking the 'key' to the case without revealing what one is doing. From this point of view, no case is banal or repetitive or obvious from the beginning.

This approach is, of course, even richer and more creative in a group, owing to the availability of the amplifying apparatus constituted by the group itself and its γ-function (Corrao 1981), i.e. the group α-function.

Carla's antidote

The 'case' is presented to me as follows: Carla, a woman of 45, is having therapy because of a court order. She says she has always been 'rejected' by her parents, who preferred her brother. She has two sons; the first she rejects because his birth was 'unplanned', while the second suffers from acid reflux and cannot keep anything down: 'he spits poison'.[2]

Carla's presenting symptom is bulimia, with uncontrollable vomiting. After the therapist has cancelled a session, she says that she puked and puked, that the house felt cramped to her, but that she now wants to wear only short, tight clothing, that she would like to set fire to the house, and that she does not give a toss about her husband. She likes going to bars, playing cards, and stuffing herself full. Then she says she can only show two per cent of herself . . . and that she would like to puke in her husband's face . . .

Of course, these few communications could have an infinite range of meanings, but the first Gestalt that suggests itself to me is the theme of incontinence. In particular – and this is the key to mystery – there is the idea of bulimia as an antidote. Owing to the 'rejection' (of the history, the internal object and the Other), Carla is faced with more and more emotions – rage, fury, anger and jealousy – which are then 'buffered' by food, all of which is then vomited up, as if she were undergoing gastric lavage after poisoning. What is poisoning her are the emotions aroused inside her, which she is unable to name, to recognize or to elaborate; she can only 'use the activated carbon of bulimia' and then evacuate them.

On a smaller scale, the same thing happens after the therapist's 'rejection' (the missed session); without a session, there is less space, 'the house is cramped', she wants 'short, tight clothing', is so furious that she would like to set the house on fire, and denies every possible need. She avoids depression by eating and then vomiting . . .

---

[2] Translator's note: The Italian phrase also means to speak spitefully.

The four twins

At the age of six, Gabriella is brought to psychotherapy after her parents separate. She is afraid to go to school, but the reason is her fear that 'Mummy might have an accident', 'Mummy might die', 'She won't come back' or 'Mummy might kill someone'.

We need to take a step back, and to know that the parents, of South American origin, had been together since they were at primary school in Buenos Aires at the age of ten; they had married very young, had the little girl, and then, in a dramatic and painful turn of events, had separated when the mother took up with another man, who was also an immigrant from South America.

Good results are obtained in the therapy, but four years later Gabriella is back with the same symptoms. The scene has changed: her father is about to marry another woman; Gabriella still sleeps with her mother, but is beginning to take an interest in boys for the first time. What is to be done?

She brings a dream to her session: she is on a trip and has to jump over a 'cleft' to join the others; someone tries to stop her, but she then decides to jump as well; she manages it, and arrives at a hotel where there are people 'in pieces'.

The problem is evidently the dialectic between symbiosis and separation. Separating gives rise to rage, fury and anxiety. However, without separating it is impossible to live. The dream seems to be saying that the 'cleft' must be confronted: she has to confront mourning if she is to live, even if she then feels that she is 'in pieces'. The onset of Gabriella's 'adolescent crisis' reactivates these issues, and a new possibility of resolving the four-fold symbiosis seems to be emerging. In this way she discovers that the father, even if he is married 'to another woman', is not lost; she is concerned about how to tell her mother that she is 'growing up' and cannot always stay with her. She realizes that she likes boys and this both 'worries and interests' her.

All this makes its way into the session, whose relational field catches Gabriella's 'illness': she must 'lose' a session to go with her father to the seaside, but would like to 'get it back'.

She then brings a dream, in which a close friend, Carlo, dies and is suddenly no longer there; but no one despaired and she herself spoke to him – for he was there as a ghost. Still in the dream, she goes to her father and confesses to him that, although he is dead, she still sees Carlo and talks to him. Her father looks sceptical, like the people in

9

the Milkana advertisement when they are told about cows and squirrels making milk chocolate to be sent to supermarkets.

It is not easy for the therapist to keep her balance on this 'ridge' between introjection of the absent object on the one hand and perpetuation of the illusion that mourning is avoidable on the other, not to mention the existence of the painful realities of life – namely, separation, mourning, absence and death.

The dream continues: there is a kiss (but is it possible to kiss Carlo?), but as she draws near to him, she 'finds nothing solid to get hold of'. One is reminded of the beautiful passage describing how Odysseus, having descended into Hades, tries to embrace his mother, who, however, 'cannot be grasped'. But in the dream, Gabriella finally manages to give Carlo the kiss (the therapist felt it appropriate to accede to the request for the session to be made up).

However, the summer holidays are approaching: 'Mummy has to go into hospital.' She sketches out her own name, saying that the 'i' looks like a suppository, because it has so many quaking or fault lines. In separation, 'someone' feels bad; separation is something to be undergone, like a suppository, and the idea makes her 'quake and explode' with rage and fear. Seeing that the sky has clouded over, she says on leaving: 'There's going to be a storm.'

Gabriella is basically a budding little Dumas, describing the transition from the *Three Musketeers* (in fact there were four) to *Twenty Years After*, in which the symbiotic nucleus of Athos, Aramis, d'Artagnan and Porthos (one for all and all for one) dissolves into the individuality and conflicts that await us all 'twenty years after'.

Which antidepressant?

Stefano, who comes from a well-to-do Neapolitan family, asks for therapy for a specific reason: he goes frequently, several times a week, to prostitutes and transvestites. At his very first interview, he tells of his tragic 'deportation' to a 'high-class' boarding school, where he endured hunger and was sent the 'foods' he constantly requested from his family. Then he tells of the severe depression suffered by his father, who has become a gambler, and says that his mother is also depressed. He works as a representative for a 'cardboard container' company. He goes on to mention the end of a relationship that had lasted for many years; he has never accepted the reality of his 'abandonment' by Mariella, his former girlfriend, and has done the most incredible things to try to win her back.

Since then his recourse to prostitutes has been ongoing and compulsive. Already at this stage, a possible narrative Gestalt begins to take shape: the prostitutes are a kind of antidepressant, which he takes in ever-increasing doses, to avoid the experience of abandonment, of 'primary hunger', of starvation, which the cardboard containers do not suffice to 'contain'. The relief is fleeting, new stimulants being constantly necessary to avoid a depressive catastrophe.

Of course, the whole story of abandonment and 'whores' may be expected to appear in the sessions, and indeed it promptly does. Whores are the professionals to whom he turns for relief in the intervals between sessions, but another 'whore' is the therapist who concerns herself with him for money, with the condom of the setting, and from whom he wants to learn the 'tricks of the trade'. For a long time, however, this entire aspect of contempt will have to remain 'in abeyance', pending the possibility of constructing new containers.

The field will promptly be infected with Stefano's problem: the end of every session is an abandonment, to be survived by means of massive doses of 'whores'; every new encounter with the therapist is actually with a mother whom he needs in order to survive, but who constantly abandons him.

A court for Marina

Meeting her therapist for the first time, Marina presents herself in the traditional costume of the Valle d'Aosta region, where she was born. She immediately tells the dramatic story of her life: twenty-five years ago her sister Nadia – their mother's favourite – died tragically in an accident while they were skiing together. Since then, life had changed for all of them: 'That nameless thing turned everyone's life upside down.'

Marina works all week and goes back to the Valle at weekends. She talks about the misfortune that occurred a quarter of a century ago as if it has just happened, conveying the impression that Valle d'Aosta – which has not yet succeeded in becoming a Vale of Tears – is a kind of enclave out of time and history, where time stopped on that fateful day. She then tells of her mother's depression, of her own fear of sliding into alcoholism and of her occasional worries about losing control.

In her first session, she brings a dream she had after reading a book about the death of the magistrates Giovanni Falcone and Paolo Borsellino, who were both killed by the Mafia: in the dream, the mother kills the two sons of a Mafia boss; she herself is an accomplice because she sent them out, so she too is guilty.

11

A possible plot now begins to emerge, although the connections between its individual elements are unclear; however, it involves violence, guilt, killings, the implicit fear of reprisals and – possibly – regret. Perhaps the Mafia mobsters Totò Riina and Tommaso Buscetta are also there somewhere.

From now on, the analysis can be imagined as turning into a trial that could not be held at the relevant time, but which, in the absence of explicit charges, condemned the patient to languish in a perpetual state of semi-liberty and expiation, with no possessions of her own for fear of reprisals. Guilt, jealousy, rivalry and aggressive fantasies and wishes (or indeed facts?) become the parameters of a court for celebrating the rite of a charge, a conviction, and possibly also absolution and repentance.

Maria Pia and the microwave

For her first interview, the seventeen-year-old Maria Pia comes along with her parents, who had telephoned for a consultation. They ask to speak to me alone first, leaving Maria Pia in the waiting room. The problem is slimming – so drastic that they are afraid their daughter is suffering from anorexia, as she has suddenly lost 10 kilos and her periods have stopped. She is doing reasonably well at a language school after leaving the high school where her mother taught.

The father is genuinely worried about the 'superficiality' of his daughter, to which he cannot resign himself. A parent of the democratic Left, he cannot understand how his daughter can want to 'vote for the [rightist] Northern League',[3] how it is that she has no particular cultural interests, and how she can claim to be ashamed of having two graduate parents and prefer a 'yob' for a boyfriend. Nor can he understand why, until two years ago, she was extremely 'bound' to him, waiting for him to play games with her every evening, whereas now she barely speaks to him. 'I would give anything for her to be a little girl again,' he concludes.

I now dismiss the parents and ask Maria Pia to come in. After a brief silence, I set the ball rolling by asking her: 'Well, tell me something about yourself.' She replies: 'I want to go to university to do PR,[4] but not as a disco dancer on a raised platform: I mean PR at the Bicocca.'[5] She then

---

[3] Translator's note: The Italian word *lega* means not only 'league' but also 'binds'.
[4] Translator's note: Although PR of course stands for public relations, in Italian it can also suggest a 'woman of easy virtue'.
[5] Translator's note: There is a double meaning here: apart from the reference to Milan's Bicocca University, the word could be construed as *bi-cocca*, or 'darling twice over'.

tells me about her school, and goes on to say that she has an easy relationship with her mother but a more difficult one with her father. She is a very good-looking young lady, like a model, although at times the features of a little girl are apparent.

I tell her that her father told me that when she was small he used to play with her a lot; this causes her to thaw out and she tells me about lots and lots of games – games with Barbie dolls that went on until two years ago. I am struck by the alternation of genuine moments of contact (for example, her answering smile when I tell her that I feel there is a secret Maria Pia whom she does not allow many people to know) with moments of superficiality and banality bordering on emotional deadness.

Finally we arrive at a dream: she is at home when a terrifying goose suddenly appears; she tries to catch it, succeeds, and puts it in the microwave. She hopes, and tries, to cook it, but the goose jumps out 'uncooked', even more threatening than before. I ask her if she would like someone to help her to 'cook this goose', and, relieved, she tells me that that was why it had been easy for her to come along. We then make the arrangements for her therapy.

With Maria Pia, a single interview sufficed to indicate the nature of her problem: she is unsettled at having suddenly become a beautiful adolescent girl. On the one hand, she does not know how to break the old bonds, and indeed she still 'de-votes' herself to them (voting for the 'League/bond' [*lega*]) to the point of even stopping her periods – with her father, and partly also with her mother, she shares the notion of remaining a little girl (the *bi-cocca*, or the *cocca* [darling] of both mummy and daddy). However, on the other hand, she also needs to grow somehow: she needs to find a way of differentiating out and acquiring a 'different' mode of being, to distinguish and separate her from her parents.

This, though, is something she is as yet unable to mourn for, because her adult identity is still somewhat spurious: every so often, out comes the superficial young girl – in the form of the 'goose' – and she feels persecuted by it, because she still lacks suitable instruments for 'cooking the goose' and for voting not for the 'League' (the old bonds) but instead for ceasing to be in league with and detaching herself from her parents – but then she, together with her parents, would have to mourn for a childhood that is irrevocably over.

Having reached the end of this group of clinical sequences, I should like merely to point out that, in all the cases described, the possibility exists of generating a (provisional) 'Gestalt' to organize facts, experiences and characters in a possible narration, thus affording a 'new opportunity' for metabolizing what could not be 'digested' in the 'then and there' situation. In each case the 'here and now' turns into the space-time where the unthinkable can finally be thought, and, as such, can eventually weave a torn fabric together again. In addition – and this is the sense and purpose of analysis – this will allow the introjection of the function of 'weaving stories' or 'narrating emotions through memories, recollections and characters' that I have elsewhere called the 'internal narrator'.

The analyst, for his part, must cooperate in the scripting of the screenplay, by introducing and modulating those characters, who often syncretize clumps of emotions; however, he must allow the patient to supply the major part of the 'skeins' from which the narrative web will be spun. In this facilitating operation, it is preferable for the analyst to adopt a posture of relative abstention rather than to force the sense by introducing threads that have more to do with his own states of mind, defences and theories than with reverie.

How to speak in order to be understood

A particular problem is presented by patients with whom communication in the consulting room becomes the central issue.

Patients who are autistic or have appreciable autistic tendencies

For these patients, as well as for the autistic nuclei of patients with other pathologies, a problem is already presented by the level of development of the 'emotional pictogram' (Bion 1962; Botella and Botella 2001; Ferro 1992; Rocha Barros 2000): the analyst's contributions must be minimal so as to avoid administering doses of sensory or other stimulation that exceeds these patients' capacity to 'alphabetize' them. There must be no active interpretative activity centred on the patient's internal world or on the relationship, as the quanta of proto-emotions aroused would give rise to their own immediate evacuation, given that the mind lacks the capacity to transform them into images, emotions, experiences or thought. For a long time, the analyst has no choice but to act like the chorus in a Greek play, confining himself to commenting on the action that unfolds on the stage.

Another important aspect is the affective tone – the emotional quality – of the voice, because it is perceived prior to any possible content. Any interpretative excess, even if 'true', will be like a voltage surge, burning out wiring that is not yet strong enough to withstand it, so that the entire communications network breaks down.

Marcello's telephone

Marcello is an autistic little boy who has found a therapist capable of calibrating her interventions so as to create an environment that enables him gradually to 'open up'; he now plays freely and sometimes sings to himself.

The therapist uses asides to comment on and describe the games that Marcello plays, varying the tone of her voice in different ways to indicate and portray various emotional nuances.

In one session, Marcello embarks on a game in which he demonstrates increasing 'faith' in his ability to let himself go: he climbs on to a little chair and lets himself fall back off it, knowing that the therapist will break his fall. The game is repeated several times and the therapist holds him physically so that he feels 'gathered up'; she comments by her tone of voice on Marcello's faith in 'letting himself go'. Marcello now turns to the toy telephone; knowing how it works, he presses the button to make it ring. He lifts the receiver and, for the first time ever, says ' 'llo . . . 'llo . . .'. The therapist avoids a direct response and even abstains from commenting directly on this new event, saying only: 'How nice to hear the phone ringing.' The game continues.

This interaction was made possible by the therapist's capacity to take part in the physical game that Marcello had initiated, involving for him the experience of being held, and for her the ability to hold him (verbally as well as physically) and to adopt a non-intrusive posture. This follows an instance a few months before when the therapist responded to a telephone call from Marcello by interpreting his 'wish to speak', after which Marcello did not utter a single syllable for months on end. In other words, the analyst must introduce a voltage, albeit at times minimal, into the field (the communications network).

The problem is, of course, different in the case of children with autistic traits; here, respect for the manifest text of the communication will suffice, with a cautious oblique description of any emotions that appear.

Luca's trains

When Luca began his therapy at the age of seven, he exhibited a number of autistic characteristics, such as stereotypies, tics, going-to-sleep rituals and a phobia of everything that was 'alive', from small insects to butterflies. For a long time he drew inanimate scenes, town plans or trains. These gradually developed into towns with street lamps and plants, while the trains began to convey explosives and foods. Meanwhile, he continued to draw road signs, particularly 'no entry' signs. Eventually, it became possible for him to draw humanoid street lamps and finally dogs, cats and horses; at the same time, he became able to experience and express 'emotions' that were more and more 'alive' and no longer terrified him.

The same development was observed in a less seriously ill boy who had a crippling phobia of anything dirty, which made him clean everything with disinfectants. He could not tolerate being 'infested' by any emotion; however, as he progressively came to feel accompanied in the encounter with things that had previously been inaccessible, he began to make contact with 'other children', with 'the neighbour's cat' and with the 'pigeons in the square'. During the course of this process, the analyst constantly exercised enormous interpretative restraint, while *always* keeping in mind the relational and symbolic meaning of these communications; for a long time she was able to keep track of their manifest text, performing the function of receiving, naming and regulating the emotions that were beginning to come to life.

Of course, the time eventually comes when what has been deposited in the analyst's mind can be shared with the patient. Again, with some patients this is undeniably possible from the beginning.

Patients with a defective apparatus for thinking thoughts

Marzia's faun

Marzia, aged 44, is an established lawyer. The problem she brings at the beginning of her therapy is her husband's severe mental illness, stated to be bipolar disorder with delusional ideas. He insists, she says, on constant, thrilling sexual intercourse, which torments her.

After one year of therapy, she manages to separate from 'Giorgio'.

Meanwhile, the story of her own childhood gradually takes shape, with a mother who was always depressed, in bed and emotionally absent. When Marzia was just a few years old and playing with her little brother, she lost a finger when it was trapped between the spokes of his bicycle wheel. This accident was followed by a series of painful operations, relentlessly demanded by her mother.

Returning to the present, a new story now comes into being, involving Matteo, a kind and sensitive person, from whom, however, she keeps her distance because he arouses overwhelming emotions in her which she is unable to 'manage' . . . When he goes away on holiday, she says she will put 'the dear departed's pendant round her neck', referring to an item of jewellery he has given her. All this, of course, takes place in the context of the approaching summer holidays.

She then decides to go on a diet of lettuce and boiled vegetables. Later in her therapy, she says that underneath her flat is a bar from which she can hear lots of noise.

However, what emerges if the situation described above is deconstructed to strip it of its status as a factual account?

Marzia's 'husband' can in the first instance be thought of as a kind of antidepressant drug, which she needs in order not to sink into depression. On another level, he can be seen as split-off forms of 'functioning' of the patient herself. Once the therapy has commenced, she no longer needs such a drastic stimulant. The analysis gradually enables her to work through the infantile depression resulting from her abandonment by an absent mother, because she too was mentally 'absent' – and the activation of this mother will call for a drama: blood must flow.

At this point Giorgio can be replaced by Matteo, who is on the one hand a transformation of Giorgio and on the other an aspect of the transference relationship. However, the separation arouses excessively strong emotions: the abandoning object is castrated, and Marzia is confronted with rage, fury, jealousy and feelings of revenge, which she lacks the mental instruments to metabolize. She feels so bad that she goes 'on a diet of lettuce', as it were turning herself into a 'herbivore'; she stays more aloof in her relationships, putting herself on a strict emotional diet that she can tolerate more easily. However, there is also the signal from the bar 'down below' that something is pulsatingly alive and that, sooner or later, she will be able to move on from 'lettuce' to 'the woods'. The name of the bar is 'The Satyr'.

With a patient of this kind, whose basic early care was deficient, interpretation and/or decoding of the need is not enough. It is if a starving person came to our house saying 'My stomach is so utterly empty' and we were to reply 'You're telling me that you are hungry' instead of giving him something to eat. Such a response might be in order for patients who are sufficiently well equipped that telling them 'You are hungry' would be tantamount to putting them in touch with a need of which they had not previously been able to become conscious, but which, having been made explicit, is no longer pressing for satisfaction, or which they have appropriate instruments to deal with. However, patients with severe early deficiencies must be 'given something to eat'; if they are merely supplied with a simultaneous translation of what they have said, they are once again not being offered food for the development of their mind. Food for the mind consists in the exercise, with and for them, of the mental functions that were previously not exercised in their history – listening, receiving, responding coherently and keeping in mind – that is to say, exercising the 'α-function' that they lacked in their history. Not all the factors making up the α-function are known to us, although we have learned something from Bion (1962), and can derive more from our experience with such patients, who demand a level of mental and emotional commitment from us that goes far beyond mere interpretation.

A brief digression on the use of the Freudian model will not go amiss here. This model is applicable when it is possible to work on the contents – whether repressed or split off – of the patient's mental life, but is totally inappropriate where there is a need for upstream operations to overhaul, sometimes to a considerable extent, the patient's actual apparatus for thinking thoughts.

This first chapter continues with some clinical examples that can in varying degrees be seen as chimeras of the different 'loci' of suffering which I have described elsewhere (Ferro 2002a).

The concreteness of Marco

Marco, an electronic engineer, is a patient whose transference communications are quite obvious, but it is impossible to interpret them to him directly. He begins a pre-holiday session by talking about the terrible pains he is suffering, as a result of which he needs to double or even treble the dose of the drug he is taking. He then mentions the death of his cat, saying also (he is in his third year of therapy) that this is the third year when he has had something to mourn for just before the summer holidays:

last year a cat, and the previous summer a little kitten. At the end of the session, he 'hiccups' violently. The therapist's attempted interpretation, about his greater need for treatment/sessions/drugs, mourning and crying for the holidays, has no effect; instead, in the next session he reports a stomach ache due to some nauseating food he has been compelled to gulp down.

A patient of this kind simply has no place to accommodate interpretations; he must be helped to 'swim' to the point of acquiring the capacity to think emotions. This can be achieved by way of the therapist's toleration of remaining, for as long as is necessary, with the manifest text, contenting himself with sharing and/or redescribing the patient's experience, until, by introjection, he has developed a gut, or mental function, capable of retaining, digesting and assimilating interpretations.

For a long time, however, the patient's *gut* can only be the analyst's mind.

The crucial point is the response to an interpretation. For example, if a patient responds to an increase in the interpretative dose by saying 'Yesterday my little boy cried all evening because my husband insisted on making him eat up all his food, although he had already had a snack not long before and he could not get any more food down', this can only be a signal of interpretative 'excess', for which no place can be found.

If the same patient were to say 'Yesterday my husband exhausted me with his caresses and never-ending foreplay', from one point of view she would be signalling her need for 'penetrating' interpretative activity; this would not necessarily be made explicit, but instead 'acted out' in the form of more incisive interventions. The first 'response', on the other hand, would constitute the 'acting-out' of a less pressing kind of interpretative timing.

A place for Attila

Alessandro is a nine-year-old boy whose parents run a centre for maladjusted persons; he suffers from enuresis and nightmares, and is intolerant of any frustration. It is immediately clear from the parents' report that Alessandro's trouble centres on incontinence – his inability to contain emotional states, which he cannot 'digest', so that they give rise to indigestion (in the form of the nightmares) or evacuation in the form of 'agonizing headaches'.

Alessandro begins his first session by talking about his dog Attila, who can never find a bitch that likes him. Then he draws a rabbit, which, however, has claws and an enormous tail that looks like a burst of flame, followed by an erupting volcano. Next he draws Uncle Scrooge's Money Bin, in which the dollar sign ($) is represented as an S, so that it looks like a huge snake that has been squeezed into a box. He thus seems to be immediately narrating what happens if the parents' minds are occupied by their own depressive problems (the maladjusted people).

Linda's A-rage-ia

Linda, her mother reports, is a little girl who lived for a long time in the Congo and in Arabia because of her father's work. She has been brought for a consultation owing to recurring enuresis and nightmares that wake her nearly every night. The mother gives a 'nunnish' impression: she wants everything to be perfect and absolutely in order, and badly misses her husband, who is currently working in a European city not too far away.

In her first session, Linda makes a pen, in which she encloses a 'frisky horse', and plants 'bombs' all round the outside. Lots and lots of animals remain outside the pen and 'run away'. Linda too plainly has a problem in relation to the containing of emotions that would otherwise 'run away', as in her bed-wetting, and which cannot be contained in dreams.

Linda gradually gets interested in the people 'living in the flat upstairs': there is surely an apartment there, and, on the basis of her pre-session explorations, she begins to describe this place upstairs: there is a door, a gate − *cancello* in Italian − and perhaps chains . . . The person who lived there must have been 'someone who went away'. This is the key to the recovery of the little girl from the Congo, from Arabia/ A-rage-ia, gated ('cancelled out') because she cannot find a place in the mind of a rigid, overburdened mother, and who is constantly evacuated in every possible way, either in dreams that cannot contain her or in bed-wetting.

Here I should like to make a brief comment on the attitude to be adopted by a supervisor: I never ask anything, but wait for the person bringing the case to be the one to 'tell me'; I take everything the supervisee says as a significant communication. For example, I never ask for the patient's name; if it is given to me, that very fact may be relevant, as in the case of Cristiana, who immediately put me in mind of Barbara − Saint Barbara [the '*barbar*ian'] becoming a Christian [*cristiana*], or Linda [spick-and-span in Italian], which immediately suggested the 'dirtiness' of the split-off part or the split-off 'non-Linda'/'non-spick-and-span', which is the same thing.

The immaculate virgin from Loano

Daniela is an anorexic student of oriental languages who engages in cleaning rituals that extend to the 'washing out' of her stomach and intestines with complex, wearisome 'lavages'. She says she comes from Loano and is 'afraid of anything new'; she must try to keep quiet and not listen to other people, so as to avoid 'being shaken by emotional storms'. So it seems that she cannot tolerate being soiled by any emotion and that anorexia is the means she has chosen to keep at bay, split off and controlled, all the emotions she knows she is not equipped to digest, of which she must 'cleanse' herself of every trace, even if they constantly reform.

With the progress of the therapy, Daniela also begins to deal with these emotions in images – 'I'm as pissed off as a hyena',[6] or 'What a shitty family I have' – but eventually she also says she is quite disturbed by 'positive ideas' of going back to school, working and having a baby. In other words, not only 'strong, negative' emotions but also 'positive' ones have to be evacuated and cancelled out as long as Daniela lacks the equipment needed to contain and metabolize them ($♀ ♂$ and α-functions), and so she starts vomiting again.

Emotion – whether positive or negative – for Daniela is something that soils her, and her only wish is to be clean. This idea of being sullied by emotions is also indicated by the fact that she comes from Lo-ano – which could be translated as 'the anus' – and for a long time all her efforts have been directed towards making herself 'immaculate'.

Stefano's sweating

Stefano, a 35-year-old engineer, seeks help for a phobia that makes his life difficult: he is afraid of 'blushing and sweating' in the presence of a woman he likes. This does not happen with other women, with whom he has frequent and relatively superficial relationships. The problem arises only with women who might appeal to him and trigger an involvement on his part. .

Still in his first session, he mentions a 'very peculiar uncle' and his fear

---

[6] Translator's note: An Italian expression.

of ending up like him. He then says how delicate his mother is and how he feels silent rage towards his father. As a child, he recalls, he could not fall asleep until his mother – a hairdresser – finished work, which was sometimes very late and on occasion even after midnight; he would wait for her lying down behind the door between the house and his mother's shop. He goes on to describe his last three significant affairs, in all three of which he had struck the woman concerned in an explosion of anger.

All kinds of images are already suggested by this presentation. My 'dream' about the patient's communications concerns his fear of relationships that truly involve him, because they give rise to passions that then overflow, setting him on fire (blushing), while the cooling system (sweating) cannot always get the better of the emotional blaze. This sometimes gets out of hand and he 'goes mad' like his uncle; he loses his boundaries and behaves unpredictably and violently, even physically attacking the people he loves.

At the next interview he reports that he has taken lots of showers (because of the sweating?) in the prevailing heat wave, and asks his likely analyst-to-be if it is true that analysts have to be 'cold and detached' (as a guarantee of a cooling function for the passions?) and whether she chose psychiatry because she 'didn't like blood' (a warning about Bluebeard?).

It is in my view important to 'dream' every first interview, in order as it were to create a screenplay or film set to organize the communications into a meaningful Gestalt, which will be confirmed or invalidated by the subsequent episodes.

Martino's sweating

To illustrate how one and the same symptom can evoke different scenes, let us consider the case of Martino, who asks for a consultation because he feels humiliated by his constant, unremitting sweating whatever the season. Every medical approach to the problem has failed.

> The son of a father who is extremely successful in his profession, Martino is afraid that he will never be able to live up to the dictates of his unattainable ego ideal.

As Martino tells me about the toils that characterize his life, in which he experiences everything as having to be done in a hurry if he is to meet his own and his family's expectations, what comes up in my mind is a classic scene from the world of cycle racing: the poor competitor on an uphill stretch, pedalling for all he is worth, exhausted and bathed in sweat. This is surely a good plan for starting work with Martino: it is surely not easy to imagine oneself as the son of a famous racing cyclist such as Fausto Coppi or Gino Bartali, riding calmly downhill, because for him the opposite is the case: every project, and indeed every instant of the day, becomes a stage in the Tour de France, with his yellow jersey every more thoroughly soaked in sweat.

Veronica's dyke

Veronica is described by her parents as a 'shy, reserved' little girl, who is 'mute', especially at school, where she does not speak to the teachers. Her mother in particular appears very worried and anxious – tired and exasperated at having to look after three small children (Veronica has two brothers), as well as go to work. The therapist says that while the mother was speaking, she herself began to think of recent reports about mothers who had killed their children.

Meagre as this account is, in my view it already enables us to postulate a possible scenario, particularly if the therapist's 'countertransference' is regarded as a place in the field. The dynamic is one of oscillation between hypercontrol (Veronica's mutism) and total lack of control (the mother who kills her children), or between the extremes of hypercontainment and lack of containment: either the emotions escape and sweep everything away like a river in flood, or they are controlled by 'dykes' that completely block the flow.

In her sessions with the therapist, Veronica gradually relaxes and talks about the 'monsters and swords' with which she plays; she then asks if 'other children' also come, draws a castle with windows through which can be seen curtains that in fact look like two profiles facing each other, and then dungeons with bars and prisoners inside; she mentions 'a little boy who got ill and died', and finally tells how her elder brother bites people . . .

If the little girl's communications are seen as characters in search of an author, it can readily be imagined that the field contains 'monsters and swords', and that the question is whether unknown or unintegrated aspects of herself ('other children') will be welcomed. In particular, will the parts that have been incarcerated or are thought to be dead (the prisoners in the castle, the dead little boy, and the doubles represented by the profiles) be able to find a space in which they can be narrated, even in the teeth of the brother's 'bites'? Will this also gradually be facilitated by the other characters that will come alive in subsequent sessions, such as 'Spiderman', 'the ghosts', and 'bears, lions and crocodiles'?

Recapitulation

Marcella: the transition from explosive sensoriality to the ability to think

The following extended case history illustrates how one and the same analysis is made up of phases that differ greatly in nature and consequently call for considerable flexibility on the part of the analyst in terms of his posture and manner of interpretation. Before presenting the case history proper, I shall outline the basic theoretical conception underlying my approach, which I shall develop further in subsequent chapters.

With some patients, a lengthy portion of the analysis necessarily involves the patient's consent to, and cooperation in, the development of the capacity to think by building a 'place' in which to 'hold' not only his emotions but also the analyst's interpretations. This task must be accomplished before one can work on the repressed material and on reconstruction of childhood history, using classical interpretations.

In the case I shall present here, that of Marcella, the pivotal part of the analysis comprised the work that I would define generally as the establishment of containments. This aspect of the analysis took priority over its actual content, since it provided the opportunity for a transformation – that of Marcella's turbulent proto-emotions and whirling sensoriality into emotions and thoughts that she could begin to manage as they took shape in her psyche. As long as she was not able to do this (a situation Bion [1962] might have defined as a lack of the α-function and of the container), her psychic activity consisted either of continuous evacuation or of a profound drowsiness, a sort of hibernation of her proto-emotional states and an emotional and existential deadening. These modes of functioning served as a sort of emotional levelling that impeded the formation of proto-emotional states, which the patient would have experienced as a source of danger because she could not contain them; she did not know how to transform them into experienceable emotions or thinkable thoughts.

It has taken me a long time to organize my thoughts on the work that I have done and that which remains to be done with Marcella. In such cases, when clinical work becomes bleak and obscure, when the patient's maladaptive patterns of psychic functioning appear unmodifiable, and when there is no obvious way out, I have found it necessary to rely on all the patience I can muster. Many of the major steps I describe in my work with Marcella took on special significance only after the event. Furthermore, a primary feature of the analysis was my own mental functioning in the sessions; for a long time, I had to compensate for the patient's inability to experience her own emotions and thoughts, until I gradually managed to pass on this skill to Marcella so that she could do it for herself.

Bionian foundations

Much of my formulation and discussion of the case of Marcella derives from the conceptualizations of Bion (1962, 1963, 1965). For him, the work done by the mother's (or analyst's) mind on the child's (or patient's) projected feelings of anxiety, or β-elements, is central. If such feelings find a mental receptor – of which the capacity for reverie is one factor – they can be transformed into α-elements, attesting to the success of the process of thought formation (or, in another language, of symbolization). The repetition of the projection of β-elements, their reception and their restitution after transformation into images (or, expressed in different language, through a process of imagination and representation) together lay the foundations for the development of what Bion called the container. This can be seen as a kind of 'basket' that provides a place for emotions and thoughts, so that they can develop and become woven into the individual's psyche.

Bion sees the mind as resembling a digestive apparatus that must be developed to enable it to digest sensory input, since what is digested will form the elements of the basis of thought. Furthermore, Bion considered the process of projective identification to be directed towards communication, and that it also has the function of projecting sensoriality that is thereby transformed into elements that can be used for thought (Ferro 2002a).

25

Marcella's analysis could be seen as a lengthy labour in the service of constructing such a digestive apparatus, before work could proceed on the actual contents of the apparatus. I shall now attempt to describe the significant phases of that labour, some of which became truly meaningful for me only after the event, and only after toilsome scrutiny of my countertransference.

Emotional turbulence: from projective identification to narration

Marcella's 'apartment below'

For a long time, the main feature of my sessions with Marcella, a young office clerk, was boredom – an atmosphere of boredom that seemed gradually to permeate the room and to take over my mind. Physically, Marcella was neither pretty nor ugly, and intellectually she had no interests whatsoever: nothing attracted her or got her involved. She had come to analysis because of an undefined and indefinable state of malaise.

Very soon, I started to perceive the work with her as heavy-going and boring, and found myself unable to make interpretations in the transference, almost as though I did not want to 'touch' her. I noticed that once I had been listening to her for a while, my thoughts seemed to become disconnected; I tended to lose contact and would stop following even the manifest level of what she was saying. All this changed when Marcella brought a dream.

> In her dream, Marcella was opening the drawers of a chest near her bed, and they were full of reels of thread, all different colours mixed together. She quickly closed the drawers, frightened by the idea of how hard it would be and how much patience she would need to sort out all those tangles.

In associating to the dream, Marcella remembered that, as a child, she used to play at the home of her grandmother, who was a seam-stress. But my mind suddenly lit up with the idea of another meaning of the Italian word for a reel of thread, *spoletta*: it also signifies a fuse, for setting off explosives. This immediately reminded me of a child I had had in analysis who used to cover pictures of fierce animals that frightened him with a thick layer of plasticine, and I suddenly understood why for so long I had not been able to reach Marcella emotionally with my interpretations: it was because I was afraid she would 'explode'. At that point, I was able to transfer with the patient to her grandmother's workroom, and to lay bare her terror of the tangled, explosive emotions she had kept shut away in drawers by means of her boredom.

The 'reels' started to unwind as Marcella's 'stories'. However, I felt that these stories could not be interpreted in any way, either in their real sense or in the transference, and that there was not even any point in trying to do so because we were immersed in a concrete setting. I therefore focused on the manifest level of the narration, sharing what Marcella had to say and trying to make my interpretations highly 'unsaturated' (Ferro 1996a, 2002b, 2002c), that is, tentative rather than conviction-driven. Above all, I had to recover my ability to think, which, when I was with Marcella, tended to dissolve, leaving me confused, disoriented and unable to make meaningful connections.

I recall a period during which renovations in the apartment below my office, which had been ongoing for a long time, started to assume significance in our work together, and Marcella began to nose around that floor of the building. This was the point when I realized that we were communicating with each other on two different levels: one superficial and totally shallow, and another via projective identifications, which had the effect of numbing my ability to listen even to the manifest text of her utterances in the sessions. As stated earlier, these projective identifications seemed to disconnect my own thought processes, and made me aware of an undercurrent of proto-emotions so absolutely primitive that they were either evacuated or became tangled in boredom.

So it was that stories surged up from the apartment below. Marcella talked about the *pastina* on the walls, referring to the rough plaster mix used by the workmen. In response to a comment of mine, she added that '*pastina* on the walls' reminded her of a very angry child. It emerged that she had had childhood tantrums when her soup, which contained tiny pieces of pasta (*pastina*), was not at the right temperature for her, and she had flung the whole plate at the nearest wall, splattering the contents.

Here I recall my reluctance to backdate the problem to her childhood, instead of finding an easy, straightforward relational explanation, for example, one concerning how the patient reacted every time an interpretation seemed too hot or too cold, and how she liked to 'splatter' the contents of interpretations.

The same applied to the Turkish divan that Marcella said she had in her bedroom, which was something like a 'bed with a backrest', thus bringing us back to the analyst's couch. Although she did not associate this with certain aspects of herself that were foreign to her and whose language she did not understand, these meanings were not lost if what she said was considered in field terms (Baranger and Baranger 1961–2; Ferro 1992). Such meanings are always present in the consulting room if they are there in the analyst's mind, waiting either to turn into plots that can be shared, or to open up fresh space in which to permit new thoughts to become thinkable.

Marcella: an emotion takes shape

After a further period of analysis with Marcella, I started to feel that I was dealing with a sort of squid, the kind that shoots out ink when threatened. Every attempt to get closer to the patient or to make even the most cautious interpretation was met with a shower of 'ink'. The only resource I could use was my patience. This stance was eventually rewarded, as affective relationships gradually started to come to light in our workplace, alongside what Marcella called her 'office connections', stories about her work as an office clerk.

> In one session, when I had succeeded in establishing a relatively tranquil atmosphere with only minimal persecutory feelings, infantile memories began to surface. These included one – Marcella did not know whether she actually remembered it, or whether her mother had told her about it – in which she was in a sort of baby-walker, in a long corridor with three doors opening off it. (It seems hardly necessary to point out that Marcella was coming to three sessions a week at that point.) In the memory, she was running faster and faster until she collided violently with the wash-basin in the bathroom at the end of the corridor. This tale brought our session to an end, and I felt pleased that this deeper, more personal level had finally started to emerge.

One day, in the ten-minute break I allow myself between patients, I was stricken by a violent headache. I wondered why, since I do not usually suffer from headaches. I started to worry about how I would cope with my 'new' patient in the next hour. I felt it had something to do with Marcella and, suddenly, I grasped the way in which my headache, the next hour and the 'new' patient were all linked. A change had taken place in my work with Marcella – not in the sense of a massive identification with the patient, but rather one brought about by the arrival of a strong emotion, a mental pain, in the field. This psychic suffering would eventually allow a leap to occur in Marcella's mental growth. I could see only its precursor at that point, but once such a presence takes hold in the field, it is never long before the patient accepts it. It later became clear that the pain appeared in response to an approaching weekend break, as well as to the break that was revealed when I told Marcella of my holiday dates. It is in my view significant that it was *I* who as it were experienced Marcella's first strong emotion, received it, and organized it as a thought.

> Some time afterwards, Marcella arrived for her session a quarter of an hour late. She was normally punctual, even though she came from out of town, but on this occasion, she told me that her train had been delayed when the *controllore* (ticket inspector) had seen a young drug addict lock himself in the toilet, and had tried to get him out and off the train. The inspector finally managed to get the boy to alight, but then he got back on to the train – whereupon all the doors were locked, and the boy was only then successfully dispatched. The whole process had taken fifteen minutes.

A scholastic interpretation would have been easy ('it's a part of you that made sure you were late for the session – showing the extreme need you feel for analysis'), but I felt that such an interpretation would have come too much from me alone. It would have been in –K, as Bion (1965) might have put it, and it would not have fitted the patient. Furthermore, this type of interpretation would not have produced insight, and might even have given rise to a sense of persecution in the patient and a resulting loss of contact.

Earlier, I mentioned my contribution to a tranquil atmosphere – but what exactly does that mean? Does the analyst pretend to agree with everything, or does he pretend that nothing has happened? My answer to both questions is a categorical no – nor can the analyst be seen as simply testing the temperature and distance of interpretations (Meltzer 1976). I do believe, however, that it is essential to respect the patient's threshold for tolerating interpretations, and to recognize that a feeling of persecution in the session is a glaring sign of excessive insistence.

> I asked Marcella to comment on the episode on the train, telling me how she experienced it. This prompted her to relate some childhood memories centring on her father's job. He had been a railway worker – in Italian, a

ferroviere. (Note that my name, Ferro, means iron in Italian, and that a railway is a *ferrovia* – literally, an ironway.) Railway workers, Marcella said, have to pay for any delays that they cause, and serious problems occur when people attempt suicide by throwing themselves on to the tracks. She then started to talk about occupational hazards for workers in other fields, mentioning a psychotherapist friend who had been knifed by a patient. She carried on talking, until I asked her: 'Is there some link between the dramatic events you are describing – suicides, knifings and drug addiction – and the fact that I told you in the last session when I shall be going on holiday?'

Marcella laughed, clearly relieved, and surprised me by replying: 'If we no longer have only "official" relations here, but also emotional ones, then violent emotions can come up, and they won't always be controllable.' In that case, I pointed out, the ticket inspector (*controllore*) might just as well not have delayed the train by his attempt to block the desperation and anger concealed in the guise of the drug addict.

Dreaming of red peppers and potatoes: names for emotions?

Marcella now talked less about what happened at her office, but when she did, she increasingly referred to the affects aroused there. One day, she told me that a colleague at work had said she had been cured of her 'affability complex', and Marcella herself proceeded to complain, getting angry about things she did not like. She wanted simpler, more immediate relationships, she said, and then brought a dream: she was meeting some friends and wanted to bring them something to show how happy she was to see them and to have them as her guests. So she took a red pepper and a potato and ran to meet them. But two animals she did not know leapt out at her and shredded the vegetables, turning the pepper into a Chinese lantern.

I asked her what those animals might be, seeming as they did to foil her intentions and to prevent her joyful, immediate meeting with her friends. (I avoided any transference interpretation, so as not to create a persecution factor that might impede our communication.) She replied: 'They're what's left of the difficulties and fears I had in relating with others', which, I added to Marcella, transform simple feelings, emotions that need a name, into strange, enigmatic things.

The 'folli-cular' tumour: a fear of strong feelings

At this stage, I unexpectedly found myself going through another long period of hibernation, when a fresh bout of boredom seemed to freeze everything. I was able to work out what it was that was sending me to sleep: Marcella was using an absolutely monotonous voice to narrate things, just stringing her sentences together with 'and . . . and . . . and', with no main or subordinate clauses to help distinguish the important communications from the less important ones. Any potential difference was masked by coordinate clauses and more coordinate clauses, all apparently grammatically equal. I was lost in this sea, lulled almost to sleep by the repetitive rhythm of the waves. Any attempt at interpreting – or even at describing – what was going on, after we had talked about emotions, proved futile, until finally, something shocking happened. Marcella said: 'My doctor noticed a swelling on my neck and sent me for tests. A few days later, I was told I had a tumour with malignant cells.'

This was the storm that whipped up the still sea. After a long string of medical investigations, it was determined that Marcella needed immediate surgery. I had to follow these dramatic and urgent communications on the level of external reality, but at the same time felt an increasing need to determine the meaning of what was going on in the analytic relationship.

Marcella told me that she might have to have a thyroid lobe removed, and added that she could not tell her mother about it because she would have trouble coping. Marcella added that the doctors did not yet know whether it was a papilliferous or a 'folli-cular' tumour. I felt at this point that an urgent operation was needed in the analysis too, and told Marcella that for some time I had in fact been wondering whether she might have something in her throat – something that she could not get out, a highly malignant thing, maybe a *folly*, and that there was something she felt she could not mention to me in case I could not handle it.

Marcella seemed at first to hold her breath, but then, in a frightened voice, admitted that there was indeed something she had never dared to tell me in all these years – which was in fact the real reason why she had decided to start analysis, even though she believed she would never be able to talk about it. She was terrified of being thought mad, she explained, but there was no longer any question about it: her house was haunted. Every time she went out, there was a little ghost of a child at the window, who waited for her when she returned, and it wandered around the house and watched her. Sometimes it played tricks on her, but it was actually harmless, and in fact kept her company. There were other ghosts, too, not clearly identifiable, who were playful; sometimes Marcella would

31

find that they had prepared food, or tidied up the house, or had hidden something in order to make her play at finding it. Sometimes they too played tricks on her.

I must confess that this account left me speechless, and I could only conclude that Marcella's deep loneliness was relieved by these 'presences', which would surely assume some meaning in her analysis. She went on to tell me that she was afraid she was a witch because she had supernatural powers, since she could foretell the future, and could call down good things and curses. All of a sudden, she asked me whether these were hallucinations. I told her that I thought they were more like daydreams – and ones that had every right to exist.

This exchange led into a series of sessions in which I discovered Marcella's world of ghosts, and my reaction was to tread fearfully among them. Sometimes it seemed to me that the patient was positively delusional, but there were also moments when I felt that she and I were playing games. Be that as it may, we could at least begin to find a shared meaning: was I, too, from a certain viewpoint, just another little ghost in the patient's life, with a significance of my own – a presence that tidied things up, prepared meals, and waited for her? I only began to wonder whether this was the case after numerous sessions in which we had simply 'toyed' with these little ghosts – while I inwardly trembled with fear.

I should add that I have had considerable experience with patients who suffer from hallucinations (Ferro 1993) or have visual 'flashes' (Ferro 1996b). But these patients all showed fear, disorientation, anxiety, surprise and a lack of explanation for – or at least a lack of curiosity about – the things they 'saw'. I had never had a patient who talked quite normally about her ghosts and her relations with them, while at the same time expressing doubts about her own sanity.

Help came to me in the form of a play I remembered, by the Neapolitan author Eduardo de Filippo. In *Questi Fantasmi* ('These Ghosts'), the main character interacts with the 'presences' living in his house, which he believes, quite naturally, to be ghosts with whom he can establish significant relations.

At this stage of the analysis, Marcella had her operation. The biopsy showed that her tumour was not follicular, but papilliferous. She was obviously relieved, explaining that, as she understood the matter, the former was very serious – a 'cold' nodule – whereas the latter was a 'hot' nodule. This brought us to the subject of passion, and Marcella explained that she considered the bureaucracy of her rather mundane office job to be one way of walking on the hot coals of passion. The ghosts also represented something hot and exciting, even though they sometimes seemed encysted; they were not cold or paranoid things. And here, I must admit, I worried that Marcella's fiery temperament might flare up before the discussion of the ghosts was fully unravelled.

The ghosts

I had trouble working with these ghosts, because I felt that I was balancing on a tightrope, poised between an inability convincingly to reassure the patient that they did exist, and the impossibility of interpreting them exclusively as detached objects or functions. For a long time, drawing on my experience of child analysis, I resorted to playing with these presences without defining them (Ferro 1996c). I gave them a place to live, hoping that, as we gathered together the emotions from which they were woven, they would eventually be free to present themselves without having to be clothed in this sort of fantastical exterior substance.

Marcella and I had been in this transitional area, in which the characters moved around and interacted, for a while when I began to realize that it was possible to reach the emotions they externalized, regardless of whether they were dream flashes or hallucinatory transformations. Then, at the beginning of a session, Marcella told me by a roundabout route that she had one of her grandfather's pictures in her home: it was a painting she particularly liked, of a landscape containing a tree, a child, and some elves (*folletti* in Italian). When she had finished telling me about the picture, I found the strength to ask her: 'And what has become of the ghosts?' As if it were the most natural thing in the world, she answered: 'Oh, they've gone back into the painting.'

Once the ghosts had been metabolized and returned to the painting, a miracle took place: no more boredom, no more drowsiness. Lively emotions came to light – bordering on violence and on the theme of 'there's no room for me'. This took us back to the patient's childhood and the fact that, although the family home had enough rooms, she was not given one of her own, but had to sleep on a folding couch in the living room – a situation similar to the precariousness of the couch in my consulting room, which also was not really hers. She mentioned her mother, who had room for her own hypochondriacal anxiety, but not for her daughter's worries and projects.

The padded cell

As had been her pattern since the beginning of the analysis, Marcella reacted violently every time a session had to be cancelled: this was tangible proof that there was no room for her, and she would lay on a temper tantrum and a display of desperation. This return to life was also mediated by a reverie of mine when she said that she felt she was throwing herself against a 'rubber wall' but no one was answering; this reminded me of padded cells in old mental hospitals. When I told her this, she was struck by the imagery, and was moved: her emotions could only be put to sleep, or contained, in a padded room for violent patients. For a long time, her bureaucratic office job had served as this padded room – deadening everything, absorbing anything that might become too violent. Subsequently, she dreamt of Zulu warriors, which frightened her, but which also confirmed that her primitive emotions were no longer bottled up. She was not crashing into a rubber wall any longer, so her emotions could be set free, even if she was afraid of them.

After the next missed session, Marcella told me of a dream in which her house keys had been broken, and in which she had felt an anxiety stronger than any she had ever known – a kind of 'black anguish'. 'As black as the Zulus,' I suggested.

Corn or chocolate

For several months, Marcella and I worked to contain and transform the Zulus, and Marcella's autistic defences (Klein 1980) – which had the function of deadening everything – gradually became less evident. During this period, the patient told me another dream: she went into a room where someone was trying to spray a deodorant, to get rid of the smell of something connected with the handle of a toilet in the next room. Then she touched a navy-blue coat and 'flakes' formed on it; when she tried to brush them away, they initially flew off, but then drifted back on to it. They were like cornflakes or chocolate flakes.

I was at a loss here, so I asked the patient what she thought of the dream. Marcella replied that the flakes made her think of something that wanted to get free but that kept coming back to its place, something to do with relations with other people. This comment lent credence to my experience with the patient, and I told her that when we first met, something seemed to close up, after which we were able to remove the flakes

34

and enjoy a good level of communication – but then we had to start all over again from the beginning.

'As if there wasn't a channel open once and for all,' Marcella said. 'That's right,' I replied, 'but the flakes are made of corn or chocolate.' 'They're biodegradable, digestible,' Marcella responded. These flakes, remnants of an old armour plating, could now be digested and brushed away, even if not yet once and for all.

I suggested that, in the first part of the dream, the deodorant was intended as a way of avoiding the need to tackle unpleasantness. Marcella agreed, and started off on a topic she had always tended to drop: her feeling that she was not wanted, that people just put up with her, and also that her femininity had never been fully acknowledged. I took this as a signal that an inner space (container) had opened up inside her, and that I could now begin to reach her with transference interpretations, without any longer having to fear emotional explosions or the develop-ment of persecutory ideas. Now, in fact, the interpretations seemed to be expected, desired, and to serve as the source of further transformational potential.

A sexual relationship between minds

My methods of interpretation with Marcella have changed, and I now interpret what happens in our relationship and her inner world and history in a much more intimate fashion, no longer worrying about intrusion or a sense of persecution in transference interpretations. In this new environ-ment, Marcella related another dream: she was on a couch with a young man who kissed her neck and started to unbutton her blouse. She wanted him, and told him to stroke her breast; his touch became more intimate. This dream, beneath its eroticism, seemed to indicate her desire gradually to make even closer contact with me, and the pleasure of the meeting seemed to confirm the patient's new way of functioning in analysis, as well as the greater accessibility of her own emotions and thoughts (Ferro 2000c).

In another dream, Marcella was making love with David, a dear friend, and in yet another, with a homeless woman who had at last found somewhere to stay. Finally, there was a dream that seemed to indicate what she wanted from analysis, in which she went to a jeweller and asked for a ring and a cameo with an angel's head. She commented on this herself in describing the dream, saying that what she really wanted was a husband and a child. But I suspect that she also wants a more stable relation with her analyst, a more fertile meeting of our minds, since all her previous relationships – starting from the one with her hypochondriacal, depressed mother – had been sources of nothing but disappointment and distress.

The journey with Marcella has not yet ended as I write these pages; there is still some distance to be travelled. The analysis so far, however, illustrates my belief that, concealed in the interpretative activity, there may always be torment in the analyst's mind (Ogden 1997), which becomes a receptor, a holder for the patient's anxieties and proto-emotional states (β-elements) that it must absorb and metabolize by means of its own often unconscious capacity for transformational elaboration. Interpretations thus become the means of 'testifying to' and conferring 'emergence' on this silent and complex work, which has much to do with the mental characteristics of the analyst and with his subjectivity (Renik 1993), which I believe comes more into play the more serious the patient's situation (Brenman and Pick 1985).

It may perhaps be useful to continue here with our previous alimentary metaphor. The patient can be seen as bringing certain 'raw' emotions to the analysis – emotions that are often violent and not manageable with his own cooking equipment – with the aim of 'cooking' them into more cohesive thoughts and emotions. The analyst is called upon to put at the patient's disposal the appropriate mental kitchen apparatus – pots, pans and oven – which will not only be utilized by the patient, but will also, through the repetition of its use (if things go well), permit its progressive introjection into the usual equipment that he has to hand. In this way the cooking implements, and hence the ability to cook, which were originally supplied by the analyst, eventually become the mental property of the patient.

This metaphor also enables us to distinguish the work done by the analyst in the 'kitchen department' (how much the analyst elaborates in his mind) from what he brings to the table in the 'restaurant department', i.e. what he communicates to the patient by actual interpretations. For this reason, I believe that the analyst's interpretative style must be flexible, that is, matched to the digestive capacity of the patient, in such a way that interpretations can function as factors of growth and not of persecution (Ferro 1996a, 2002b; Guignard 1996).

With Marcella, prolonged and silent labour in my 'kitchen department' has been necessary to permit the elaboration and transformation of the psychic areas that lacked the capacity to experience emotions. For a long time, she had used quasi-autistic nuclei as defensive armour to protect her from any excess of feeling that she could not metabolize in thought (Tustin 1990). Marcella had to develop her own α-functions in order to manage her proto-emotions, rather than merely resorting to evacuation – that is, turning her proto-emotions into hallucinations (her ghosts). She accomplished this through repeated micro-experiences of being in unison, of emotional sharing (Bion 1962, 1963, 1965). Now that she has reached this stage, the analysis can proceed along the rails of a mind that is adequately mapped. Analytic work on the repressed and on reconstruction of the infantile experience can thus take centre stage. Let me again emphasize – this time by a Freudian metaphor – that with some patients the 'mystic writing-pad' must be reconstructed before the erased text can be revealed.

In this clinical example, I have opted to concentrate on the development of the transference-countertransference relationship in the analytic work, so as to give coherence to my presentation and to limit its overall length. Other stories and characters, viewed from alternative vantage points, could of course also have been described, and would permit a more complete view of the work done with this patient.

2

Digressions on interpretation

Many analysts believe that the specificity of analysis lies in *interpretation*, that is, offering a discourse different from the patient's so as to reveal the deeper meaning of his communication. I have concerned myself with this issue for a long time, starting with the paper I wrote together with Michele Bezoari (Bezoari and Ferro 1989) and extending to my more recent reflections on the analytic field as formulated first by Willy and Madeleine Baranger and subsequently by Francesco Corrao.

However, with many patients a strong interpretative approach is out of the question; with them, for very long periods, the need is for a response that, while centred on analytic and transference-based listening to every one of their communications, assumes a 'homogenized' form whose vector is their own language. For a long time, all that is possible with these patients is *reformulation* of what they themselves have said.

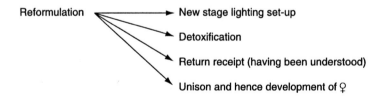

If a patient responds to an interpretation by saying that her saucepan makes a noise, or that if she does not get a concrete offer of work she will leave her job, or that she is fed up doing a useless kind of work, instead of thinking of the whole range of possible interpretations from envy to the intolerance of dependence, I ask myself: how must I speak today in order to be fully understood by this patient?

39

Such a patient – like someone who thinks he can speak, say, French or German instantly – does not of course have any knowledge of the language of analysis, but can, I believe, be led by the hand to acquire it for the first time.

> A patient talks constantly, and with anxiety, about his adolescent son's problems at school and the son's affective and emotional difficulties. It is perfectly obvious to me that he is talking about aspects of himself with which he cannot make contact in any other way, but by consenting to stay with the text as narrated ('the son's problems'), I am able to work on these problems with him and thereby even to share other points of view with him; for instance, the son's great sensitivity and, in particular, the sense of being assailed by more external stimulation than can be absorbed and mentalized ('I remember him when he was very small, with his eyes wide open to the world, jumping out of his skin at every single sensory impression'). The patient's comment at the beginning of the session that his son's brain contained non-negotiable areas, one of which was made up of the traumas he had suffered, enabled us to open up this sequestered area, which was actually part of the patient himself, who now described some incredible traumatic experiences of his own. However, this was possible only after he had had the experience that what he felt to be his most urgent problems were being listened to, albeit in the guise of his son's problems.

In terms of a theory of the *analyst–patient relationship*, a given session could be imagined as having the following configuration:

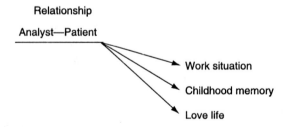

Here, certain emotions and affects have to do with the analytic couple, whereas others concern other significant relationships (for example, work relationships, affective relationships, relationships of daily life, or relationships from the patient's history or childhood).

In terms of a *theory of the field*, the diagram would assume the following form:

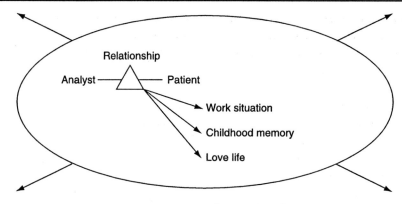

Space–time prism and expanding field

In this case, a space–time prism diffracts the relationship into other relationships that will remain in different screenplays (work–related, affective, historical, etc.) as partial aspects of the analytic relationship. All this takes place within a field, represented by a possibly expanding curve, which includes all possible diffractions and stories.

In this way we can stay with the manifest meaning of the patient's text or one of the collateral stories, while at the same time remaining within the 'psychoanalytic field' that is the locus of transformation. Sometimes the communications can remain 'in the field', whereas on other occasions they may be transferred to the place in the field that we call the 'relationship'.

When a patient begins to speak, he talks about contingent facts, his history and his relationship with his wife and colleagues. Our ears are bound to act as vast collectors of all these communications, which will inevitably be situated within the 'analytic field' and – as an exercise – in the 'analytic relationship'. All this can sometimes be returned to the patient direct, but in some cases it must remain in the field pending subsequent small transformations.

Martino's fears

On her first meeting with Martino, a little patient-to-be, a child therapist says: 'Mummy brought you to me because you are good when you are away but very naughty at home.' The child is disorientated and then draws 'a mouth blowing out a lit candle', 'a scratching finger', 'a dinosaur jumping over a wall' and a series of characters out of Popeye the Sailor, all of whom have been hanged, have committed suicide or have had their heads cut off. It seems to me that all these 'productions' can only be seen as the child's response to the therapist's comment. It is as if he were saying: 'What you told me is something that banishes all my hopes, something that scratches me, terrifies me and plunges me into despair.' It is surely not meaningful – for the time being – to understand these communications in any other way.

The child uses the next three sessions to work through this 'difficult' beginning. I take particular note, in supervision with this therapist, of her telling me 'with the indignation of a teacher' how Martino is allowed to play computer games at home, and in particular an adult game in which aliens suddenly appear and invade the Earth: in desperation, Martino cries out for his mummy. The therapist then says she is worried because the child has told her about seaside trips with his father involving the use of an aqualung.

Here, the significance of these communications in terms of the present relationship has gone totally unnoticed: the sense of being invaded by alien emotions and of not being helped, followed, however, by the recognition of being accompanied by the therapist in taking a look at the 'submerged world'. The therapist has as it were been infected by the parents' uncontaining and thoughtless world and acts it out in her relationship with the child.

The nub of my argument, as already presented in a number of contributions (Ferro 1996a, 1996c, 1999, 2000a, 2000b, 2002a, 2003a, 2003b), is that the specificity of psychoanalysis, as it were in pure culture, lies in the sequence of sensory impressions and proto-emotions constantly produced by the mind and then transformed into images. The resulting film, made up of emotional pictograms (or, in the language of Bion, 'sequences of α-elements'), is substantially unconscious, and we can know only its 'narrative derivatives'.

In a given sequence α → α → α, the narrative derivatives may either be very close to the sequence or progressively depart from it, sometimes to an extent involving extreme distortion. It is up to the analyst to bring the narrative derivatives back into proximity with the basic emotional and pictographic sequence. This notion differs in two important respects from the 'conventional' view of the Kleinian formulation, one theoretical and the other technical.

The first difference is the idea that every mind produces α-elements and sequences of α-elements in a manner absolutely specific to that mind, unlike unconscious (or primal) fantasies. This is exemplified by the following picture, taken from an exhibition held in Arezzo in

2004, in which one and the same subject, the 'human face', is portrayed in radically different forms by three masters of painting.

The second difference is that the 'narrative derivative', however distorted and remote from the pictographed sequence, must be followed and received in its manifest meaning too, and gradually brought back stage by stage to the basic sequence, which is unknown to us; that is, both to ourselves and to the patient. It is rather like searching for a saucepan and its contents by following the smell that reaches our nostrils, however remote and distorted it may be, until we track down its origin together with the patient.

A more serious problem of course arises in the case of a deficiency upstream of the sequence of emotional pictograms, in situations where the capacity to form these pictograms is damaged (or, in the language of Bion, where the α-function is defective).

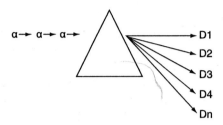

Distorting prism (defences, literary genres)

In this diagram, D1, D2, D3, D4, D*n* . . . represent the narrative derivatives, which can be chosen as literary genres, these too being the fruit of the defences deployed against the emotional truths of the mind. For instance, a problem of *rivalry, competition* and *jealousy* could be pictographed by the following waking dream thought sequence:

A mediaeval tournament → Two cyclists sprinting → Medea killing her children

This sequence, which remains unconscious, could announce its presence in increasingly concealed fashion on the basis of a dream, a memory of childhood, a diary item, a story heard, a film seen and so on: there is no limit to the possible narrative drift. Analyst and patient must work together with a view to gradually coming closer to the original waking dream sequence.

A further complication in analysis is that, however stable and thoroughly analysed, the analyst's mind is necessarily a variable of the analytic field and, depending on its functioning, contributes to the generation of the events taking place in the field. The analyst's self-analytic function is the resource customarily deployed to cope with all situations involving an excess of suffering that has to be metabolized in order to ensure that the analyst's mind does not contaminate the field.

At a time of suffering, which affects my analytic work in the form of reduced receptivity and increased interpretative activity, I dream that a Mafia boss in a helicopter lands on a block of flats and kills his son who has been costing him a lot of money; the son is a painter, who also looks after his friends financially. Then I am in a train with a doctor friend of mine who is an important anti-Mafia judge.

I reflect that the 'Mafia' are trying to hush up the cost of the suffering by simply eliminating it, but that this causes me to lose contact with my creativity, which after all costs me a lot; the presence of the doctor allows me to hope that I might be able to treat the suffering instead of eliminating it, and at the same time the anti–Mafia judge suggests to me that action is already in hand to deal with the short cut of eliminating the suffering. This dream not only puts me back in contact with myself, but also enables me to work receptively and creatively again.

In the corridors of psychoanalytic congresses people are often heard to make comments about colleagues belonging to different schools such as: 'That's not psychoanalysis!' This is in fact quite a significant issue. It seems to me that such a remark could be reformulated as: 'This way of doing psychoanalysis is *different* from my way of doing psychoanalysis.'

Various groups, at various times and in various countries, have defined 'genuine psychoanalysis' in various and sometimes diametrically opposed ways. In many subgroups, what is deemed to confer 'analytic' status on an analyst's interventions is the approach of constantly working with 'transference interpretations' without regard to the degree of transformation or persecution thereby generated. This is rather like deeming only – say – intravenous injections to constitute a 'medical act': the medical repertoire certainly includes both simpler and more complex actions, and it would be ridiculous for a doctor to say: 'If it is not an intravenous injection, it is not medicine.' That would be reminiscent of the miracle cures described by Molière in *Le Malade Imaginaire*.

Conformity with a supposed orthodoxy – which will inevitably lead in the long term to mannerism – is often held to be more important than the modicum of 'artistry' that every true analyst must possess, and I believe that this is one of the main factors in the present crisis of psychoanalysis. However, let us return to our subject.

The analyst's ear must in my view be like a funnel:

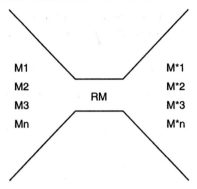

What the patient says must be transferred to a form of relational listening involving the whole field. What is at 360 degrees must thus be situated on the 'current relational axis', passing into the analyst's mind, crossing it and being deposited in it to varying degrees, after which it must emerge – enriched and transformed – as if through an inverted funnel. What comes in as messages M1, M2, Mn . . . has to be compacted in the 'relational message' (RM) so that it can emerge and be returned to the patient as M⋆1, M⋆2, M⋆3, M⋆n . . . – that is to say, as a message transformed by its passage through the analyst's mind.

For example, if a patient talks about a 'new business' that he would like to set up, the 'profit' he expects from it, the 'new economy' and so on, these messages must necessarily be regarded as relational messages (RM): the patient is saying that he experiences his analysis as a business that he must deal with, from which he expects a profit, and also that there is a new economy in his approach to the link, etc. Without suffocating the patient by reducing him to a mere simultaneous translation, we can only return these messages to him through his own narremes, with a view to their transformation and development.

The situation may, of course, differ from the above. Sometimes the narrated problem 'throbs' so intensely in the consulting room that it must necessarily be interpreted strongly and univocally along transference lines.

If a patient with relationship problems announces before the holidays that she wants to leave her boyfriend because the more she commits herself to the relationship, the less involved he is and the more she feels his absence – and when the boyfriend arrives, he expects her to be there for him, whereas she is full of rage and frustration – there is no alternative to severing the narrative knot in the only possible way,

like Alexander the Great, by cutting it with a transference interpretation to reveal and demonstrate to the patient what her affective and
defensive attitude is.

However, even this is not a hard-and-fast rule.

> A severely depressed lawyer has a dream featuring the phrase 'banana
> republic' and the FBI. To 'banana', he immediately associates the word
> 'chimpanzee'. I then take up this word when he eventually mentions
> his rage at anyone who neglects him, describing it as the 'rage of the
> chimpanzee'. At this point I find myself at an interpretative parting of the
> ways. I could say 'The FBI seems to me to be over the top for an angry
> chimpanzee,' thereby alleviating the manifestations of the superego, per-
> secution and guilt; or, conversely, I could demonstrate the intensity of the
> rage, which might then turn back on him like a boomerang and give
> rise to an ultimately crippling depression. I opt for the second alternative
> and say in a light-hearted, 'joking' tone of voice: 'Perhaps it was not a
> chimpanzee but a serial killer in the form of an orang-utan.'
>
> The patient replies: 'I've just remembered a dream in which my mother
> phoned me, or actually turned up, and that for me was a natural disaster.'

In other words, my choice of the second alternative has been experienced by the patient as inappropriate, persecutory and invasive. I
could interpret accordingly, but I take care not to do so – that would
be like the natural-disaster mother turning up once again – and
instead, using the patient's narremes, I 'cook' the 'persecution' that
I activated with my interpretation. I pick up the anxiety, the experience of intrusion and the fear of having *beside* him such an invasive,
devastating mother, until a new figure comes to life: Lucilla, a nanny
who was able to relieve his anguish and calm him down when he was
small. In this way, the session is constructed in real time in accordance
with the constant signals furnished to us by the patient, or by any
other place in the field (such as the analyst's countertransference or
reveries, the patient's or the analyst's soma, or the setting).

At this point, it is worth considering in detail Corrao's (1991)
concept of 'narrative transformation', which is described as follows by
Baruzzi and Nebbiosi (1995):

> Corrao begins by considering the ability of mythical narration to
> combine 'various minor functional units that can be called nar-
> remes [. . .]' in a manner conducive to transformation. He then
> states that myth, 'by virtue of its narrative form [. . .], unites the

elements of a story in a manner reminiscent of the arrangement of the elements in a deductive system. No single element can be understood in isolation – that is, independently of its relationship with the other elements' [. . .]. This argument is considered further in terms of the group character of myth [. . .] and the specific ability of narration to effect a chronological reversal in which the recombination of the elements of the narration constructs a *narrative series* [. . .], and culminates in the fundamental formulation of *narrative peripeteia*: 'A narration may be linear and be resolved without peripeteias, or it may be complex, proceeding by peripeteias, to which it conforms because it contains recognitions that arise out of the very structure of the narration. On the other hand, the narrative peripeteia, in the categorial sense, is the central dimension of the great narrations that have been handed down to us; it is the change that takes place in a direction contrary to the current situation, constituting a *metabole* – that is, a reversal of time. Not only history but also philosophy and the exact sciences lack this capacity for *metabole* – for chronological reversal – which, on the other hand, is inherent in the structure of narration and has certainly been inherited from myth. So mythical knowledge would appear not to have waned and disappeared [. . .] but to have transmigrated into narrative structure in the function that resembles truth.'

At the beginning of the 1990s, the confluence of these themes, which, as it happens, are thoroughly interwoven throughout Corrao's oeuvre, led him to formulate a general and fundamental postulate:

[. . .] *case histories, interpretations during analytic sessions, and explanatory or hermeneutic theories of the analytic field all belong together in the category of transformational groups with a narratological or narrative character.* Although the performance of narrative transformations of a literary, historical or exegetic kind admittedly by no means amounts to the bringing about of analytic transformations, the truth of the contrary can nevertheless be assumed – that is, that analytic transformations possess the narrative dimension to an extremely high degree. This should be regarded as one of the fundamental parameters of the analytic field, or a fundamental analytic category.

All this differs radically from the situation in which the analyst has in his mind a thoroughly saturated theory and a precise diagnosis about a patient, from which he derives his interpretations, instead of

48

'listening humbly' to what the patient is trying to communicate. It is against this type of epistemic arrogance on the part of the analyst that Bion invoked the celebrated vaccine of being in the session 'without memory or desire'.

> A female adolescent patient dreams that she is in the house of her paternal grandmother, running round and round the table in the dining room pursued by a man and getting more and more terrified. She falls, hurts herself, gets up and continues to run.

While bearing in mind the various levels presented by the dream (Tuckett 2000), what is immediately evident is, I believe, an initial communication of the following kind: 'I feel pressured, pursued and terrified by my analyst's pressing interpretations; it is like being led to the crucifixion.'

This reading could be communicated, or could serve as a timing regulator; instead, however, led astray by the ideas of his particular school and the notion of a patient with a substantially hysterical structure, the analyst regards the dream as clearly of a 'sexual nature', interpreting that the patient felt guilty about having done something bad and expected to be punished for her thrilling and infectious attachment to her father. The patient responds to this interpretation by mentioning an air disaster with many fatalities and then absents herself for ten days.

It seems obvious to me that the analyst is here espousing a theory of his own, leaving no space for listening to the fact that the patient experienced the dream interpretation as a 'disaster', thereafter restoring a minimum of hope and consonance by skipping her sessions. This happens while the analyst continues to defend himself like a terrified child clinging to the theoretical skirts of his metapsychological mummy.

Hence, an analyst whose approach is to demonstrate to the patient, say, penis envy, castration, the primal scene or the Oedipus complex could be likened to a travel agency that organizes a world tour in which clients are allowed time to photograph the Eiffel Tower (so it is now Paris), the Sagrada Familia (so it is now Barcelona) and the Statue of Liberty (so it is now New York) without any trip actually having taken place; what we have here is a mere parody of an analysis.

What kind of 'driving' for Licia?
Licia is a patient who is becoming progressively more capable of

expressing her emotional experiences. She begins a session before the summer holidays by saying that she has a 'bad backache', which came on suddenly after she kissed a departing friend goodbye. She then immediately reports a dream: in it, she went into the therapist's 'new consulting room', which, however, was also 'one of her old homes'; she then had to leave in the rain and without her shoes, and, as she walked, she noticed with fear and surprise that hair was growing on her legs before her very eyes.

The patient immediately draws attention to the 'pain' of separation, but then, in the dream, she seems capable of forging a link between the new consulting room when she meets up with the therapist again after the holidays and the old consulting room, or home, from before the holidays; she also draws attention to the bad time, or bad weather [*tempo* in Italian means both time and weather], when she is left without the necessary requisites – the shoes represented by her sessions – and to the rising within her of a 'bestial rage', turning her as it were into Mr Hyde.

The therapist picks up the rage and describes the other affective movements in detail. In the next session, the patient brings another dream, in which she was in a car with a woman friend, who, however, was driving very fast and ultimately taking risks.

The dream can obviously be associated with the analyst's 'high-speed' interpretation of the first dream in the previous session, but, once this has been realized (and so far the problems are in the field of technique), there is the subjective problem of what to do with what has been understood – and here the problem is one of 'art'.

The first possibility is to give a saturated interpretation of the dream, along the lines of 'Perhaps you felt me to be something of a dangerous driver because of the way I interpreted your dream in the last session . . .' Alternatively, one could opt for a less saturated intervention, such as: 'The dream suggests to me that you would be calmer sitting beside a careful driver.' In my view, neither of these approaches is right or wrong; it is a matter of taste and sensitivity and, above all, it will be of fundamental importance to listen to the patient's subsequent communications. For instance, if, in the first example, she were to say 'Yesterday at the circus, a hippopotamus was jumping out of the ring and people could have been trampled underfoot', this would indicate that the analyst's interpretative activity was feared to be excessive and invasive; if, on the other hand, in the second example, she were to say 'Yesterday I was invited for a meal by some friends, but ended up almost starving', this would point to a need for a more explicit interpretation.

In the actual case, the therapist in fact skips over the dream and the patient talks about her friend 'Barbara', a borderline who alternates between periods of closeness and remoteness. This once again draws attention to the problem of the holidays and separation: from our patients' point of view, we are often 'barbarians' in that we look after them with close attention, only to leave them to their own devices when we go on holiday, or when they feel that we are on 'interpretative holiday'.

The patient ends the session by remarking that she really needs to wear a 'collar' for her back pain, but does not do so; she adds that she will go to the swimming pool, but will allow her friends to carry her 'bag'. In this way she seems to be modulating her own capacity to separate: she says no to being on the leash, acknowledging the relationship of dependence (which is perhaps too close), and yes to the help represented by going off with someone who will bear the 'weight' of her bag.

Duilio's spring water

It is interesting to compare this with the work done by the same therapist at about the same time with Duilio, a lad with many autistic characteristics but whose emotions have now been greatly mobilized.

Duilio begins a session following a week's break in the therapy by saying, as if talking to himself: 'Is there something wrong?' The therapist promptly responds: 'There were a few days when we didn't see each other, and that's what is wrong.' Duilio plays at drinking from a little bottle, saying: 'I'll drink some natural mineral water; it's so nice to drink this spring water.' He has manifestly felt the therapist's intervention to be absolutely on his wavelength and his comment is in line with this idea. Before the one-week interruption, he played a game in which he took away the therapist's shoes – thus symmetrically paralleling Licia's dream of 'being left without her shoes'. Whereas the boy plays an acting-out game that means 'This is what it feels like to have your shoes (sessions) taken away; I want *you* to feel it too', the adult patient says the same thing in a dream.

In the session, Duilio goes on to construct a magic wand (no doubt an omnipotent defence against separation, involving disavowal, but also demonstrating the capacity to create a game); he says: 'You must use this to build the little house.' Assisted by Duilio, the therapist starts building the house, which has three walls (Duilio has three sessions a week). This game corresponds to Licia's dream of the 'new consulting room' and the 'old homes', representing the possibility of thinking of a space within the therapy as the patient's own.

Maura's Russian doll

A young woman of nineteen is approaching the end of a six-year therapy. She takes a sheet of paper and divides it in half; then she divides the halves into further halves, and so on, until there are six pieces, which she places first side by side and then on top of each other. I tell her that it reminds me of a Russian doll. Maura now asks me for some adhesive tape and sticks the pieces together. I wonder how to convey to her the idea of the possible coexistence of infantile and increasingly adult aspects, as has actually been achieved in the years of therapy, and whether to work on the integration of parts, aspects or kinds of functioning, or to work not on space but instead on time, with a view to achieving 'chronological' integration.

I begin to say: 'There are six pieces of paper, and we have been working together for six years . . .', but am immediately interrupted by Maura, who takes out a 'mouse' drawn on a phone card and says: 'Isn't it disgusting.' So I decide against this explicit interpretation and look for a different way of drawing attention to the passage of time.

As stated earlier, a frequent technical problem with patients with severe affective deficiencies is that abstinence – the failure to answer direct questions and to ask questions ourselves – is 'classified' in the same category of traumatic behaviour as the patient's experience of a parental lack of interest and affective remoteness, so that the setting not only causes these traumas to 'live again' but increasingly becomes terribly traumatic in itself.

The only way out, in my view, is first to draw attention to the bringing back of the traumatic situation into the present, to reconstruct the traumatic situation, and then – something that is absolutely essential – to introduce 'shock absorbers' to soften the rigidity of the setting. These must be calibrated individually for each patient, bearing in mind that the ultimate aim is to eliminate them (although this may not always be feasible). With these and only these patients, this may entail, for example, answering their questions 'with analytic good sense' and sometimes accepting a modicum of disguised self-disclosure (it was, of course, Winnicott who was the pioneer in this respect, in his paper on hate in the countertransference). In particular, one needs a technique sophisticated enough to hide any 'trace of interpretative technique' in the way one talks to the patient.

Of course, given the need for these shock absorbers, all the rest of the analytic apparatus must be rigorously respected: not a single communication must be read by the analyst's mind as not being transference-related; no concessions must be made as regards strict observance of the setting; and there must be no relaxing of the analyst's analytic posture in the session.

The patients concerned are those who lacked care and affection and who are imbued with a fundamental distrust that is likely to emerge immediately upon any 'imperfection' along the analytic path. All this must be the subject of constant 'work', but in the (seeming) absence of any technique. André Green (1993) has written about such patients with rare mastery.

The above observations enable me to distinguish two ways of being an analyst, which can be likened to two ways of being a cook. Some rigorously espouse recipes of one kind or another, such as 'Envy must be interpreted immediately'; 'Envy must not be interpreted prematurely'; or 'Interpretations must be given immediately, and must only be transference interpretations'; 'Interpretations cannot be transference interpretations for a long time, and certainly not immediately'; 'The content must be interpreted immediately'; or 'Make sure you develop the container first!'

Some constantly sample their concoction during the course of the process, creating a 'special' analytic recipe for each individual patient: 'With *that particular* patient on *that particular* day, I felt it right to interpret in the transference and it seemed to me that it was working'; or 'I had to change tack and give only a tangential interpretation.' These analysts/cooks have no faith in recipes, but instead a taste for, and faith in, the 'sense' of the kitchen. They run the risk of people mistaking their approach, which has a great deal to do with their way of being an analyst, for a 'recipe' and imitating it. What can be taken from them is the method, not its content and the way it is applied. We cannot ask all cooks to be like that; it is acceptable, legitimate and human for there to be some who espouse recipes, and we must to some extent tolerate their being more faithful to the form than to the spirit of psychoanalysis.

Analysts of the first kind are full of certainties and know what is right or wrong. The second group have doubts, and are therefore able progressively to explore new solutions, in the knowledge that these will involve much more effort. The former are plunged into crisis by a patient who does not like 'cheese' (if included in the recipe!) or transference interpretations, while the latter enjoy working with atypical patients because they permit the creation of new and unexpected recipes. To become an analyst of the second type, one often needs to have belonged to the first type for a long time and to have visited many kitchens. For this reason, I am concerned, as regards the future development of psychoanalysis, by how little time many analysts currently devote to psychoanalytic practice proper, because only in this way is it possible, with the gradual passage of the years, to evolve an original and individual way of being an analyst that is not merely 'academic'.

Another peculiarity is that two analysts of one and the same school adhesively reinforce each other's positions without any development, whereas two analysts belonging to different schools will clash, again without any development, each convinced of the correctness of his own school and the falseness of the other's. Conversely, two analysts who are 'recipeless cooks' not only understand each other but succeed in mutually enriching each other. However, why is it that even analyses of the first type often work?

The answer, I believe, is simple: it is because, in analysis, we use our minds to carry out many more operations than we are aware of, which thus belong in areas of functioning not covered by schools, whereby transformations are effected without the analyst being in any way conscious of them. For instance, if an analyst is capable of listening and reflecting, he will, even if he espouses an old-fashioned drive-based model, receive β-elements and transform them into α, in the belief that he is reconstructing the patient's childhood.

However, let us return to the subject of interpretation.

A woman patient begins her session by saying that someone in the street wanted to swindle her by collecting money for children suffering from AIDS, and there were also other people who were trying to take her in, whom she could not figure out. The analyst eschews the easy response of transference decoding and takes up the patient's message, summarizing it and adding that such experiences are bound to give rise to rage and disorientation.

In our earlier diagram of the two prisms, this 'rage and disorientation' is precisely the additional 'x' contributed by the analyst. In effect, the patient's communication (a) has been summarized in the analyst's communication (a1) with the addition of the piece 'x' that gives rise to transformation. The patient comes along, let us say, with a set of message segments that are first 'organized' and to which an additional segment ('x') is contributed by the analyst.

This approach is most effective if the session proceeds on the basis of dialogue, in which what happens is not the 'squeezing out of the last ounce of meaning' by the analyst, but a succession of operations:

$$a \rightarrow a1 + x, \ b \rightarrow b1 + y, \ c \rightarrow c1 + z$$

that allow a virtually uninterrupted sequence of microtransformations concomitant with the development of the spiral dialogic progression.

The contribution of 'x' is, of course, the transformational factor, which must conform to the patient's capacity for absorbing it. As stated, the patient will signal any excess or deficiency.

After a session that developed well, a therapist considers that he can give a strong, decoding interpretation centred on the patient's internal world. The patient begins the next session by talking about his 'boss, who is always shouting and bullying at work', and adds that he does not like *his* style of working: he is always in a hurry, and the patient is sometimes afraid that his boss wants to kill him by making him have an accident. The therapist immediately realizes what has happened, abstains from interpreting it, and in his subsequent interventions 'receives' what the patient says, at the same time describing the emotions involved. The patient then mentions a girl he knew, with whom he immediately felt on the same wavelength, and he emerges from the persecutory climate induced by what he experienced as excessive interpretative pressure.

A young patient tells his woman analyst that he often sees prostitutes in the street and that, apart from the fact that they disgust him because they are dirty . . . 'Well . . .' he adds, 'I don't know how to tell you this.'

The analyst desists from giving an academic interpretation, which would be only too obvious and, developing what the patient himself has said, adds: 'And you feel attracted and tempted to go along with them.' The patient replies: 'I see you understand me.' In other words, instead of interpreting the contempt, attack and disparagement, she helps the patient to become aware of his wish for an encounter with the analyst, who is also disparaged, but who is thereby 'transformed' from a prostitute into someone who understands.

For the analyst, it is, I believe, very difficult to forgo the role of the holder and decoder of emotional truths and instead to espouse the more modest function of an 'enzyme' of transformation – but no analyst should forget Winnicott's well-known remark about all the changes he prevented from taking place in patients on account of his own need to interpret, instead of being capable of promoting the creative capacity of the patients themselves.

I shall now give a detailed account of some analytic sessions to illustrate different interpretative modalities matched to individual patients' capacities for metabolization and digestion, as constantly signalled – as I shall never tire of repeating – by their responses to interpretations.

Four sessions with Lisa

Lisa (Ferro 2005b) is a 34-year-old patient in her tenth year of analysis, on which she embarked because of panic attacks and severe agoraphobia sometimes accompanied by experiences of depersonalization and derealization. In the first years of the analysis she was often assailed in her sessions by quasi-hallucinatory states – waking dream flashes rather than true hallucinations – that resulted in confusional states. She had given up her studies and lived shut up at home with no relationships at all.

Simultaneously with the analysis (four sessions a week), she had commenced drug treatment as prescribed by an analytically trained psychiatrist who kept track of the analytic work and was called upon to deal with any problem arising outside the analysis.

The first years were extremely difficult – even getting Lisa to accept the need for a setting with sufficiently established rules. After a few years, Lisa finally agreed to lie down on the couch, which had previously caused her such unbearable anxiety that I had had to accept the face-to-face position; in the session after the one when Lisa lay down for the first time, she dreamed that she was on a child's slide made of sharp blades that cut into her – so agonizing was the loss of visual contact with me.

During her childhood Lisa had been traumatized both by the lack of the most elementary care from her parents and by the violent intrusions of a seriously disturbed brother. This caused me quite a few technical problems: in Lisa's eyes I was always in the wrong, doing either too little or too much. For a long time I felt myself to be treading a fine line between her overwhelming alternate catastrophic anxieties of abandonment and of violent intrusion.

Prolonged work carried out with commitment, passion and pain on

Lisa's part as well as my own gradually enabled her to develop a capacity for containing emotions instead of allowing them to inundate the field: she had innumerable dreams of flooding, rivers bursting their banks, or Venice under water. Eventually she began to go out again, resumed her studies, got her degree, married and began work first as a school librarian and then as a temporary teacher in a vocational training college.

Lisa then had her first child; on discovering that she was pregnant and feeling much surer of herself and her mental stability, she agreed with the prescribing psychiatrist that she would stop taking her medication. It is interesting to note that this also led her to accept the analytic setting more readily. For a long time in the sessions, Lisa had needed two *drugs*: the need, first, for me to reply, however tangentially, to her questions, and, second, to 'burst the banks' of her sessions by often going on for several minutes over time. Her decision to give up her medication and to respect the setting constituted a mental rebirth and a dawning of the awareness of time within the analysis.

Over the many years of the analysis I felt that I was confronted with a jigsaw into which new pieces constantly had to be fitted, or with a Russian doll containing an infinite succession of smaller dolls.

Now that the possibility of termination of Lisa's analysis is perhaps in the air, in retrospect I can discern previously unseen connections that can be summarized in the following diagram:

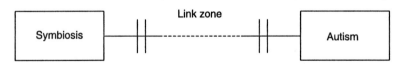

This is a schematic representation of a constant oscillation between attempts at symbiotic fusion (the conflicts over the setting, the intolerance of frustration and of not getting immediate answers to questions or requests) and a kind of autistic withdrawal (when frustration was excessive) that led Lisa to collapse into a state where she could communicate neither with herself nor with me, often through the device of pseudo-sessions filled with empty words and non-relating.

For a long time we worked on these symbiotic 'clods' – all attempts to break these up being met with panic attacks that burst on to the scene like eruptions of uncontainable lava-like emotions – as well as on the autistic withdrawal in which she took refuge.

57

We devoted years to talking about her 'brother', in whom characteropathic evacuations alternated with autistic manifestations, which it became possible only with difficulty to see as the way Lisa herself operated in alternation with her symbiotic functioning.

A significant turning point occurs in about the eighth year of Lisa's analysis, when, after a short absence, I return to find Lisa utterly desperate, regressed and incapable of speaking. Slowly she tells me that for many years she has been silently desperate and furious because the *door* in my waiting room that leads to another room that I use as an office has always been closed. For several sessions I naturally interpret this closed door in all possible ways: exclusion and the resulting rage, my absence, my mental non-availability, and all the metaphorical meanings of a 'closed door' that I could think of. She adds that even if I were to open the door it would mean nothing because I would be doing it only because she asked me to.

The monstrous thing in her eyes is that for years I have not *heard* her request. At this point the patient herself realizes with amazement that this request – to have the door opened – has never been expressed, and *that is why* I have not heard it. She immediately goes on to say that if I were really fond of her I ought to have been able to hear her request even though she never actually expressed it to me.

The day after this session she telephones me – this is unprecedented – to say that she feels very, very bad and asks if I can 'see' her the next day for an extra session (something I never agree to!).

I sense that an extremely important match is being played here, and I manage to accept what I see as a difficult violation of my setting and say 'yes', because it seems to me that something concrete has to 'happen' – that a door needs to be opened: in my mind I transform the closed door of the waiting room into the opening door, outside the usual setting, of my consulting room. I do this in the conviction that without this interpretation, this acting-in, there will be no possibility of transformation.

Next day Lisa arrives smiling, saying that this time I 'heard' her request even if she had to express it: she had been quite certain that I would answer 'no'. It is the first time – she says – that I have actually 'heard' a request of hers, and adds that up to now it has always been as though a baby was crying desperately and no mother ever came to its aid. This time the mother said 'eh' – that is, she has actually answered – but Lisa wonders only why her call is answered with the word 'è' (is) – why with a verb? (The usual Italian response to a call is 'eh?', as a

58

sign of acknowledgement that the message has been received.) The word play between the response 'eh' and the verb 'è' (is) suggests to me that the meaning is: 'Only a mother who responds *is* a mother.'

We go over all this on the basis of the work done so far, and a kind of fog that enveloped this maternal transference, which we have always 'known' about but never actually experienced, seems to lift.

My acting-in gave me much food for thought; perhaps it was not necessary, but it brought down the last barrier in a tunnel dug out over a long period from both ends. Now Lisa and I talk about termination, aware that we still have to throw light on the area linking the Scylla of symbiosis with the Charybdis of autistic functioning, while making it possible to inhabit the area of the link in which trust in the object begins to be recognized.

This work has greatly stabilized Lisa on the emotional level: on the one hand, her dreams are richer and less disjointed, constituting a particularly valuable channel of communication and transformation, and on the other her relationship with her husband has become more solid. They still quarrel periodically, but the quarrels are increasingly containable. Quarrels with her husband often draw attention to something wrong in the analysis.

Her second child – a girl – was born recently and the possibility of termination has been in the air for several months and is being seriously planned for.

I shall now present a flashback to two sessions from the third year of Lisa's analysis. The first dates from a period of hospitalization when Lisa was allowed out to attend her sessions. She was sent to hospital by the psychiatrist owing to the risk of self-harm and to establish the right dose for her medication.

Session 1
The patient is still standing in the centre of the consulting room with an air of defiance. She has come in without using the entryphone, having been given a key to the street door of the block where my consulting room is located on a busy main road, so that she could come up immediately in case of a panic attack.

Patient. If you're angry with me, tell me right away.
Analyst. Why should I be?
Patient. Because I opened the street door myself without ringing the bell.

Analyst. I expect you had a good reason.

Patient. Yes, it was raining and I was afraid I would end up with an ugly face, my lipstick might run and my hair might get soaked.

Analyst. You were afraid your makeup might disappear and reveal an 'ugly face' – perhaps a very angry one.

[*With a slightly less combative air she lies down on the couch.*]

Patient. Yes, I am angry. You must say something nasty to me, then we'll be quits, after what I said to you yesterday.

Analyst. That was what we call 'Paolo'. [*Paolo is the name of her disturbed brother. In our language it also stands for the mode of functioning of the patient herself, blocked and violently incontinent by turns; she had hurled violent insults at me on the previous day.*]

Patient. Yes, but you mustn't say that: 'Paolo' is what I hate most in the world; you can't tell me I'm like that; I don't want to hear any more about him; he's hateful. They told me I was aggressive in the hospital too.

Analyst. Well, maybe 'Paolo' has reasons of his own from his point of view; he might be that way because he's wounded, very frustrated . . . like your 'boxer' that time [*a reference to a childhood memory when her dog bit a cyclist who had run over and hurt it*].

Patient. Yes, I remember, when an animal is wounded it's unapproachable. I feel like someone who's been out in the snow, in the cold, and then even tepid water feels scalding.

Analyst. We know there is snow and cold far away from here, and if your feelings for me are not even affectionate, but just tepid, that hurts you – it feels scalding.

Patient. I don't understand how I feel; it's as though half of me was in a swimsuit and half in an anorak. I am fond of you, I need you and I hate you – well, not you actually. I hate Dr 'Battaglia' [*Dr Battle*], he's terrible. This morning again in the hospital Dr Battaglia said no tranquillizers because they would be covering up a symptom; we have to find the right medication and I can't manage any longer without a bit of 'tranquillizer', but I realize he too is right; then I come here and you see everything differently, you're more understanding. The two places – the hospital and here – are so different. The hospital is full of ill-treatment, violence and incomprehension, and the doctors are incompetent . . .

Analyst. It seems there are 40 kilometres between me and Dr Battaglia, like from here to the hospital. But maybe one reason why you're in the hospital is so that you can tell me about a place where terrible, monstrous, inhuman things happen . . . I am understanding . . . available . . . but Dr Battaglia is like how you experience me from another point of view – that is, as cruel, as someone who doesn't give you a 'tranquillizer' – the hugs and kisses you want – which you yourself are basically prepared to give up.

Patient. I understand what you are saying: so my stay in hospital is not so useless, it serves a purpose, at least for understanding a part of me that I don't know, the part you call by the name I don't even want to speak [*Paolo*]. But apart from that you haven't understood anything about me: I'm absolutely not prepared to give up hugs and kisses, I want them, I must have them . . . otherwise I'll go mad; I *must* find someone to hug and kiss me . . .

Analyst. I think you can find *me* – not that way, but instead through being together and understanding together; I think you must give up the idea of getting those things concretely here.

Patient. I had a dream: a mother had a baby, and there was a festive atmosphere, but soon afterwards the baby died and she was absolutely desperate . . . just like me waiting for you finally to show some affection towards me, and you are doing that, but I need physical contact, caresses, embraces, what I have never had and what you make me realize I have never had; I have never wanted anything else – you talk about it to me, but you don't give it to me . . . it's like going to a restaurant and looking at the menu but not getting any food to eat.

Analyst. Perhaps I still haven't found a way of making you feel something with more life and truth than a menu; I give you a bit of warmth, something is born, and then I immediately disappoint you.

Patient. No! Don't you understand, I want concrete things, hugs and kisses, and I know even the dream says so, I can only cry for what I lose, for what I have lost . . . it's all hopeless . . .

Analyst. Well, perhaps you're meeting Dr Battaglia *now* – someone who is utterly strict, a doctor who ends sessions, leaving you in terrible pain, after the terrible pain of lying down on the couch . . . as well as the festive atmosphere of seeing me and then straight away losing me, so you can't eat me with your eyes.

Patient. Well, incredible as it may seem, I must tell you that in the hospital too I saw a room with an analyst's couch.

It is some months later, after she leaves hospital and has begun to come along unaccompanied. The Monday session reported below comes before one I told her I would have to cancel on the following

Wednesday. Owing to Lisa's symbiotic structure, any change in the setting always upsets her terribly.

Session 2

Patient [*curling up on the couch*].   Who was the person I met on Friday? He is persecuting me; wherever I go I see him; I go to a concert and he's there; I go to a lecture on psychology or psychiatry and he's there; last time he said he was having analysis . . . I can't stand his being there . . . he says hallo to everyone . . . he's always in a good mood . . . . he must be a student of psychiatry . . . or psychology . . . maybe he wants to do this work here . . . I've already seen him come up here . . .

Analyst.   I think you are continuing what you were saying on Friday: perhaps it's the plan that you yourself have, which has been on your mind for quite a time, to enrol for psychology once you've got your philosophy degree, and also the idea of fully accepting the idea of *having analysis* properly. And I must tell you that the person is Dr X; I'm telling you this so that you aren't put out if you should ever need his help. [*We had agreed that during the summer holidays when neither I nor her usual psychiatrist was available she could go to a colleague, who was in fact Dr X.*]

[*Lisa throws herself to the ground, screams, bangs her head and hands on the floor, rolls over and over, rushes round the room and finally kneels beside the couch.*]

Analyst.   I see that has upset you.

Patient.   How can I trust you; you would have sent me to someone with a face like that . . . how can I trust you . . . I hate and detest that person – I know it's nothing to do with him, he's probably good and honest, it's me who is upset and not well . . . I've had nightmares and I wanted to talk to you about them. Now shut up, or I'll smash your consulting room to bits . . . Totò Riina [*the Sicilian Mafia boss*] is nothing compared to me; I nearly cut my cat's throat . . . I want to kill someone. Here are my nightmares: a puppy was trying to get to its mother, but there was a sort of glass panel between them . . . then their noses touched . . . now I thought its mother would make a fuss of it, but instead she slit its throat and ate it. Then on Saturday I had a panic attack; I had gone out with Piero, there was a baby crying, it was terrible . . . then I dreamt that my whole room had been turned topsy-turvy . . . and when I lifted up a piece of cloth there were mice and snakes . . . and then a hospital . . . they asked me if I was the inspector and I said no . . . and I couldn't park the car . . . there were people on drips . . . like dead or alive . . .

62

people with holes for breathing tubes . . . and then terrible needles they put in like drips . . . needles that really hurt.

Analyst. I seem to recognize myself in the mother who eats her puppy instead of showing affection for it, just as I am eating Wednesday's session. I frighten you and make you suffer when I open my mouth: when I say 'having analysis' [*in the sense that the patient wants something concrete from me, rather than 'having analysis'*], it infuriates you and makes you cry. And then the topsy-turvy room – it's just like the analysis this week. You decide not to be the inspector, like when you kept asking me questions and demanding answers . . . and then you discover suffering, the hole left by the Wednesday session . . . the resuscitation unit, and there too, just like what I'm telling you, for now my treatment is more like needles that arouse fear and pain . . .

Patient. In Pavia there's a famous criminal doctor who doesn't give a damn about other people's pain – it's Professor Y, the transplant surgeon . . .

Analyst. I think my operating on your feelings makes me like Professor Y in your eyes – partly because I am excising the session on Wednesday.

Five years later, Lisa has completely given up her medication because she has decided to have a child, and is now three months pregnant. In the session before the one reported below, Lisa mentioned her terror at the idea that anyone might know she was having analysis. I tried to understand this fear better, but in a persecutory crescendo 'the primary school teacher who forced her to read things she did not know how to read' had immediately appeared, so I had abstained from going into this material in greater depth. She then said how ashamed she would feel if her neighbours saw the mess in her house, and I interpreted this communication in the transference. Next to appear was her husband, who, seeing her undress, said: 'What horrible big legs you've got.' The image of an enormous gorilla arose before me in a reverie. In the next session Lisa called her old way of functioning with drugs 'Europe', while 'Rwanda' was her new way of existing without them, in which she was a prey to new and violent emotional states that no longer belonged to her. Other characters make up a family lexicon of this analysis. The session described below takes place on a Monday after I have had to cancel the Friday session.

Session 3

Patient. I've been feeling absolutely awful, panic attacks again . . . I was

terrified . . . I wanted to run away . . . but I couldn't move. I couldn't go
to work . . . I was in total panic.

Analyst. What do you think might have happened to you?

Patient. I really don't know, something to do with home, I don't know . . .
not the analysis . . . my husband is far away . . . away from home . . .
I'm relieved that he's not there . . . but terrified because he's not there.

Analyst. Your feelings seem to have been all mixed up and conflicting:
good feelings because he was away but also bad ones because he
was away [*for the time being I avoid a possible transference
interpretation*].

Patient. Then I saw two films on television – *Krakatoa East of Java* and
King Kong (the black-and-white version) – and I couldn't sleep at night
either.

Analyst. Certain situations seem to set off a volcano or arouse a gorilla,
and then you run away or are left paralysed, or at any rate terrified. It
seems to me that the volcano and the gorilla stand for emotions that you
weren't able to 'read one at a time', and when they all appeared
together they terrified you. I thought that was what you were really
saying in the last session when you talked about the teacher who forced
you to read things that you didn't know how to read – which is what *I*
was doing by insisting on trying to get you to say why it would be so
monstrous for anyone to know you were having analysis.

Patient. You surely haven't spoken to me like this for a long time; I think
you've understood me and are close to me. And I've had three dreams.
In the first I was on a motorway and had to go from one place to
another, but there were flyovers, forks and junctions. I couldn't understand anything and was panicking. In the second dream Angela, my
maid, had taken some shitty sheets to the laundry; I felt utterly
ashamed; it just wasn't possible – and then the laundry didn't clean
them but sent them back dirty. The third dream took place in the country, where they were cutting a tree down – it was the tree of life, how
could they do such a thing, it was quite agonizing and yet they were
doing it, and I felt desperate . . .

Analyst. What do the dreams suggest to you?

Patient. Nothing. I used to know how to comment on dreams, and lots of
ideas came to me, but not any longer. I don't know what to say . . . I
feel as if I am lost in Rwanda and don't know which way to go . . .

Analyst. I think that after so much Europe where you understood and
helped me, it's important to be in Rwanda, because that's where
we have to improve our reading skills. Perhaps the teacher really is

necessary. The first dream seems to me to be connected with our missed session: in Europe, you feel 'This damned analyst of mine absolutely infuriates me – oh well, I'll see him on Monday', but in Rwanda it's all confusion, you can't find the right road or, even worse, you're in a jungle which you have to get through from Thursday to Monday.

Patient. That's what I felt: I was terrified and lost; I can recognize myself in that, but I haven't a clue what to say about the second dream – perhaps just the sense of disgust.

Analyst. The second dream reminds me of the previous session: you showed me things you are ashamed of, you mentioned 'big legs' (fat, ugly legs), and you were afraid I might say you had ugly parts that were horrible to see, and telling me you had never laid yourself bare . . .

Patient. [*interrupting me*] No, no, that's wrong. Those would be mature thoughts, not ones from Rwanda. What I feel is different. Maybe it is shame and embarrassment at what I told you . . . it goes much, much deeper, it's fear and shame about the thoughts I don't express, the ones even I don't know, which *you* can't 'launder' because they haven't been expressed.

Analyst. Perhaps they are unexpressed, dirty and impossible to confess, and I'm not up to the job of laundering them.

Patient. No, it goes even deeper; for now we don't know what they are – they are thoughts that I still don't know how to express.

Analyst. And they're like shit that can't be cleaned away, but perhaps it's shit that needs to be 'analysed', and that's what terrifies you – the fact that we know we have to analyse the shit and with it your needs.

Patient. There's something in that, but what about the tree of life?

Analyst. The third dream suggests to me that on one level we missed a session and you don't like that, but on another level cancelling the session is like cutting down the tree of life – a catastrophe that causes an eruption of emotions, rage, fury and despair.

Patient. Well, I don't really feel that.

Analyst. Perhaps it's too painful to feel.

Patient. Yes, this time you're right, the teacher's reading is correct. I was thinking I felt relieved to be coming here today; I saw a TV programme where relatives met up again after 49 years . . . and I felt some emotion . . . I was a bit tearful, as I am now.

Analyst. Perhaps it was the emotion about today's session: you feel as if the time from Thursday to Monday was not just a few days but 49 years . . .

Patient. No, that's not right, except what you say about time. In Pavia you can get anywhere by car in five minutes if there is no traffic, but not in the jungle: time is different there. But I told you what I did because I really felt an emotion when I saw you again and you saw me again, and I was really moved. On the subject of time, tell me, could we have a session in jungle time, lasting four, five or six hours – just answer me. If you say no, and I know you will, my hate for you will know no bounds.

Analyst. Maybe you are asking me this on purpose to bring on the hate now that we are about to part: you would rather have the gorilla with the big fat legs and the volcano than feel your need for analysis and for me. We are your life, but as a piece of homework you could read about what this gorilla is made of, and everything you didn't want to feel again – the pain at the tree of life being cut down.

Two years have passed.

Session 4 (part)

Patient. Beppe [*her husband*] has come back, but is going away again soon . . . The children need set times . . . hard and fast rules . . . and Beppe often doesn't understand this. Well, I've had two dreams. In the first I was at home: my daughter opened the door without asking who was there and a dropout walked in – one of those with beer bottles and their ears pierced . . . I was afraid he would hurt my children, so I woke Beppe and he managed to get him out of our house. In the second dream I was in a train, telling myself I would get off as soon as the time was right.

Analyst. What do you make of them?

Patient. The first dream puts me in mind of the negative thoughts I have about analysis, about you – that you are not a relative but an outsider, that you are not my father, but *only* my analyst. I can't bear this idea, but then I have resources I can rely on so as not to spoil the good things that I do have. The second dream is about the termination: as soon as I can manage it, I'll get off and then . . . that will be that.

Analyst. You said first that rules and set times are important for children. Now I think the dropout is the wish to overturn all the rules, for me to be not just your analyst. If this thought gains a hold you feel it is dangerous, but now you have the resources to cope with it even at weekends. In the second dream it almost seems that analysis is something to be run away from – and that it won't be possible to set a date when the time comes.

Patient. I know you're happy to be my analyst, but I don't know if I'll ever be able to accept this. I'd like you to be a member of the family, a friend, a relative I can go on seeing for the rest of my life even after the analysis is over.

Let us now bring the story up to date. Lisa is mourning for her acceptance of the fact that I am *only* her analyst. She often dreams of out-of-order telephone lines that are repaired, and stable communication has now been established between us. The idea of life after analysis raises many problems. She recently dreamed of a house that was icy-cold and full of deep-frozen dead bodies, and when she approached a second house there was a killer with a gun who wanted to kill her, but then the police arrived to rescue her. Finally, there was a tiny house, which was well built, a bit sad, but with flowers. How she had toiled to have just a small house, even if it did have a solid floor and new walls!

We work on the dreams together and see them as representing both the course of the analysis and three mental states that she has negotiated: deep-frozen emotions of loneliness and emotional frost; and then fear when over-keen emotions make her feel terribly in danger and persecuted until the police arrive: Lisa associates the police (the third state) to my answering her call and responding with 'eh/è'. The last dream, Lisa says, puts her in mind of all the analytic toil involved in arriving at the point described by Salvatore Quasimodo with great simplicity and humanity as follows: 'Everyone stands alone at the heart of the world / pierced by a ray of sunlight / and suddenly it is evening.'

A session with Nicola

The patient in this session is in the process of reowning the possibility of experiencing and expressing his emotions.

I regard all characters mentioned as characters of the session, any external reference being only a seeming one. There are no characters whom I do not see as included in the field and generated by it. This idea resembles Widlöcher's '*co-pensée*' or Ogden's 'analytic third'. Moments with relatively unsaturated interventions alternate in the session with ones in which the interpretations are more focused and saturated.

Patient. Life at the hospital is getting harder and harder. Yesterday I tried all morning to go to the toilet: I went to the downstairs toilets, but they were absolutely disgusting . . . all filthy and blocked . . . It's absolutely shameful. I really got very, very angry.

Analyst. And then?

Patient. I didn't go, and wrote a letter to the head of health and safety – a letter of protest. My colleague Marina said 'You should talk to the head of the department about it first' and I answered '. . . Are you a revolutionary, then?'

Analyst. Everyone basically has the right to protest at an annoying situation like that.

Patient. I should think so! I wasn't able to relieve myself because the bogs were so filthy and revolting!

Analyst. [*jokingly*]: Well, you can't expect me to be lucid and brilliant all the time; sometimes the *sanitari* [*the Italian word has a double meaning: either toilets or doctors*] do sometimes get blocked. It's perfectly understandable if you get angry when that happens.

Patient. I was called to the obstetric department for a termination certificate; there was a woman who didn't want to give birth to a potentially malformed child . . . but it wasn't definite; the child might actually turn out to be normal . . .

Analyst. I wonder if perhaps you are afraid that you might have to 'abort' any critical thoughts or grumbles about me. Maybe you were wondering whether you could allow yourself to think certain things – whether that's normal or not.

Patient. . . . it's not easy for me; I always had to behave myself, to do things properly, to behave the way I was expected to behave. It's hard for me to believe that I can think such things and come out with them. The other day, my boss had drawn up the holiday schedule and I would have liked to say to him '. . . What the fuck are you up to?' I didn't, of course, but afterwards I felt as if I was getting an ulcer . . .

Analyst. A 'well behaved' boy wouldn't tell me: 'What kind of a fucking holiday are you taking this year? Even your summer holidays are different from usual!' If you can come out with that, then perhaps 'cutting comb and wattles' [*a reference to earlier sessions*] will stop forming part of your morning toilet like shaving.

Patient. . . . if only . . .

He leaves with a broad smile.

In this session the movement of the field is evident from the linkage between the various characters: how I really did feel unavailable (slow on the uptake) in the previous session, how the patient draws my attention to this, and how I am now able to accept his protests as legitimate.

A session with Filippo

The patient in the next session is Filippo, who is nearing the end of his first year of analysis. He has to steer a course between a general need for pacification so as not to lose the affection he needs, and a wish for greater autonomy that impels him to assert his identity. He feels very persecuted by saturated, direct and transference-based interpretations (after one of which he said: 'My computer was struck by lightning and completely burnt out and it doesn't work any more!'). Consequently, my style is very narrative, indirect and allusive, and will remain so until the field signals the possibility of more precise interventions, which must not, however, break the container.

> *Patient.* Today I am full of rage at my mother; it was only when I came here that I was able to calm down.
>
> *Analyst.* What happened?
>
> *Patient.* My mother wanted me to go and vote – for the candidate she favoured, of course.
>
> *Analyst.* So you didn't feel able to make a free choice.
>
> *Patient.* Precisely. I can't decide to go for one party or another. My mother would like me to vote for the Lega, or else for Formigoni [*an arch-conservative politician*] . . . but look at all the harm he has done to the health system!
>
> *Analyst.* Two unacceptable ideas, which are just the opposite of what you feel.
>
> [*Meanwhile I recall that this week the patient is increasing his number of sessions from three to four: how much of a free choice does he have in this? Does he think I want to tie him up (the Lega, or Northern League, is a secessionist party, but in Italian its name means to bind, to tie or to tie up)? I then remember that in the last session I was colder and more detached than usual, owing to personal concerns that had nothing to do with Filippo's analysis.*]
>
> *Patient.* Last night I had a dream: I was on a road and arrived at a refurbished house. I didn't like the refurbishment, as the whole thing was cold. There were lots of bathrooms, one for each bedroom.
>
> *Analyst* [*I imagine he is describing my mental functioning in the last*

session – cold and impersonal – and I avoid giving a transference interpretation]. So it's more like a hotel than a house – cold, but with one bathroom for each bedroom.

Patient. That's right! I even remember a four-star hotel in Paris, the Carlton, which had the same effect on me. Everything seemed perfect, with brasswork [*oh dear, if only I had a less metallic surname than Ferro, which means iron*], but it was impersonal. At one time, I often used to go to Paris on business, with a female colleague. She would always bring candles and photographs to personalize the hotel room.

Analyst. So you 'need' a 'house' with a little fireplace and a stove [*a reference to material from earlier sessions*].

Patient. Yes, not a hotel but a comfortable house, like when I was small and we lived in a 150-square-metre house [*three 50-minute sessions?*], full of love and warmth. Then we moved to a larger house . . . It's true, there were four of us children . . .

Analyst. Did you feel a bit lost?

Patient. Yes, it was less intimate.

Analyst [*avoiding any interpretation about our change of setting and my reduced mental presence in the previous session*]. Anyway, in the commercial [*one currently featuring on all Italian television channels*], ET says 'Phone, home' and not 'Phone, Carlton'!

Patient [*laughing, reassured, warmer, as if the usual climate had been restored*]. Now I remember a second dream I had. There was a schoolmaster, a cross between Baglioni [*a well-known Italian singer*] and Maldini [*a football coach*]; he was teaching a class of children and doing it well, very well, explaining everything very clearly.

Analyst. And the children felt that someone was by their side while they were learning.

Patient. I sometimes have moments of depression when I feel all by myself, but it doesn't take much to warm me up again . . . My girlfriend bought me a Boublet record which I really liked . . . he sings 'Gonna go to my home . . . my home . . .'

Analyst. The pleasure of finding your way back to a familiar, warm place [*I feel that we have found our way back to each other and that emotional contact has been re-established; the session continues with alternating accounts of the patient's childhood, old houses, removals and the pleasure of having a space for oneself*].

Analyst [*at end the session*]. We two are refurbishing things this week. Hopefully you will not miss the little stove and the fireplace. As for the photographs you are going to bring along . . . they are all welcome!

He leaves with a smile.

At the beginning of the session, I try to encourage the field's expanding movements by seemingly attributing great importance to the manifest meaning of the patient's account. Guided by his anger, I then succeed in making contact with my own experience and as it were working through my countertransference (Brenman and Pick 1985). The restored emotional contact with myself opens the way to the patient's affects connected with my coldness or our change of setting. In this way, these emotions, searching for a way to be put into words, find a possible path, perhaps for the first time, towards emergence and definition, to the extent that they can ultimately be made explicit.

Of course, this material also contains infantile themes. Once transformed, these will inhabit the internal world differently. Progressively, and after the repeated operation of *Nachträglichkeit*, they will radically rewrite the history of the patient's childhood and family romance. Many themes which have not yet emerged (for example, the maternal function, or idealization) constitute the narrative threads to be eventually woven into a fabric.

3

Psychosomatic pathology or metaphor: problems of the boundary

This chapter is intended not to supply answers but as a part of the process of working through a problem that is still too complex to admit of any exhaustive solution. My hope is only that 'working' on the problem may help us to take some steps in the right direction.

Minimum certainties

The problem I wish to address is whether, given a patient's communication, 'what is communicated to us' is causally related to a particular mode of being or doing on our part, or whether what we are told is just one of the many possible ways of recounting to us what is happening on the mental level.

Let me explain. After a very 'heavy', 'spicy' interpretation of mine, in the next session the patient reports a stomach ache. Is what *is relevant to me* as an analyst the causal explanation that my interpretative overdose has given him a stomach ache, or is it the fact that his chosen way of drawing my attention to the overdose is the account of the stomach ache, and that, failing the stomach ache, he could have described the same emotion to me otherwise? For instance, he might have said: 'In a film I saw, some prisoners were forced to eat yucky food,' or 'I dreamt that a cloudburst flooded the town so you couldn't cross from one part to another.'

In other words, what is the analytic status of the character 'stomach ache' within the analytic session? Is it a 'character' that I must consider on the 'realistic' level, as a 'thing' or 'fact' (and, in this sense, an aggregate of β-elements), or can I see it instead as a narrative sub-unit that already signifies something and awaits the assignment of further meanings (in my idiolect, this subunit would be a *narrative derivative of the α-elements* of the session at the moment of its narration)?

Gabriella's fishes

Gabriella, a postgraduate student doing a PhD in mathematics, is unable to accept and use the cautious, measured interpretations given by her young analyst. She responds by mentioning a female acquaintance who has herself written a 'thesis', of which she is envious: she does not understand the thesis, but merely thinks that she herself would not be able to write it. Clearly, the interpretations, at least in the form in which they were 'prepared', are not a factor of growth, for they prove to have been a 'thesis' of the analyst that arouses envy and feelings of inadequacy.

Immediately afterwards, the patient describes a little room with a computer (again in the house of someone she knows) – a room that was also full of tanks containing fishes and other marine creatures; there was in addition a small tank with turtles that were trying to get out. She felt rooted to the spot as if in a horror film. She adds that she likes fishes, but if, for example, she goes to an aquarium, she comes out in a state of fever. Gabriella goes on to say that these were living beings that she could not control – beings with a life of their own that don't do what you tell them to do. And they might get out of the tanks, jump on her and terrify her.

Next, she says that on her own computer she has installed a screen-saver showing a 'sea-bottom scene' . . . although she is afraid of water and cannot swim. It seems obvious to me that she is talking about her 'own submerged world', about how it is full of living emotion-fishes she feels unable to manage, which 'are there', alive and capable of jumping out and terrifying her . . . So they are stripped of their affective content, flattened and managed by means of the computer.

I forgot to mention that, at the beginning of the session, Gabriella had mentioned a 'rubbish dump' with a treatment unit, but there was still a risk of pollution. So the other way of managing all these emotion-fishes was to evacuate them, because they could not be cooked. This is illustrated by the following illustration, which relates to a project for promoting literacy in Russia as an alternative to seeking easier ways of managing anxiety such as alcoholism.

The task of the analysis will therefore be to supply the patient with the instruments – the α-function on the one hand and the satisfactory operation and development of ♀ ♂ on the other – that will enable her

to 'metabolize', 'cook' and 'experience' these emotion-fishes. Plainly, it will not be a matter of simply interpreting all this; instead, the analysis will have to become the place for reactivation – or perhaps activation for the first time – of the (mental) functions that are not up to the task of handling the patient's emotional needs. Again, it is hardly necessary to say that, as regards her attitude to food, the patient's behaviour is borderline anorexic: she can eat only 'crumbs'.

But why is it that, in this patient, everything remains on the mental level, or at least on a level capable of narration, whereas, in others, the same situation *could* give rise to the development of a psychosomatic illness, in which, for example, the place of the 'rubbish dump' might be taken by an attack of colitis, or indeed by a bout of Crohn's disease?

A provisional answer might be that we are dealing, after all, not with the actual discharges of colitis or of Crohn's disease, but with the *telling* of these, so that the 'rubbish dump' or 'Crohn's disease' are characters of the session – and, just as the real rubbish dump *is irrelevant to me*, so too is the real Crohn's disease, and consequently I shall be interested only in the story, in the entire complex of 'narremes' that will allow me to activate thoughts and transformations.

The problem of the 'rubbish dump' or 'Crohn's disease' might well subsequently be solved in the analysis, but only secondarily, and that is perhaps all I could know about it.

Anselmo's high-voltage electricity

A patient mentions 'closeness and warmth' and 'arrow shots that cause epileptic fits' – two entities that he sees as opposites. The latter are felt to be accumulations of high-voltage electricity that seek discharge and lead to the loss of consciousness and convulsions. However, can what the patient is talking about also be thought of as an epileptic trigger, so that whenever an excess of emotional voltage arises in a patient or indeed in anyone else, 'epilepsy' supervenes, and do we then have an *ethical obligation* to remain on the transitional level of the narration?

My point is that the risk of interpretations that saturate *à la* Groddeck is always lurking round the corner, and that it is very tempting to succumb because they soothingly assuage the need for a response.

Baldassarre's haemophilia

A patient describes his haemophilia, saying how it constantly exposes him to risks, to bleeding, swellings or paralysis of the joints. The 'illness', he says, also causes him to adopt a whole range of defensive measures, such as avoiding even the smallest trauma and the tiniest wound. He has embarked on a course of preventive therapy, in the same way as he deploys a range of preventive behaviours to act as an upstream 'tampon' for any possible trauma.

However, does what the patient says tell us any more about the 'haemophilia' or its pathogenesis, psychogenesis and psychosomatic and somato-psychotic aspects? Or must we undertake a narcissistic renunciation, in the belief that, in our psychoanalytic laboratory, 'haemophilia' means the patient's tendency to bleed and to be vulnerable on an emotional level, so that he avoids traumas, conflicts and fights, which he forestalls by avoiding dependence? In that case, 'haemophilia' would be regarded as the character of the session most capable of conferring 'narratability' on what is happening in his internal world and relationships.

In analysis, 'haemophilia' can in the end be seen simply as the most immediate 'narrative derivative' that best corresponds to the sequence of α-elements that constantly pictograph the patient's mental state

– without any possibility of making inferences about the disease of 'haemophilia' as it exists outside the analyst's consulting room. Furthermore, the analyst is free to believe that, failing the narreme – and narrative derivatives – of 'haemophilia', the patient could have found other ways of 'narrating' his vulnerability and the defences or preventive actions he constantly deploys. Ultimately, in my view, the more capable the analyst is of performing a metaphorizing function, the more he will be able to enter into contact with the pictograms upstream of the 'narrative derivatives'; but, at the same time, the more he will run the risk of believing that his metaphorizations are meaningful outside his consulting room, and of thereby practising 'wild psychosomatics'.

If, for example, a young patient experiences the maturational explosion of an autistic nucleus and exhibits a mild form of epilepsy with a 'freak storm wave', we might have an aetiological and pathogenetic explanation of forms of epilepsy – however mild – along the following lines: the explosion of the autistic nucleus puts into circulation as yet unmanageable proto-emotions that can be evacuated by a fit, which involves a 'freak emotional wave' or, in other words, violent emotional conflictuality (the storm).

Alternatively – in our laboratory – we can be certain *only* that, by his account of an *autistic nucleus and epilepsy*, the patient has found suitable 'narrative derivatives' for placing the problem of unthinkability on a narrative level, and then for activating proto-emotions that are sometimes evacuated because they are not yet 'thinkable'; but this can tell us nothing about the 'epilepsy' outside the consulting room, which is another matter.

The seductive power of an all-explaining metaphor is of course very great, but I believe that analysis is now a sufficiently mature science to be capable of mourning for the possession of a specific field of application – namely, mental life in the present.

There remains the problem of boundary areas, of the possible applications of psychoanalysis, for instance its intersection with the neurosciences, but this takes us into quite different territory, almost all of which still remains to be explored. As I have said elsewhere, analysis exists where there is a patient, an analyst and a setting.

However, what are we to make of the so-called psychosomatic illnesses, and how far does their realm extend? Again, how are we to explain the beneficial effect analysis sometimes has on the course of certain diseases? And indeed, what of the adverse effect that analysis can equally well have? Or are these merely cases of the failure to distinguish between *post hoc* and *propter hoc* to which Hume drew attention?

When can an illness be regarded as an evacuation of β-elements into the body, as an expression of asymbolia or alexithymia? To be honest, we must in my view confess that we know very little about these matters and that for the time being perhaps even psychoanalysis cannot offer much enlightenment. It may be that more information will accrue from 'applied psychoanalysis', given that reductionistic explanations are always immediately to hand like Sirens. However, we must also remember the other meaning of 'siren', as an alarm signal warning of the risk of extending the application of psychoanalysis beyond its specific field.

The same applies, for example, to a child's asthma: possible psychosomatic formulations are one thing, but asthma as a narration in the consulting room, considered as a 'narrative derivative', is another. An extreme formulation of this kind is given by Chiozza (1986), who claims that even the most serious diseases, from multiple sclerosis to cardiac infarct, can be mapped psychosomatically.

This is tantamount to asserting, for example, that if an analysand is suffering from leukaemia and mentions 'analyses' revealing the presence of immature, undifferentiated cells, we are automatically entitled to believe that the leukaemia is due to immature, undifferentiated emotions, instead of considering that the patient is referring, in his analysis, to immature and undifferentiated aspects of himself, which the 'narreme of leukaemia' enables him to narrate in all their dramatic, invasive proliferation.

Failing this narreme, this patient could have found other 'narremes' or 'narrative derivatives' to express the same sequence of α-elements. If this were not so, psychoanalysis would have found a magic key to every 'fact' of the entire species, both psychic and somatic.

From an entirely opposite vertex, an analyst, in the process of analysis, cannot in my view doubt the communicative value of even the most seemingly realistic facts and events. For instance, if a patient says during his session that he is suffering from Crohn's disease, my psychoanalytic vertex will inevitably suggest a situation of evacuative bleeding, which will induce me, say, to prescribe 'an appropriate interpretative diet' or to apply 'cortisone treatments'. These will continue pending a transformation, which I as an analyst can expect, of the patient's Crohn-type mental functioning. That is my analytic concern, rather than the 'fact' of Crohn's disease, which belongs to a different therapeutic scenario.

Even so, outside the consulting-room situation, I can still put questions to myself about the frontiers and interconnections between psychoanalysis and the neurosciences, as recently described with great clarity and precision by Mancia (2006).

Moreover, it is virtually impossible to make any prediction about the 'choice' of a symptom; it is only after the event that we may be able to reconstruct the route that has led to the choice – which is not really a choice, as it is highly determined – of one symptom rather than another. As long as we are unable to make sensible forecasts of symptomatic choices and are dependent on 'hindsight', I therefore believe that the appropriate attitude is one of great humility. We can then admit to ourselves how little we know, and shall be encouraged to undertake new journeys and explorations, while curing ourselves of the terrible disease of 'orthodoxy', which belongs to religions, academies and bureaucracies – rather than to science and art – whereby everything is seen in terms of the already known, which is fetishized.

If a patient claims to be allergic to gluten – that is, that he is suffering from coeliac disease – and has to avoid any kind of flour that is not gluten-free, what are we to think? In my view, we are then caught between the Scylla of believing that we can 'only' concern ourselves with the form assumed by the patient's emotional reactions to this pathology and the Charybdis of simply assuming the existence of a psychosomatic condition.

Steering a middle course, we could 'suspend all our knowledge' of this situation and begin to see *what* the 'gluten' in the session *also is*; we could then determine what type of approach or interpretation would be 'gluten-free', as opposed to the type that gives rise to intolerance. In other words, it must be possible for the 'gluten' to be seen as a 'character' of the session. We need to observe when and how it makes its appearance in the session, and which 'ingredients' of the analytic bread and dough the patient is intolerant of. In this way, 'transformations' of the patient's experience and psychic life can potentially be brought about, and it is only at a later date that we may be able to discover whether they have perhaps also had some effect on the 'real illness'.

Martina's dirt

Martina is a patient with a severe dirt phobia that severely restricts her social and work contacts and compels her to observe a whole series of cleanliness rituals. She also claims to suffer badly from leucopenia, which greatly increases her risk of infection and fever if she does not meticulously 'clean' everything she comes into contact with. Indeed, Martina 'sterilizes' not only objects but also, as far as possible, the emotions potentially entailed by any relationship: she says that the arousal of any emotion or intense affect can seriously infect her, make her ill and give her an emotional fever.

As Martina's analysis proceeds, she eventually begins to dream of animals of gradually increasing size, of enclosures she can build, and of children she can look after without any longer falling ill; in other words, thanks to the analytic work, she is introjecting the functions that now allow her to experience and contain the emotions that previously had to be obliterated. At this point, she mentions that the leucopenia too is progressively improving.

If the analyst were now to succumb to the temptation of claiming that the leucopenia represented the somatization of, say, identity problems or insufficient self/not-self differentiation, he would in my view be guilty of a 'logical leap'. In Martina's account, the 'deficiency of white corpuscles' stands for a deficiency in her apparatus for protecting herself from and containing virus-emotions. The same content could have been expressed by a description of a farm without enclosures for the various animals; by an infantile memory in which a child suffering from leukaemia had to stay in germ-free rooms to avoid bacteria; or by an account of the daily lives of some prosperous friends in Brazil living in guarded gated communities who were afraid when left unprotected by a strike of the security staff. In other words, the patient forms α-elements, of which we can know the narrative derivatives, which may belong to a wide variety of literary genres.

The communication about the proliferation of white corpuscles, or the ending of the security guards' strike, tells us something about the 'inside' of the session, but nothing about 'leucopenia' or the 'socioeconomic situation in Brazil'. The possibility that an analysis can have effects on the soma – by pathways whose outline we are only just beginning to discern – is 'another story'.

Stefania's abortion

I am working with a supervisee on the analysis of Stefania, a 35-year-old biologist at a research institute, who has had a 'missed abortion'. In the session before this painful event, she tells the analyst she did not feel like talking about her pregnancy to her friend Carla, as she was afraid that Carla might be envious because she was working too hard to have a child of her own. In the next session, the patient reports on arrival that there have been serious problems with her pregnancy: she has had a 'missed abortion' calling for 'uterine curettage' – the technical term for scraping out the womb, she adds. The analyst manages to get very close to Stefania, who tells her of a colleague who remarked to her: 'What with all the dying that goes on in hospitals, it's really great that something is born there too.'

Stefania then mentions the cold demeanour of the sonographer and the fact that the child's heartbeat was no longer detected. She goes on to express her fear that she might convey something 'negative', and reports a dream of a horrible plant with its leaves cut to a spiky point. On the phone to the head of her laboratory, the patient said: 'I terminated the pregnancy,' and her astonished interlocutor thought she had done so voluntarily.

The emotional climate of both patient and supervisee is imbued with guilt: the patient says she is conveying something negative, and then there is the phrase she used to her boss; the analyst too wonders where she has gone wrong, what she failed to see, and in what respects she has proved inadequate, even considering turning everything round and talking about the patient's 'destructiveness'.

It seems to me that this situation is very germane to our subject. First, I believe it can help us to rid ourselves of the omnipotent fantasy that we are responsible for what happens to the soma – ours and the patient's – and that there might be such a thing as a simple, naïve psychosomatic reading code whereby, in a kind of delusional *Nachträglichkeit*, everything can be explained in psychoanalytic terms. Second, it can help us to avoid shirking our responsibility as analysts in regard to patients' 'communications'.

This patient had begun her analysis with severe hypochondria, expressed through intense fear of a tumour, mostly located in the breast; syncretized in this way, this had turned into the various malignant and benign tumours in the children's cancer ward with which she had begun to collaborate on a genetic research project. At a certain point in the analysis, it appeared that, alongside the cancer ward (proto-emotions and β-elements still awaiting thinkability?), an obstetric ward (for giving birth to new thoughts and emotions?) might also be opened. The cancer ward somehow unexpectedly includes the obstetric ward: even the new entity that was in the process of formation 'dies' and must be expelled.

However, it is vitally important not to assume that the abortion takes place *because* the anti-growth parts of the patient have prevailed over the pro-growth parts. Instead, we must 'dare' to adopt a radically psychoanalytic vertex in relation to the patient's communication: in other words, what makes it possible for the 'event' (the abortion) to be narrated with all the associated drama is the fact that the 'tumoural aspects' have prevailed – for the moment – over growth and development and that Stefania has found this 'event'.

That is to say, the patient could perfectly well have proved able to continue with the pregnancy and found a different way of expressing the prevalence of a disorganized over an organized form of emotional development. For instance, she could have mentioned the plight of her husband as the councillor responsible for public works, who is unable to enforce the planning guidelines because unauthorized buildings are constantly being erected in violation of the regulations, and who is threatened by the Mafia into the bargain; or she could have dreamt – as she in fact did – of a plant that was unable to develop because its leaves had been cut off or else she could have brought an infantile memory in which her garden was overgrown with weeds and the plantlets she wanted to see growing were never able to develop.

Nor does it make sense to invoke destructiveness on the part of the patient (rather than regarding the destructiveness as the confused proliferation of proto-emotions that for the time being give rise to the cancer ward, among which we are beginning to glimpse envy), or to interpret the 'missed abortion' as due to these hostile forces. Instead, aware of her present anguish, we should give her hope, once again patiently working 'in the cancer ward' while waiting for an organized development of emotions increasingly to take the place of their massive, confused proliferation.[1]

The ideas presented so far suggest two possible avenues for reflection. Let me now try to describe what happens in situations when the analyst is mainly called upon to work on the verbalization of what the patient can transform into 'visual pictograms' even if he has lost contact with what generated them.

---

[1] This would be the 'symmetrical' opposite of breast cancer: lyophilizing the anxiety that is in search of a narrator and turning it into a 'thing'.

Consider, for example, the case of a patient whose mental climate includes the following sequence:

Anxiety → Terror → Fear → Hope

Let us assume that he has formed the following 'visual pictograms', i.e. α-elements whose sequence gives rise to the waking dream thought:

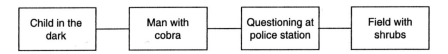

These would of course remain unknown, but could be inferred from their narrative derivatives (ND), which, as we know, belong to the relevant literary genres and may be distorted to different degrees.

> ND1: *an 'infantile memory'*: 'I felt terrible without my mates; I remember I once dreamt I was being pursued by a lion: I ran into a cave, and then, luckily, my mother woke me up for breakfast.'
> ND2: *a sexual genre*: 'After unprotected sex, I was very frightened and then I had an indescribable feeling when I came out in red spots, but they disappeared after a few days and the world then seemed different again.'
> ND3: *a diaristic genre*: 'I couldn't believe it watching TV and seeing the terrorists' planes smashing into the towers and the fire brigade rushing to the scene, but I was greatly comforted by Mayor Giuliani's speech.'

The narrative derivatives may be so 'remote', and sometimes so (seemingly) imbued with reality, that it is difficult to 'trace the path back' to the emotion pictographed by the α-elements and subsequently diluted in the narrations. The pattern might be as follows:

Anxiety → Terror → Fear → Hope

Through the narrative derivatives (ND1, 2, 3, . . . *n*), the analyst succeeds in giving a voice to the emotions and in restoring contact with the waking dream thought.

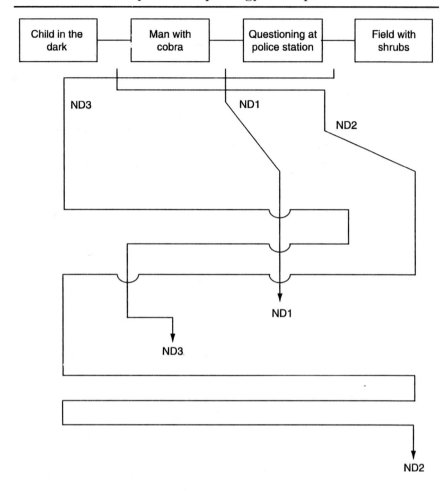

This is the case with a patient who reports that her son is allergic to something in his diet (after a session with many transference interpretations); or a male patient who mentions an acquaintance suffering from coagulopathy in whom any trauma causes bleeding of the joints resulting in several days of paralysis (the patient then misses a session). In these instances, the 'narrated illness' takes the form of a 'narrative derivative' (which could have been a different one).

The analyst will then work forward from ♀♂, Ps ↔ D and NC ↔ SF, in the sense that the emotion has already been pictographed by the patient and the analyst must weave it together – as when, for example, a patient at the beginning of the week mentions experiences of abandonment or agonizing separations.

Maximum (optimistic) aspirations

The situation is very different if the patient only partially succeeds in transforming proto-emotions into α-elements. In this case, there are agglomerations of β-elements which the patient is unable to alphabetize (these are sometimes 'undigested facts' of his history and sometimes undigested transgenerational facts).

The proto-emotional states are still too scattered and unelaborated; they are:

$$x \qquad y \qquad q \qquad z$$

The patient's α-sequence is silent:

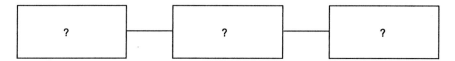

or present in outline only (in the form of what I have called 'balpha'-elements):

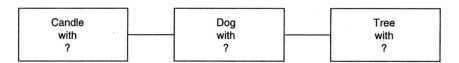

It will then be up to the analyst's mind to furnish the receptive capacity for attention and dream-type organization (α-function) for the acceptance of, and assignment of meaning to, what reaches it in the form of projective identifications – say, x, y, q and z.

In other words, the analyst must himself perform operations upstream of ♂ ♀, Ps ↔ D and NC ↔ SF, and form α-elements from agglomerations of β-elements (or more often, balpha-elements), as follows:

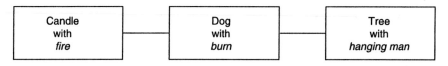

The analyst can get in touch with these α-elements either by means of his reverie or progressively through dialogue and the exchange of emotions (even with small quanta of β → α) constructed in the relationship with the patient. Eventually – to continue with the same example – he may postulate that intense jealousy inflames the patient so much that he wants to kill someone or to commit suicide.

Of course, either this can be communicated to the patient 'as is', or a prolonged process of transformation may be necessary first.

It is *perhaps only on this level* that possible therapies for psychosomatic disorders can be considered. For if these pathologies are regarded as evacuations of β-elements, 'discrete' alphabetization of quanta of β-elements may shift the balance from evacuation towards symbolization and thinkability. It must always be borne in mind that an excessive communication of content may result in fragmentation of the container, which will then be violently evacuated. This may be the underlying cause of much pathology arising during the course of therapy (Ferro 2002a).

Maria and her fits

A competent young analyst brings me a long clinical sequence.

Maria, a young mathematics and physics teacher at a scientifically oriented secondary school in a small country town, has just begun her analysis. She starts the week by reporting that her father irritates her by constantly trying to teach her things or by his recurring rows with her mother; on one occasion, she was so exasperated by their noisy quarrelling in the bedroom that she 'threw a hammer at the sideboard'.[2] She then mentions a 'cousin from the south' who lives in Sicily: although he is aggressive, she is not afraid of him.

Before the next session, the analyst, somewhat debatably, telephones the patient to say that, owing to unforeseen circumstances, she will not be able to make that afternoon's session and that, if the patient wishes, they could reschedule it for the late evening. The patient agrees. At the beginning of the session, the analyst apologizes for the 'bother'; Maria replies that the change of time was convenient for her too and that the 'shift' [*spostamento*] was no problem. They go on to discuss the need for perfection and any 'slight flaws' there might be in the analyst's own conduct.

Maria then complains that she can 'never manage to say no'. The analyst asks: 'Not even to me?' 'Not at all,' the patient answers, and then

---

[2] Translator's note: The Italian word for sideboard is *credenza*, which also means belief.

goes on to talk about some unpleasant things that have happened 'at work': 'It's all right this evening, but Carlo must never behave like that to me again' . . . 'I think I have to do everything he wants in double-quick time, and that doesn't suit me.' Next she says she does not always like her work, even though she now has a new, younger colleague, who is very nice, not a conformist, but actually very free and easy; it seems that her 'nice workmate doesn't make problems for himself,' and she herself would like to be 'dragged out of my own way of doing things: a bit of spice in my life would not do any harm, and in fact I'd like to let the brakes off.'

Let us consider these exchanges.

In the first session, the patient already demonstrates an intolerance of anything educational, as well as her own 'incontinence' resulting from the weekend's suspension and exclusion, which gives rise to a loss of control: 'throwing the hammer' at the 'faith (the belief [*credenza*] I have in you)', without taking fright at this violent-cousin aspect of herself.

Her initial response to the analyst's request for a change of time (which was basically an aggressive act on her part) is submissive: she says there is no problem, on the contrary . . . But then she complains about not being able to say no, and having to give way and accept other people's needs.

Maria then seems to recover a positive aspect from what has happened, in the form of the 'young colleague', who stands for the free-and-easy, non-academic side of the analyst, who has contributed a bit of spice and who seems not to have any inhibitions – the inhibitions that afflict Maria in regard to food, as well as sex and relationships – and she would even like to 'let the brakes off'.

In the next session, Maria shows how far she has moved on from having been 'a perfect, well-behaved little girl', by neglecting the work she should have done to prepare for exams. She then mentions her father's total lack of interest, while admitting that 'he has changed a bit since I had the fit' (Maria has had an epileptic-type fit). She reports the arrival of 'a letter from my cousin accusing my mother of having stolen some jewels' and asserting that 'there should be a trial that forces the guilty to pay'; he also told her to 'save yourself while there is still time', but she was not bothered because she 'knew that her cousin was not only from the south but also mad'.

Some further reflections are appropriate at this point.

Maria has allowed herself to be 'influenced' by the free-and-easy manner of her analyst; she is more relaxed, and does less preparation for the exam (the session), and then there is the reference to 'letting off the brake'. So if the handbrake is less firmly on, the 'cousin part of herself' can emerge – the part that experienced the change of time as something that 'put her out'[3] (made her lose control): the analyst stole the session, which was an injustice worthy of prosecution, and the patient must save herself from the clutches of such an unreliable person. In other words, the after-effects of the 'shift' [*spostamento*] of the time of the session are now being felt. Her faith (the *credenza*) is still fragile: the weekend and the change of setting unleash uncontrollable aspects of herself if her hypercontrolling guard is lowered even for a moment.

However, what are we to make of Maria's 'fits' – of her epilepsy? There are at least three possibilities:

1   *Epilepsy as a character of the session*: 'If I do not inhibit myself, I am afraid I might "let the brakes off", and sometimes I do just that.'
2   *Epilepsy as a fact of external reality*: Being outside the field, this does not fall within our competence.
3   *Epilepsy – between the two previous possibilities – connected with the hypothetical psychosomatic space*: Here, in addition to being an account of an inability to contain or of a neurological 'fact', the epilepsy could also be seen as a way of dealing with hypercompressed and hypercontrolled aspects which, in the absence of any possibility of modulation or alphabetization, are evacuated by the fit – although they have found a channel of 'expression' in the 'cousin's letter'. This last aspect proves to be the most complex, and marks the limit, the wager and the hope *that the analysable will be transformable*.

Continuing my open-ended and perhaps even contradictory exercise – this is the time to put out the nets, but not yet to haul them back on board with the catch – I should like to consider the possibility of an intestinal model of the mind, borrowed from Bion, in which, say, a 'mental colitis' would be expressed by the alternation of symptoms of constipation and diarrhoea. The constipation would correspond to

---

[3]   Translator's note: The Italian verb *spostare* can mean to shift as well as to put out – see before. *Spostamento* is the equivalent noun.

inhibition, mutism and hypercontrol, and the diarrhoea to all the various forms of incontinence, including every type of evacuation, from enuresis to characteropathic acting-out and various somatic diseases.

Marcella's enuresis

Marcella was a very lively child in her family circle but socially inhibited to the point of exhibiting selective mutism at nursery school, as if she had her handbrake on. What remains to be understood is whether and how psychotherapy, at one session a week, has 'released her brake' to such an extent as to give rise to serious enuresis.

The first 'somatic' symptom in Marcella's history was minor vomiting when under stress; this was followed by mutism and then by enuresis. However, why did Marcella often opt for 'somatic' symptoms? What led her to evacuate through the body rather than on the level of behaviour or disturbed psychic functioning?

Since childhood, her father had suffered from diarrhoea for months on end, which no medicine had been able to cure permanently.

Is the inhibition in Marcella's history a way of hypercontrolling a sort of 'tiger'? Marcella has a phobia of cats, whose very appearance terrifies her: she is absolutely unable to draw a cat. Is the enuresis a way of evacuating this 'tiger' (as a state of mind)?

In Marcella's case, it seems to me that the transition from inhibition to evacuation also entailed the putting into circulation of parts of the 'tiger'; that is to say, 'ti-' has entered into circulation, activating her rivalry with her numerous brothers and sisters, while '-ger' is evacuated by the enuresis. An analysis might perhaps allow further deconstruction of '-ger' to the point of allowing more letters to begin circulating, the ideal being that there would be no further residue to evacuate. In other words, if '-ger' could also enter into circulation and be alphabetized, there would be no further need for evacuation.

Why, then, are there some situations in which the 'tiger' is evacuated in acting-out or other forms of behaviour and others in which it is 'evacuated' by discharge in psychosomatic pathologies? Why do some individuals manage this situation through, say, anorexia (an attempt to split off and starve the tiger), or a phobia (for instance, of knives) or obsession (e.g. religious rituals) or an explosion of symptoms (panic attacks) rather than through psychosomatic evacuation?

One possibility might be to consider whether the 'tiger' is a 'blind spot' or an instance of myopia – and on what scale? – in relation to that blind spot. It may be that, the more something is denied, split off, unknown, alien and remote, the more it potentially lends itself to psychosomatic expression – and that, the more it is partially visible, the more likely it is to be expressed psychically.

However, what determines the quantitative degree of symbolization? I believe it is the other's 'look' – its breadth and depth – and not just the particular subjective defence mechanisms deployed voluntarily or spontaneously by the individual concerned. Psychosomatic illness is the positive side of the other's absent look; what the other fails to mentalize is 'made flesh', embodied in the psychosomatic illness: the affect, the unthought emotions. Given these presumed psychosomatic pathologies, the problem can be considered on various levels: first, the *illness* itself, and everything it involves in medical, affective and psychological terms; second, the *narration of the illness* as such, as a 'narrative derivative' of the waking dream thought that conveys something *other* than actual reality; third, the *psychosomatic and/or somato-psychotic* level: how a powerfully evacuative situation is constructed in and through the body; fourth, the *neurochemical, genetic and environmental level*: how environmental situations give rise to neurochemical modifications or cause latent genetic possibilities to become manifest; and fifth, the *therapeutic* level – from 'physical', symptom-directed therapy to 'psychoanalytic' therapy, whose approach is to seek pathways of thinkability rather than evacuation and to find ways of integrating split-off aspects.

Let us now return to our young teacher, Maria.

> As her analysis proceeds, she says she had her first epileptic fits – which have ceased since she began taking the medication she is still on – at the time of the illness and death of her aunt, who had still been young and like a mother to her. She remembers the difficulty she had in 'putting thoughts into words', and then 'a roaring noise and falling'. She also remembers coming to on a stretcher. Next, she returns to her 'aunt's death', recalling her MRI scans and the 'embryonic residues in a cerebral ventricle'; then she mentions 'aggressive outbursts' and throwing things at everybody, which could have done some real harm.

Maria is meanwhile coming to realize that she is particularly sensitive to *changes of setting and separations*. Here Bleger's (1967) concept of the 'agglutinated nucleus' comes to our aid – a notion that is surely related to Ogden's (1989) autistic contiguous position and Tustin's (1981) autistic nucleus. This nucleus is stratified in the setting, as if cats (or tigers?) were stacked in layers when falling asleep and squeezed tightly together, ultimately forming a smooth, plush surface, like a fur moquette. Then comes the 'shock of the change', which wakes them all up so that they are no longer 'manageable'; it then becomes essential to 'evacuate' them (by the fit?), as they cannot be metabolized.

In the same way, the patient proves to be highly sensitive to separations; she often operates in adhesive-identification mode, in which the 'cats' (or proto-cats/proto-emotions) are flattened out in a submissive 'the way you want me', only to explode again at the next separation.

> At the beginning of one session, Maria mentions a school inspection due on the following Monday (it is now Friday, the last session of the week): 'I am very calm,' she claims. Remembering that Maria's first fit coincided with a time of great turbulence, but also with a time of seeming 'calm, when you no longer felt any emotions', the analyst draws attention to the patient's denial, saying: 'Calm, but you are talking about it.' The patient replies: 'It's not how I said at all: I'm terrified I might have a fit . . .' The session continues, leading eventually to the emergence not only of anxiety about the following Monday's session (the social phobia she is to describe later and the reference to her experience of the session as a ministerial inspection), but also of separation anxiety, which is 'narrated' by the description of a 'one-metre'-deep swimming pool, which has a 'big drop', after which one loses touch with the bottom (contact is lost), there being a 'four-metre' chasm.

Another metaphor of the explosion of the agglutinated nucleus, this time in the language of Bion, might be the explosion of the container, which becomes the *evacuated invasive contained*. 'Evacuated' may mean 'evacuated into the other's mind', but *only* if that mind is receptive and available; otherwise the contained may be evacuated in acting-out or in a psychosomatic illness. The ultimate cause of the explosion – using the analogy of a coal mine in days gone by – is an 'outpouring of firedamp', perhaps due to the failure of walls between which it was compressed, which then explodes, causing all or part of the gallery to collapse so that part of the container is either damaged or collapses in turn, or the container itself explodes.

In those old coal mines, small amounts of firedamp had to be blown up gradually in harmless small explosions; in other words, proto-emotions can be alphabetized only a little at a time.

Another metaphor, this time using the language of Anzieu (1974), is that of the containing function of the psychic skin.

What I believe happened to Maria was the activation of split-off proto-emotions, which exploded and had to be evacuated. The other's reverie had not been sufficient to receive and transform them. So the analytic task now is to render the remaining firedamp harmless and to strengthen the gallery walls – that is to say, to metabolize the contained by a process of progressive alphabetization and to increase the elasticity and strength of the container.

A further metaphor is suggested by the Jodie Foster film *Panic Room*. The encysted autistic nucleus is like the situation of the heroine and her daughter, who take refuge in the panic room, which is equipped for prolonged resistance, as a defence against invasive, unmanageable proto-emotions (the violent burglars who break into the house); all this happens after the heroine has divorced her husband. If an emotional event that cannot be metabolized – e.g. separation – activates unmanageable proto-emotions, which one fears might 'destroy' one, an extreme defence mechanism is the formation of an 'autistic shell' in which to seek refuge. The problem is that if aspects of oneself (living parts) are shut in, albeit with a view to saving oneself, after a while it may be necessary to emerge on account of claustrophobia (from which the heroine suffers) or to obtain sugar – libidinal supplies (for the diabetic daughter) – and this involves exposure to risk. In this case, however, there are comings and goings into and out of the panic room, so that it is a question of 'autistic withdrawal' rather than an autistic nucleus, which would suggest a more stable structure.

A different and in some respects less serious situation for the possibility of mental functioning is when, at a certain point, it is not vital aspects of the self but the very proto-emotions by which the subject feels threatened that are walled up in the panic room. However, it is virtually impossible for these vital aspects too not to remain 'shut in', again as in the film I have arbitrarily chosen as my model, in which the burglars are shut in the panic room together with the heroine's daughter. As soon as the door is 'opened' to track down the aspects imprisoned within, the proto-emotions break out and devastate everything they find; this situation is more reminiscent of the level of the hyperobsessive, hypercontaining management of proto-emotions, which then burst out uncontainably. In this case, autistic modes of managing the proto-emotions are in my view a less regressive, less drastic defence mechanism than the forms described above.

Another significant point in Maria's analysis comes when her analyst has the fantasy: 'Perhaps she was attacked by her cousin when she was small.' Although the analyst adopts a *realistic/historical/reconstructive* approach, this is unimportant; what matters is that, in her own mind, the analyst has built a bridge between the 'abused patient' and the 'abusing cousin' – in other words, she has put the patient's suffering together, in one and the same scene, with the abusing contact with a split-off psychotic part of the patient's personality.

A few sessions after the analyst has this insight, Maria mentions both her asthmatic brother and the fact that she herself always needs to keep the windows open, even in winter; immediately afterwards, she *unexpectedly* mentions certain odd, mad kinds of behaviour by her cousin and 'his' violent, persecutory aspects. The analyst does well to follow Maria's manifest text, and a few sessions later the patient comes along with conspicuous tattoos and her ears pierced. Peripheral aspects of the 'cousin' who previously had to be kept 'shut in' and who made his presence felt by the suffocation of asthma (within the claustrum) or who was evacuated through the always open windows (the fits?) or was 'chilled', are embarking on the path of integration, and are beginning to find expression in 'Tortuga-buccaneer' aspects of the patient. In this way, the 'psychotic-cousin' part can come to be treated differently, no longer necessarily being isolated, controlled, split off and evacuated, but instead integrated, albeit slowly.

Such problems can in fact be expressed and solved in a variety of different ways, and may have a variety of origins.

Tiziana says that – perhaps – she was attacked by her father; she also suffers from bruxism. She explains that she was often 'knocked to the ground' by her violent father, who is disrespectful and invades other people's space, even when 'they take refuge in the loo'. Her relationship with this 'father' is one of terror. At the same time, he is described as very religious.

She goes on to describe her various boyfriends: Giovanni, an expert in women and prostitutes, who forced her to have 'oral sex'; Marcello, with whom she was really in love, but who became violent, jealous and possessive after drinking; and 'Gennaro the trucker', who was also very violent. After these episodes of 'violence' of which she is the victim, she 'switches off' in order to recover; she shuts herself up in her room and does not speak for days on end.

In such a case, Bion's concept of 'hyperbole' is in my opinion more useful than that of splitting. Here, projective identifications, which have not been picked up and metabolized, go into orbit and in effect form aggregates of β-elements (the betalomas described by Barale and Ferro [1992]) or aggregates of balpha-elements ('balphomas'), which periodically succumb to the effects of 'gravitational attraction' and rain down violently and intrusively on the subject. In terms of Tiziana's mental functioning, these characters – the father and the various boyfriends – can be thought of as a way of narrating the abuse and violence to which she is subjected by these 'aggregates', which, having been expelled at some point in the past, periodically return to invade and abuse her.

Another important point is that, when a violent projective identification fails repeatedly to be picked up by a function of reverie, not only does 'something' go into orbit, but an 'autistic' scar remains in the place previously occupied by the expelled entity. Therapy may give rise to a 'reconnection' with what was violently evacuated, and in addition, if this entity should come to inhabit and partially de-collapse the autistic scar, it may be continually expelled, perhaps also somatically, resulting in a wide variety of psychosomatic manifestations, at least until the autistic virtual space becomes stably three-dimensional.

When this occurs in Tiziana's therapy, a flood of dreams and memories are unleashed, putting back into circulation everything that had been projected into space. In the absence of therapy, such reconnections with orbiting entities split off from the ego trigger violent and unexpected forms of acting-out of which no one would have thought the individual concerned capable.

To return to the case of Maria, it is interesting to observe how the further integration of split-off aspects (which, as stated, had found an outlet either in the claustrum – asthma – or in evacuation) takes place inside the analyst's mind, giving rise to fear and surprise. One day, Maria's analyst finds herself terrified by the idea of a possible meeting between Maria and the next patient – a 'madman' who, the analyst fears, might attack or even kill Maria. It is not difficult to see in the

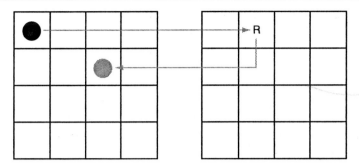

Projective identification and its return to the patient after transformation by
reverie (R)

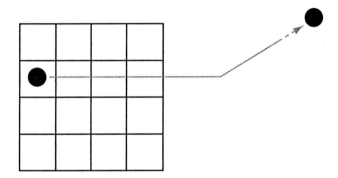

Projective identification declined

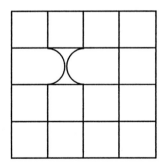

Residual autistic scar

analyst's 'terror' – 'Whatever am I doing, telling the patient not to
stay in the waiting room any longer and to avoid all contact with
this man?' – as a new and updated version of her fantasy about the
abusing cousin: the split-off contents are drawing near, orbiting in

ever-decreasing circles as they come closer to the patient's mind, so that the analyst fears that this approach–cum–integration might present a grave danger.

> After a few more months of analysis, Maria says she cannot understand why she sometimes feels that she frightens her mother, just as her mother fears the uncontainable behaviour of her nephew (Maria's cousin); that is, she is afraid that he might stab her husband or kill him in some other way. Maria then mentions the 'bestial desires' that one of her suitors exhibits towards her, and finally reports two key dreams: 'I got out of my car and there was a madman with a gun who turned into my nephew's cat'; and 'I was in a dual-control car with my cousin; then there was a cat with its throat cut, and, still in the dream, I cried out: "It could have been me!"' Evidently, something that could previously only be evacuated has gradually drawn closer and can now find a 'place', accompanied by representability and narratability, in dreams.

Dario's Western
Dario is a four-year-old boy characterized by uncontainable and afinalistic turbulence with evacuative tendencies. After just one month of analysis he plays games that indicate an incipient recognition of certain 'notes', or rather 'basic rhythms', of analysis: a 'cuckoo' game, a game with marbles that meet, collide and separate, and games connected with the sequence $1\rightarrow2\rightarrow3\rightarrow2\rightarrow1$ corresponding to the number of sessions. These moments of 'stillness' are violently interrupted by 'onslaughts' in which he not only turns the therapy room upside down but also tears along the corridor without restraint and overturns everything in the waiting room.

The analyst's reverie is of scenes from a Western: a cowboy sets to work at the ranch, tills the land, and so on, until, as in the classic script, along comes the gang that sows panic and destruction in the small community. The analyst is now clearly called upon to perform the function of a sheriff who not only *contains* but also *limits*.

That night, the analyst has a series of countertransference dreams which he cannot connect; they are fragmentary, made up of single images and colours. How are we to interpret this situation if we abandon the metaphor – the Western myth – and row C of Bion's grid in order to conceptualize what is going on? No doubt we could say that in his sessions the patient is beginning to display forms of functioning in 'D' as well as the more frequent manifestations when 'Ps' is unleashed.

In another language, we could say that there are moments of alphabetization of proto-emotions that hold fast and work as they should: we are witnessing the formation of little lumps of sense, of narrative – or, if you will, play-related – derivatives, of short sequences of α-elements and of a waking dream. Then come whirlwinds of β-elements that sweep away everything in their path, and can only be violently evacuated.

The analyst's dream shows us how the process of alphabetization – or, if you will, the creation of 'literacy' – takes place; although under bombardment, he is at work, transforming quanta of β-elements into small oneiric fragments, as yet still with sensory characteristics, which constitute short sequences of α- or perhaps balpha/α-elements.

As stated, a major problem is certainly that of the reversibility or otherwise of the psychosomatic symptom. Such a symptom is after all a successful defence, albeit harmful to the organism, but nevertheless a way of 'evacuating' something that was not otherwise manageable. The opposite process, the transition from evacuation to thinkability – or, depending on one's idiolect, to symbolization or alphabetization – is an uphill task, involving the sacrifice of a laboriously achieved solution, the reopening of suffering and the full experiencing of the difficulty of the path towards mentalization.

This is very conspicuous in Maria, who, at the beginning of the third year of her analysis, makes autistic, affect-stripping choices when faced with the possibility of closer contact with suffering areas of her psyche. As she herself puts it, she can no longer bear any contact with her boyfriend, whom she feels to be a 'beast' with violent passions he wants to get rid of; she would like to sit at her computer without the problem of relating to the children in her class; and, in particular, she is afraid of immersing herself in the work with the problem children who are sometimes entrusted to her because they often exhibit a violence, aggression and impulsiveness with which she cannot cope. So she would rather avoid all these upsetting things by doing secretarial work, seeking a calm, 'quiet' life in the collection and statistical processing of data, a task that would not arouse her emotions. Unable to stand the daily contact with the children, perhaps she could instead do research in the statistics department of a university far away from the town where she currently lives, even if this meant that she would have to break off the analysis.

97

Maria is clearly at a parting of the ways: she must choose between the downward slope of evacuation and the corresponding computer-like, affect-stripped mode of functioning, and the arduous uphill path from the (evacuative) symptom to the alphabetization of proto-emotions. The quality of the analyst's mental functioning will be one of the variables determining her choice.

However, let us see how things turn out, and to what extent the analyst's mind becomes the mill that can push the water back against the flow.

Maria says she is fed up with being well-behaved; she now thinks the cousin from the south is very similar to herself and, like a child, wonders: 'Who are you to tell me to sit still at my desk?' She then adds that she would like to work in civil defence, rushing off to places that are evacuated when there are floods, to shore up the dykes.

So Maria seems to have got in touch with the rebellious little girl she was never able to be, and is moreover integrating the 'cousin' aspect: she wants to shore up the banks of the emotional rivers and become skilled in the management of the emotional floods that trigger evacuations (her fits?).

The analyst initially takes fright, fearing acting-out, but at length – after Maria says she is not interested in behaviour therapy – understands the superego element that has dominated her and succeeds in allowing space for Maria's rebellion – and Maria mentions the title of a book: *Good Girls Go To Heaven, Bad Girls Go Anywhere.*

A new space is thus also opened up: the space of the forest, of the animals that dwell in it, of the work of protecting its various endangered species, and of the wish to work on 'limiting the forest'. This seems also to imply an opening up to long-denied emotions that must be safeguarded, protected and allowed to develop. So what was previously 'evacuated' can now, it appears, live in the forest – even the intense and indeed violent emotions that are coming alive in Maria.

This sequence from Maria's analysis reminds me of a game invented in a session by a hyperadapted little girl, involving treasure. In the game, a sheet of paper served as a lid on a jungle populated by every kind of animal; whereas the manifest game involved guessing where the treasure was underneath the cover sheet, in reality the cover sheet acted as a window opening on to the – that is, her – inner jungle, and stood for the possibility of emerging from an autistic protective bubble like the one enveloping the hero of the film *The Truman Show*.

Here are some more clinical examples.

Piera's evacuations

Piera is, one might say, a 'psychosomatic' patient *par excellence*, who 'evacuates' her anxieties, great and small, into every organ and apparatus of the body: she ranges over the entire gamut from skin disorders via stomach troubles to hypertensive episodes, headaches and so on. She also seems to be afraid of contact (with the emotions she is constantly evacuating into the body?), so that she avoids ever acquiescing in her analyst's custom of shaking hands at the beginning and end of a session.

A possible sequence for a psychosomatic disorder might be as follows:

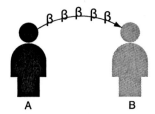

Here, β-elements are transmitted to the other's mind (by projective identification), but that other is not receptive to them, fails to metabolize them and shuts himself off from them.

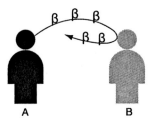

The β-elements then return in gigantic and accelerated form to the transmitting person, who has no choice but to evacuate them. A possible route of evacuation is projection into an organ.

Of course, the second situation, which belongs to the patient's history, gradually comes to be introjected as an unreceptive 'internal object' – in favourable cases – or indeed as a 'reversed reverie'.

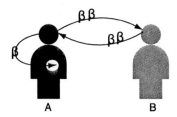

With these patients, the central issue is then 'not what to say but what to do': the most vital requirement is the mental receptivity of the other to what is said and to his own emotions:

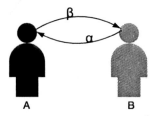

What is progressively returned to the patient must also be based on receptive functioning (Meltzer's toilet-breast), and the return must be 'minimal', undertaken in ways that can be tolerated by a mind that does not – yet – have a capacity for introjection. It is like a person with severe diarrhoea: what matters is to find a suitable toilet, capable of containing and having its lid open. What to give the patient to eat, and when, will follow later. If any 'rehydration' is necessary, this will certainly not be achieved by interpretation of content, but through dilution in metaphors, images and 'asides'. Sometimes the field must fall ill of the patient's problem, pending the possibility of transformation.

Alessia's restaurant
After a session with many accurate transference interpretations – but remember Bion's warning that accurate interpretations arrived at on the basis of thought are likely to be evacuated as β-elements if they exceed the patient's capacity to contain them – Alessia dreams that she is in a smart French-cuisine restaurant with some homosexual friends. Another friend then arrives and throws things at her, and although they are nice they hit her and make her feel ill: she feels giddy and vomits.

I suggest that the field in this case could be represented, in terms of β- and α-elements, by the following diagram:

100

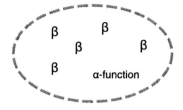

That is to say, it is a hyper-β field with an inadequate α-function.

The hyper-β stems from the patient's history and internal world, as well as from the analyst's approach, which inclines more to interpreting than to receiving.

In terms of the apparatus for thinking thoughts, the situation could be represented as follows:

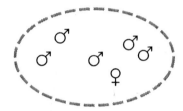

Here, ♂♂ stands for the homosexual relationship that lacks receptivity, while the contained (♂) does violence to the possibility of ♀ and is therefore evacuated.

These diagrams, which are based on the history and represent the patient's internal world, also describe the present field. This can constitute the starting point for its gradual transformation into a field in which ♀ and the α-function will assume greater significance – that is, a field with a greater capacity for reception, metabolization and digestion on the part of the analyst. If this new configuration can be achieved in the here and now of the field, it will eventually inform the internal world and the history.

This will also call for tolerance of the narrative genre chosen by the patient, which will sometimes be remote from the α-sequences of his waking dream thought.

For instance, one and the same sequence of α-elements from a patient's waking dream thought may lead to the following situation:

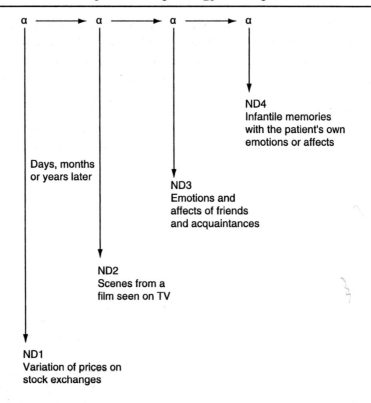

Eventually, if the patient's narrative scenarios are respected while trusting that the analytic work will gradually 'metabolize' them, new scenarios that are less remote from and less distorted than the originals will emerge, thus giving rise to the following sequence:

$$ND1 \rightarrow ND2 \rightarrow ND3 \rightarrow ND4$$

which embodies the analyst's patience and trust as well as the Keatsian negative capability invoked by Bion.

Let me end this chapter by describing, without comment, some clinical situations that perhaps raise more questions than they answer – as is in fact my intention.

Luigi's losses

Luigi is a seven-year-old boy who has been brought along for a consultation because he is '*losing* his hair' – 'after the *loss* of his uncle and grandfather, to whom he was devoted', as his mother, who has come with him, reports. It should be mentioned that the grandfather lost all his hair when he died. 'He found it all terribly painful,' the mother continues. Now Luigi has bald patches on his head, which constantly come and go. The mother goes on to say that Luigi did his best not to cry, even when he was very small, and that even now he is unable to express what he is feeling.

These initial indications already suggest some explanations. The mother herself seems to sense that the deaths of the grandfather and the uncle, of whom he was so fond, are somehow connected with the hair loss. Perhaps the problem *lies in the pain* which *he has been unable* to feel. The coming and going of the bald patches on his head seem to point to a blocked mourning process, which is constantly represented but never resolved – as if Luigi were attempting a kind of symbolization, with and in the body, of something he is unable to experience – namely, loss.

On his first meeting with the therapist, Luigi reports that he has been beaten up by his mates and that this was followed by some pranks, in which he lifted up the bench or his mates themselves. He then makes some drawings.

The first drawing features some crosses. The tower of the church in the picture has small windows that look like huge tears. In the second drawing there are also trees with tear-shaped leaves and branches. His third drawing shows himself with his father and mother, as well as his uncle and grandfather. Finally, the graves of his uncle and grandfather in the cemetery are depicted in the fourth drawing.

Luigi, then, manifestly feels assailed by emotions which he is as yet unable to metabolize – by anguish due to the conflict between the still blocked process of working through mourning, which is for the time being blocked, and the impossibility of mourning, or in other words between loss and its disavowal.

Carlotta's pain

Carlotta takes us over some familiar analytic ground, which makes for a calmer climate after many arduous and conflicting digressions in the direction of what we know and what we would like to know. What we have, then, is a 'functional disorder'.

A colleague telephones me in great alarm about the plight of some friends whose nine-year-old daughter developed a paralysis of the legs within a few days and is now totally unable to move. She has been hospitalized several times, but to no avail. Carlotta's father is a diplomat stationed in a country on Italy's borders and her mother is a well-known journalist.

Carlotta, the parents say, had chickenpox and then a *pain* in one of the trigeminal rami, which was followed by the onset of the leg paralysis. Despite two spells in two different hospitals with first-class neurology wards, nothing organic was diagnosed. This was no great relief to the parents, as the girl has been confined to bed and unable to move for four months now, with a flaccid paralysis of both legs.

The mother also tells me that she had been wondering for some time whether to continue with her work because she was finding it very stressful, and that she had also received threats; perhaps it would have been preferable for her to have a pause for reflection. In view of the new situation at home, she had had to give up work for the moment to look after Carlotta on a full-time basis; this she had also done when Carlotta's elder brother was born: then she had not yet been working full-time for the newspaper but only occasionally.

I am alarmed by this account and feel that great responsibility and great expectations have been vested in me: after all, Carlotta's parents have travelled hundreds of miles to consult me. I decide to have a few meetings with the parents and see how things develop.

There are, it seems, two aspects. The first is the mother's problem with her work, which has been 'solved' by Carlotta's illness, so I start working with the parents on this point. The mother would like to avoid the subject, but feels compelled to address it by the expectations of her husband, who is taken aback and says he has nothing against his wife's choice of staying at home to look after their daughter, but if she didn't feel obliged to do so, she might want to work for the paper again. In this way we begin to disentangle this problem, which was threatening to consolidate an unconscious alliance between mother and daughter.

The second aspect is that of *pain*, which I try to understand in terms of the metaphorical sense of this communication: what kind of pain might Carlotta be suffering or have suffered at this time; what kinds of suffering have gone unnoticed; and how much rage might this have unleashed?

Carlotta's parents are not only highly intelligent but also possess great human sensibility, so that they have no difficulty in embarking on this new path.

To sum up, we have four meetings at fortnightly intervals, developing the aspects they bring me in connection with the *pain* and the mother's professional choices. They also invent a game, a kind of pain graph, along the lines of the bedside charts that record hospital patients' temperature and blood pressure, which signals a gradually decreasing trend as the parents take on board the various problems that make Carlotta suffer.

I try to make sense of what is happening and I compare the situation to a flooded control room where, as the waters retreat, the various sections dry out and start working again. Carlotta in effect quickly passes through the stages whereby children learn to walk: first she crawls along the floor, and then, with difficulty, crawls on her hands and knees. Eventually, on our fifth meeting, the astonished parents tell me that after one pain-graph drawing and a subsequent additional one showing the rage level tending towards zero, Carlotta has started walking again and has even arranged a 'ballet' with her friends to celebrate the event.

Carlotta will of course have psychotherapy to enable her to express her remaining, not yet 'untied', suffering and problems in other ways, and her mother has opted to work part-time.

There is not always a gulf between saying and doing: Sergio, Licia and Piero

I shall now present three clinical vignettes that seem to extend over the entire range from an account of a psychosomatic disorder in an analytic session in a field other than that of the patient, to an account of a psychosomatic disorder by the patient himself.

In the first case, a session with Sergio ends with a reference to jealousy and the rage it can unleash, and a mention of firearms. The patient begins the next session by reporting that his small daughter has had a serious allergic reaction to what was actually good food: the reaction was so bad that she had to be taken to A&E.

For a few sessions I try to reduce the antigenic level of my interventions, until the daughter who has made a full recovery appears. The patient now talks about the 'Grand Cherokee' (the well-known 4×4) he would like to have but cannot yet afford, and, referring to the Indian tribe, I say it needs to give way to the little Cherokee.

The 'little girl' can tolerate the food if it is administered tangentially.

Of course, the problem of listening to the patient's listening is complex, and an even more complex problem is deciding what to do; that is, to interpret the response to one's interpretations or instead to modify the quality of the interpretative food.

The second vignette relates to a young woman, Licia, who – according to the colleague who discusses her case in supervision – appears 'all too mature', and is constantly quarrelling with her slovenly, untidy mother. The conflict between the two protagonists seems irremediable and often revolves around beauty and ugliness, clothes and beauty care, and on many occasions it is acted out intemperately.

With Licia's successive boyfriends, too, it is always a tale of rows and conflicts about appearance and ugliness. The key to all this is ultimately furnished by a dream of the picture of Dorian Gray, which indicates that beauty is the antidote to the decomposition-imbued depressive states with which contact is abhorred. Furthermore, Licia goes on to mention frequent allergic episodes in which she comes out in swellings or buboes – the disavowed part of herself? – which have to be treated with high doses of cortisone; she then gets better, but the cycle is promptly repeated.

Piero, a patient suffering from Crohn's disease, is the subject of the third vignette. His symptom of violent evacuation has shown a distinct improvement, connected – chronologically or causally? – with the progress of his analysis, in which he is managing to reown disavowed or split-off aspects of himself. After studying psychology he had decided to become a librarian instead, but then gradually came to think he might return to the idea of 'treating the insane'. Eventually, he discovers that he himself is afraid of the dark because it seems to 'harbour monsters, ogres, bogeymen and devils', and that he also fears that his wardrobe might contain a murderer who could emerge at night and kill his entire family. In addition to attending his psychiatric training course, he now begins to draw cartoons of terrifying aliens, who thereby find space, containment and representability.

4

Homosexualities: a field ripe for ploughing

This chapter, like its predecessor, is intended not as an organized compilation but as an extended series of examples of work in progress. Based on clinical or supervision experience, these eventually permit the gradual emergence of a previously unforeseeable attempt at conceptualization – namely, the idea of considering the various types of mental functioning observed in terms of 'homosexuality', irrespective of the subject's biological sex. The only claim made for this kind of conceptualization is that it constitutes a piece in a jigsaw that admittedly calls for further in-depth reflection and the contribution of additional material. I shall begin with an attempt at provisional 'mapping'.

1 One form of homosexuality entails a manner of relating and of tranquillizing a part of the self that feared to be very violent and uncontainable, and which is sedated by masturbation, fellatio or being sodomized; in this last case, the part that is, or is feared to be, uncontainable is projected on to the Other. In other words, the functioning of the subject's internal world can be seen as ♂ – what I call a 'hypercontent' – and can be managed only by splitting it off and then 'tranquillizing' it; this is a form of management of psychotic or primitive aspects of the mind which the subject is not equipped to deal with in any other way.

2 A second type of homosexuality consists in a kind of defensive self-cuddling, which may extend from the narcissistic extreme of a homosexual relationship with oneself that disavows the absence of and need for the different Other, to highly excitation-laden forms in which homosexuality and the entire retinue of

anxiety, guilt and self-reproaches act as a 'drug' – a powerful antidepressant, or rather a thought-banishing stimulant (what Esther Bick [1968] called a second skin).

3   A third kind of homosexuality shades off into transsexualism; here, a part of the self feared to be violent and uncontainable is 'oestrogenized'. This excess of $\male$ is managed in various ways, ranging from 'feminization' to fantasies of 'submission' to the object or person that 'personifies' it. This is the situation with Sandro, until he dreams of 'a gorilla dressed in yellow on a skateboard'. The appearance and recognition of this gorilla represent a turning point in Sandro's therapy, enabling him to progress from suicidal plans – which also constituted the ultimate defence against the invasion and unmanageability of the 'gorilla' – to aggressive and violent fantasies; however, this is possible only once he comes to experience the analysis as a kind of 'zoo with a keeper' in which the 'gorilla' can begin to be 'held' without running the risk of non-containability, as in the well-known Italian song by Fabrizio De André about what happens in a small town when a gorilla escapes from the zoo. The hypercontent $\male$ can now begin to seek other ways of being contained and metabolized (through the setting, or the Other's mind), as the creation of links with the Other's receptive mind comes to permit the development of the container. I therefore tend to consider this type of homosexuality too as a form of management of 'violent and invasive psychotic anxieties' that have not found any other way of being kept under control or transformed.

4   Yet another type of homosexuality is feminine in nature ($\female\female$), and consists in an undifferentiated harmony deployed as a barrier against proto-emotions, which the subject feels are likely to burst violently on to the scene and which are thereby 'lethargized'.

There remains the problem of the choice of symptom: why this type of homosexual defence rather than obsessive control of the 'gorilla', or a phobia of, say, animals or fur, or characteropathic explosions?

The situation may be likened to an impounded lake with a failing dam. How the dam responds to the flow of water will depend on the nature of the surrounding terrain: the result may be the formation of a stream, a pool, a flood and so on. Other relevant variables might be the size of the crack in the dam, the pressure of the water and the depth of the lake.

However, whereas an engineer might well be able to devise a formula to 'predict' the possible outflow, we for our part – partly because of the characteristics of the 'living matter' with which we are working – can only use 'hindsight' and make an *a posteriori* reconstruction; predictions, other than extremely general ones, are out of the question.

Following these general reflections, I shall now present some clinical examples.

What is missing with Dino?

A competent therapist in supervision with me brings the case of Dino, saying that the patient's *real* name is important. She tells me of Dino's fear that he 'might be a homosexual', of how he presents himself with his 'emotions supercontrolled' and of his tendency to 'avoid any conflict'. Turning to Dino's way of tackling problems, she quotes his own words: 'I smash them to pieces and then take a bulldozer to them.'

The session she now describes demonstrates a 'bulldozing' type of interpretative activity whereby the therapist in effect attacks the patient's defences with a power hammer; he then asks (as if aware of the concept of projective identification or of the β-screen): 'Do patients usually make their therapists act like parts of themselves?' Now the puzzle for me is substantially resolved: my reverie about the importance of the name Dino immediately focuses on the missing piece: '-saur'.

The subsequent communications bear out my theory: a part (or form of functioning) of the patient that is split off, primitive, violent and felt to be uncontainable is 'acted out' or, if you will, received and personified by the therapist herself with her interpretative hyperactivity: hence the patient's question about whether patients usually make their therapists act like parts of themselves.

The homosexuality was obviously a defence and at the same time a way of managing and masking the 'violent -saur'. The circle is closed by a description of delicate and ailing parents whom the patient has had to support since he was small, without ever being able to express rage or dissent towards them.

The situation constitutes an alternative version of the case of Dr Jekyll and Mr Hyde, in which, instead of the protagonists alternating in their roles in mutually exclusive fashion, Mr Hyde is engaged in a homosexual relationship with Dr Jekyll, who submits to it passively.

The search for, and personification of, the split-off characteropathic (or psychotic) double is reflected in the plots of numerous books and stories, and even more dramatically by the final act in the life of the film director Pier Paolo Pasolini, who was murdered in mysterious circumstances in 1975.

Paolo's comforter

Paolo's constant self-torture about being a homosexual, transsexual or paedophile soon proves to be a kind of cruel rumination that distracts him from his fundamental problem – namely, that of not mattering to anyone, of having no value or weight. This obsessive rumination can be likened to a comforter saturated in chilli pepper – or bile – which both distracts him and somehow protects him from depressively catastrophic experiences; having come into contact with these, he has no option but to attempt suicide, thereby ultimately 'opening up' the dramatic scenario that was blocked by his ruminating.

Martino's noose

The fear of 'sodomization' and of passive homosexuality observed in some patients is attributable to terror at the prospect of being sodomized by their 'own psychotic part', whereas the fear of being a paedophile manifested by other patients or at other times in the therapy has to do with the fear that the 'psychotic part' might 'force its way' into the healthy part, which is felt to be smaller and defenceless.

Martino was a patient of this kind; overwhelmed by the pain inflicted on him when 'sodomized' by his psychotic aspects, he killed himself with a 'metal noose for slaughtering pigs'.

In patients whose 'homosexuality' is thus characterized by violence emanating from a huge primitive part ♂ that forces its way into an inadequate container ♀, the point at which the intrapsychic becomes relational is of paramount importance.

In the case of Dino, described above, the therapist lapses into a kind of 'role-playing' in which she unconsciously acts out this violent, uncontainable part of the patient through her interpretations. However, this enables the patient to feel relieved of the burden of this part

110

and to experience the overwhelming intrusion in the relationship, where it is able to become visible, livable and thinkable.

This is indicated by the session following the one with the violent interpretations. He begins by saying that he has been to a dentist, who violently inserted all kinds of 'hardware' into his mouth, rummaging through it with forceps and pointed instruments and making him bleed. The therapist sees this as a transference communication, saying that he himself sometimes 'puts implements into his own head' in clumsy and unsettling fashion, and he responds by talking about another patient, who killed a psychiatrist. It then becomes possible to get in touch with the rage, fury and sense of violent intrusion that characterized his infantile history, now experienced through internal objects and proto-emotions with which he was not equipped to cope.

This allows a start to be made on metabolizing (in, and by virtue of, the relationship) the hypercontents ♂ by which he felt 'sodomized'.

Mario's attractions

As stated above, the moment when the intrapsychic becomes relational is very important and foreshadows the possibility of significant future development, because from then on we shall be more likely to succeed in unravelling the fantasy structure that has hitherto persisted unchanged. Incidentally, this also explains why the relationship and its vicissitudes, and interpretations centred on the relationship, mobilize the patient's fantasy life more than interpretations 'about' or 'between' his internal objects.

> At the beginning of a session with Mario, while following him from the entrance to the consulting room, I am surprised to catch myself thinking: 'What a lovely big arse he has.' This fantasy then leaves the stage, and it is only after the session is over that I realize that I have taken up the patient's entire time with intrusive and premature interpretations.
>
> However, this enables me to reflect on how I have 'fantasized' and then 'personified' the violent and intrusive part of Mario, by which he himself often feels 'assaulted'. I can then begin to unravel the tangle relationally – something for which there would not have been enough 'space' if we had remained on the intrapsychic level.

Giulio's 'Negro'

In a moment of depression, Giulio tells his analyst in dismay that, while alone in a distant town, he had homosexual fantasies and was distressed

111

by the powerful temptation he felt to act them out. It is not difficult to understand, in the session, how he was thereby seeking antidepressive stimulation and how – in particular in the fantasy of a homosexual approach to a big strong 'Negro' – he was attempting to 'recharge his batteries' from a kind of primitive womb represented by the life force of the 'primitive Negro'. The story ended with his having a few 'Negronis' (gin cocktails) at a bar.

Pino's grieving

In Pino's analysis, images of homosexual relationships in which violence is inflicted on him lessen the more capable he becomes of experiencing feelings that he previously evacuated. The feelings are of pain, loneliness, and in particular a state of mind that he calls 'grieving', bound up with memories or fantasies of children alone, children from Northern countries 'with their house keys hung round their necks' because there was no one waiting for them at home, because everyone was fully occupied with work and had no time to care for and show affection for them.

Domenico's 'drugs'

Domenico, once a pilot for a well-known airline, immediately presents himself as 'gay'. He says he suffered a lot because of a relationship with an artist living in Rome, and mentions 'agonizing memories of what it felt like when his partner left Rome'. Promptly, however, he is confronted with two problems that he sees as more dramatic. The first is the bulimia that leaves him no peace, and the second the feeling that his 'penis is too small' and that he is 'poorly endowed'.

He seems to be living out the drama of an unhealable split between, on the one hand, artistic aspects of himself (possibly idealized) and, on the other, a 'poorly endowed' part that causes him to work as an odd-job man, as he feels unable to take on more demanding duties. He is tormented by this sense of inadequacy – the impossibility of integrating artistic and poorly endowed aspects.

The outcome of the torment is a homosexual promiscuity, which acts as an antidepressant, compounded by drug use and compulsive gambling. However, the homosexual relationships seem also to reflect the hope of a possible reconnection between his impoverished South and the wealthy North featuring in a dream.

In his analysis, if the intensity of interpretation exceeds a certain level, he begins to vomit and skips sessions. The only possible strategy seems to be to take charge of the poorly endowed part, because 'liposuction' and a lightening of the burden can enable him to find the receptors whereby he will be able to integrate idealized, split-off and potentially functioning aspects.

This 'excitational and antidepressive' modality is not specific to homosexuality but also characterizes other possible forms of perversion, such as fantasies of paedophilia, of orgies and of inflicting violence on persons of the opposite sex. These manifestations extend over a kaleidoscopic range, their common feature, as stated earlier, being the hypomanic, thought-banishing aspect. They constitute a kind of alkaline buffer to counteract painful 'acidity'. Rather than picking up and interpreting content (either in the internal world or in the transference), it is therefore important to discern its 'function' at a given time in the particular mental functioning of the patient.

A fog for Emanuele

In Emanuele and patients like him, homosexuality and a whole retinue of miscellaneous perversions are used as a kind of defensive 'fog' in order not to see the persecutory monsters that would otherwise threaten. The counterpart of this fog is the psychoanalytic theories that Emanuele's therapist deploys symmetrically, causing them to 'descend' in the sessions. Bion is very clear about such situations: there is always the temptation, for both patient and analyst, to remain in column 2 of the grid; that is, on the level of lies, so as to avoid the impact of often 'monstrous' emotional truths.

> Before the holidays, Emanuele loses emotional 'contact' with himself and his therapist, who, as stated, in turn defends himself with theory-based interventions. Eventually, speaking in the past tense, Emanuele says that he 'gobbled down feelings he did not like', immediately adding that his penis did not work, that he was absolutely furious with God and that he was attracted to women's clothing.
>
> If Emanuele senses that his feelings are not being recognized and received, the only course open to him is to banish them to the depths, otherwise he will find himself impotent and absolutely furious with his therapist; and if *those* feelings are in turn not received and transformed, he can only resort to a kind of emotional 'oestrogenization', in the form of women's clothes and the pretence that nothing is the matter. He then says he would like to smash someone to pieces – to destroy someone.
>
> Once again the therapist fails to receive the signals, and Emanuele

returns to the subject of homosexuality, this time partly in the sense that the other is not receptive towards his anxieties: if the other is not receptive, the relationship is indeed ♂ ♂ and not ♂ ♀. Emanuele says he would like to meet up again with an old girlfriend (♀) who he felt understood him, whereas in reality the therapist is too full of concerns about him to be truly receptive.

Eventually, however, the therapist does pick up Emanuele's sense of loneliness and understands how this gives rise to bomb-like, explosive emotions. Emanuele immediately notices the therapist's greater permeability and responds by describing how he got to know a boy in an internet chatroom, who, however, seemed to be a girl. Encouraged by this feeling of having been partially 'received', he brings a dream, which reveals what was concealed by the fog: 'There was a monster that tore boys to pieces and raped girls.'

In Emanuele's eyes, the therapist who decides on the holidays and their dates although he knows that his patient is at risk of suicide is inevitably a monster that tears him to pieces and abuses him; yet the therapist, failing to pick up this communication, talks about the 'slavery' involved in the dream image, and Emanuele starts talking about homosexuality again . . .

My point is that, on the one hand, homosexuality and transvestism appear whenever communication is interrupted, while, on the other, homosexuals, girls and transvestites in turn take the analytic stage as signals of the qualities of the mental mating occurring in the sessions: ♂♀, ♂ ♀, ♂ ♂ etc.

Drawing the various threads together, we can postulate that both men and women exhibit forms of mental functioning characterized by male homosexuality or female homosexuality.

What I mean by male homosexuality is a problem complex concerning the management of mental hypercontents ♂, in the form of ♂ ♂: the problem concerns the tranquillization, weakening and sedating of the hypercontent, for which adequate containing capacity is lacking. This is the situation in most of the cases I have described so far. Another example is that of a patient with a long analysis behind him, who said that, as a child, he covered himself completely with a duvet when he went to sleep, even in summer, to protect him in case somebody leapt out from under the bed. I asked out of the blue: 'Who were you afraid might jump out?' The reply came without hesitation: 'The werewolf.'

Female-type homosexualities, on the other hand — I repeat that these may be exhibited by both men and women — are those in which the predominant form of functioning is ♀♀; that is to say, the quest here is for total harmony in order to avoid the leaping out of unmanageable hypercontents. This form is in a sense even more archaic and persecutory, because it involves phobic avoidance of the hypercontent ♂, the 'leaping out' of which must be prevented. *In the 'male' form, on the other hand, it has already 'leapt out' and the problem is how to manage it.*

Cristiana's tranquillity
At her very first meeting with her therapist, Cristiana tells of her constant need for total harmony and of how she was terrified, as a little girl, by the 'whistle of the locomotive': she seems to be saying that harmony can be shattered by the irruption of a train of overwhelming and uncontrollable passions, as will indeed emerge during the course of the therapy. She dreams of idyllic landscapes in which terrifying spiders suddenly appear, while in reality she has sudden explosions of rage and jealousy, the only alternative to these situations being perfect understanding.

However, the harmony, or rather tranquillity, must not be disturbed by beautiful experiences either, because these too interrupt it — as in a dream in which a woman friend showed her a beautiful landscape, but she was unable to tolerate so much beauty. While this could be read in Meltzerian or Kleinian terms, it seems that Cristiana's α-function is overtaxed even by positive afferences. Beauty, enjoyment or a positive passion are also sources of ill-being, because they shatter her 'tranquillity'.

There is a possible link here with the autistic areas of the mind in which a hypotrophic α-function precludes any alphabetization; the situation is one of 'hyper-β' in which the α-function is lacking, and the corresponding defence is a blanket of tranquillity.

As stated earlier, if homosexuality is seen as bound up with the functioning of minds and of their interrelationship, the notion of male or female homosexual functioning is extended also to situations not involving actual sexuality.

Mariella and her cuddling
Mariella has been married to Stefano for many years, during which time they have had intercourse perhaps ten times. They like to embrace in bed,

cuddling or stroking each other's backs. They are living out a totally pacified emotional situation, without shocks, peaks, conflicts or violent emotions, immersed as they are in a climate of mutual tenderness and affection.

This remains the case until their intention to adopt a child is approved: Mariella now explodes, saying that they have managed to deceive everyone into thinking that they are something which they are not. This explosion is followed by a second one, in which Mariella falls in love with a nuclear physicist whom she meets by chance and with whom she embarks on a passionate relationship.

Her husband at first 'pretends' not to notice, then does not want to know, and finally weeps at the idea of separation. The family romances of Mariella and her husband are full of mourning and losses that have not been worked through, just as all the violent emotions aroused by those enforced separations have never been worked through.

They spent their wedding night 'crying' because of the separation from their respective families. The many years of holding each other tenderly by the hand then began.

In my view, the functioning of their minds was characterized by female homosexuality, with a relationship of the ♀♀ type, in which affection and the elimination of any difference or possible conflict served the purpose of keeping all the unthinkable emotions (♂) split off and out of the field, so that they remained like hurricanes in remote seas, not even mentioned in weather reports.

But they were then likely to burst on to the scene without warning, as with the need for emotional truth and the passionate love affair; in other words, a ♂ form of functioning enters the field and subverts the old ♀♀ system (♂ being completely split off). The irruption of ♂ gives rise to intense turbulence owing to the relative inadequacy of ♀ to contain it.

Later, the situation with the new boyfriend becomes more complicated, in that he too becomes more tender and affectionate, so that Mariella wonders if *she* is the kind of person who castrates men – that is, whether she attempts to manage ♂ emotions by performing a kind of 'castration', in which ♂ becomes ♂, subsequently being split off or oestrogenized into ♀♀ functioning. However, the emotions make themselves felt again: catching her boyfriend with another woman, she has a violent explosion of jealousy. Mariella thereafter reports to her therapist: 'I uncovered myself and ran after her like a puppy.'

Not only do the emotions explode, and not only does she un-cover herself in the sense of showing herself, but she also dis-covers herself and discovers how dependence, linking and relationships attract genuine and intense emotions. 'I'll make him pay for this' – so she also discovers rage, violence and the wish for revenge.

In effect, she has emerged from a kind of 'paradise on Earth': having eaten the apple of knowledge and lost the Eden of non-conflictuality, she has now moved on to heterosexual forms of relating (♂ ♀) in which she is confronted with proto-emotions and the ability/inability to manage them (container/reverie). By virtue of this 'inability', she has as it were fallen from the Garden of Eden into a kind of proto-emotional jungle in which emotions are like wild beasts that attack and bite people, as in a dream in which she was pursued in terror by panthers, tigers and leopards.

Sometimes she feels that she would like to go back to her husband and resume her 'peaceful', if soporific, life with him; however, she feels that it is good that Luigi, her new boyfriend, 'dragged me out of the situation', even if it is not easy 'to be at the mercy of all these emotions'.

In conclusion, it seems to me that, in strictly psychoanalytic terms, we need a new nosography based on the patient's mental functioning and not on behavioural epiphenomena. For example, male homosexuality characterizes a patient who claims to be 'Ace gentle stain remover' – whereas harsh bleach remains inside him, as well as, perhaps, sulphuric acid – lest the Other is burnt. So the situation is reversed: the patient turns himself into 'gentle Ace' and makes himself the victim of bullying by the Other, who uses corrosive acid on him. In this situation we have a ♂♂ relationship that lacks a test tube for H_2SO_4, which is oestrogenized and feminized into 'gentle Ace' (♂ → ♀).

Psychoanalysis could in fact advantageously lead us to consider the existence of couples who are heterosexual on the phenotypic level but in reality substantially homosexual, or to investigate phenotypically homosexual couples who are in reality more heterosexual than officially heterosexual couples. This would provide us with a revolutionary vertex, from which we could think of psychoanalysis too as something genuinely capable of opening up 'scandalous' vistas of thought that turned out to contain truths that were more true than they seemed: *if it seems that way, it is that way!* As 'someone' has already said, psychoanalysis can be a plague!

In my preferred language, sexuality in the analyst's consulting room could be said to be either a narrative derivative – that is, a way, equivalent to any other, in which the patient tells us of his mental functioning or dysfunctioning – or a description of something taking place between the minds of the patient and the analyst (Ferro 2006). In the one case we have a narration and in the other the 'event', or fact, of different forms of mental mating with the Other and ultimately also with ourselves.

One type of mating is of the kind ♀ ♂, which constitutes a psychic heterosexuality, in which one party penetrates and the other is penetrated, and in which one receives and the other asks for and obtains reception, in a constant mutual alternation of roles. Then there are functioning of the type ♂ ♂, in which neither party is receptive and available to the other (or in which parts of the self are irreconcilable with each other); and functioning of the 'fusional' type (♀ ♀), without penetration or receptivity, but involving instead a kind of undifferentiated sharing without specificity. In this case, the hypercontents ♂ generally remain split off and liable to burst on to the scene, giving rise to situations of the type ♂ ♀ ♀. Similarly, in the previous case, there is always the possibility of the configuration ♂ ♂ ♀ – that is, of hypercontents with a hypocontainer. The first of these two forms of functioning could be called a masculine and the second a feminine type of homosexuality between minds.

These configurations can make their appearance in the analyst's consulting room in various forms and have little or nothing to do with the protagonists' biological sex. Biologically heterosexual couples can function in a male homosexual register (with constant conflicts) or its female counterpart (with a kind of fusional symbiosis).

Hence biologically homosexual couples (whether male or female) too can function in all three of these ways; biologically homosexual couples can also function with heterosexual forms of mating ♀ ♂; and so on. This, then, is the bewildering reward, or gain, obtained by humanity for the constant prevalence of the mental over the biological as a 'neoformation' of our speciation.

In the analyst's consulting room, *all* of these forms of functioning can be narrated in ways that have nothing to do with sexuality. Again, from another point of view, it could be said that biological homosexualities have nothing to do with psychoanalysis – and at this point in our speciation, it could be agreed that they do not constitute a problem. What is a problem is the functional/dysfunctional ways in which we mate mentally, because they and they alone lie at the root of all kinds of symptoms, in whatever way – that is, in whatever narrative genre – we narrate them.

A child who projects β-elements that are not received by an available mind finds himself in the ♂ ♂ situation of an emotional 'plenum' that encounters another emotional plenum, so that no mental mating or transformation can take place. Conversely, a fusional type of relationship without the circulation of strong emotions gives rise to a ♀ ♀ situation, with intense emotional states that remain split off elsewhere, until one day they perhaps burst on to the scene as symptoms or emotional tsunamis.

So the protagonist's biological sex has little, or indeed nothing, to do with such situations, which may therefore concern relations between men, between women or between men and women, as well as, for that matter, between adults and children, and may include all categories of abuse. Men and women, then, can have homosexual relationships of the kind ♂ ♂ or ♀ ♀, while – why not? – it is surely quite possible for homosexual couples to have fertile and creative ♀ ♂ relationships.

Some further examples that illustrate aspects of the foregoing now follow.

Luca and the civil code

Luca is a lawyer in his forties who is a university lecturer in civil law. He was very much a wanted child for his parents, but when he was two years old his mother contracted a blood disease, which resulted in long periods of hospitalization and gave rise to an intense depression, partly due to the medication she had to take. The father was immersed in his work and, while an affective presence, was unable to make up for the physical and sometimes also mental absence of Luca's mother.

Immediately after his own marriage, Luca finds himself living a double life: his shared existence with his wife and children is paralleled by a secret life, in which he abandons himself to nocturnal homosexual forays, which seem to fill the desperate vacuum by which he at times feels invaded. The time, however, comes when this double life appears to become radicalized, as if there were a 'civil' Luca and another, absolutely 'non-civil' counterpart, who take turns with each other in dramatic fashion. The former's family and university life is seriously jeopardized by the 'non-civil' Luca, who enters into a passionate relationship with a sadistic homosexual, Manolo. He submits to Manolo's pleasure in sado-masochistic orgies, during which, according to his reports, wounds and bruises are inflicted, while also subjecting himself to every possible type of humiliation. This is the point at which Luca asks for analysis.

It immediately seems clear that Manolo stands for a split-off part of himself – the part that failed to be received and transformed by his care-givers' minds and therefore remained thoroughly imbued with violence. Luca submits to this violence in the two-fold register of tranquillizing it (even if he cannot contain it) and of rediscovering his own lost proto-emotional states.

The consulting room, too, promptly appears in Luca's narrations in the form of two places split off from each other: on the one hand, the chambers of the lawyer, a serious professional, and on the other, the darkened red-light establishment where Manolo exhibits himself. The analyst can not only see Manolo as the split-off part of Luca (as well as one of Luca's ways of seeing his analyst) but can also break him down into the emotional subcomponents of which he is an aggregate. This disaggregation is achieved through the recognition and description, in various scenarios, of the rage, jealousy, vengefulness and violence of . . . Manolo.

This eventually enables Luca to speak to his 'wife' (the receptive part of himself ♀ and the analyst ♀) about his double life.

Before this, Luca has a dream in which he remembers a cinema in his home town where there were two auditoria side by side. Sometimes a romantic film would be shown in screen A and a Western or war film in screen B, and on occasion the shots or cries from the film in screen B could also be heard in screen A.

The narration continues with a serious illness contracted by Luca: an uncontrollable form of diabetes, which, however, proves amenable to an experimental pancreatic cell transplant procedure devised by the Karolin-ska Institute in Stockholm.

Manolo can be seen as a kind of uncontainable aggregation of 'ketonic bodies' that resulted in the invalidity of his 'civil' life; but the analysis is becoming the transplanting of cells, or of the α-function, that enables him to metabolize his proto–emotional states of rage, fury, jealousy and despair – until Manolo, having no further need to exist, leaves the stage.

Luca will be able to have an accepting relationship with his own proto-emotions and will achieve a ♀ ♂ relationship with himself, emerging from the sadomasochistic relationship and from homosexuality. However, all this has nothing whatsoever to do with sex: the protagonists could have been of any biological sex.

A part of Luca's mind had found acceptance and transformability, and had achieved $\male\female$ relationships, whereas another part ($\male$) had remained untransformed, in the guise of Manolo, and exerted pressure to be received and transformed. Luca's therapy permits the further development of the α-function and of $\female$, so that 'Manolo' can be disaggregated into his component subunits, 'digested' and transformed into emotions and thoughts.

Laura and the lies

Laura (A. Ramshorn-Privitera, 2006, personal communication) asks for analysis owing to the despair into which she plunges without knowing why. She also suffers from crushed vertebrae. Her affective life has included some homosexual episodes, first with Lucia and then with Martina. The relationships with her partners are utterly affectionate and relaxed, but this is achieved on the basis of a lie: everything that might cause conflicts, clashes or quarrels simply remains unsaid or is 'settled' in such a way as not to arouse conflict.

Laura's emotional situation could be represented as follows:

$$\female = \female \qquad\qquad \begin{matrix} \male\ \male \\ \male\ \male \\ \male\ \male \end{matrix}$$

Here, the fusional homosexual relationship is shown on the left, while the right-hand side represents the constantly disavowed and split-off proto-emotions, which come to inhabit a parallel universe, but with which there is no communication.

The analyst initially accepts a degree of collusion with Laura, agreeing to provide her with certificates enabling her to receive payments from her health insurance fund, which actually only covers the cost of neurological treatment, by certifying that she is receiving neurological and physical/rehabilitative therapy for the pain of the crushed vertebrae; these 'partial falsifications' enable Laura to afford the 'cost' of having analysis.

In so doing, the analyst is guided by her memory of the phrase 'To the pure, all things are pure' pronounced by Father Cristoforo in Manzoni's *The Betrothed*; but when Laura obtains a position that enables her to pay for her analysis herself, the therapist decides to stop issuing the desired certificates to her. This is the moment of truth about the analytic work done. Now that the wall of disavowal and lies has been penetrated, will the emotions that burst into the field utterly destroy the capacity to contain them, or will the joint work of analyst and patient succeed in containing the emotions activated by the analyst's refusal to collude any further? (I, in fact, see the analyst's collusion as only apparent, because she felt that her certification of the pain and physical/rehabilitative treatment was actually a metaphor of Laura's sense of being crushed by desperation and pain and of the analysis as a 'physical/rehabilitative' treatment.)

The analysis trembles on the brink; the explosion of anger, rage, jealousy and revenge is unbridled, and Laura at one point even threatens the analyst over the 'false' certificates. Ultimately, however, the analysis holds up and Laura, accompanied by her analyst, succeeds in owning all the proto-emotional states that she had always kept at bay by lying.

The analyst realizes only after the event that the field had to catch Laura's illness – the lies and connivance – in order subsequently to reveal whether the analytic work carried out had made it possible to overcome the lying and to confront increasing doses of emotional truth. That, as it turned out, was what had been achieved.

Here again, the biological sexes concerned are irrelevant except as a way of narrating the transition from the original form of functioning to one between ♀ and ♀. In this case, the analysis basically seems to have permitted the construction of a digestive apparatus whereby it was possible for the split-off proto-emotional states to be digested. The notion of the 'digestive apparatus' could be replaced by the formulation 'α-function/container'.

Remo and Lucio: a 'lite' homosexuality
Remo (Ramshorn-Privitera 2006) is a computer engineer who has a homosexual relationship with Lucio. They have been together since they became aware of a mutual attraction at secondary school; however, the familiarity between them is such that they are like brothers.

The mothers of Remo and Lucio met and became friends in the waiting room of the psychiatrist who was treating them for 'depression'.

122

Both mothers seemed to have minds in a state of partial indigestion, so that their sons' proto-emotions could be only partly received and transformed; excess amounts remain, giving rise to the 'double', which becomes the way in which these lost parts are managed.

A kind of psychic twinning is evident, in which a high proportion of the proto-emotions were picked up and metabolized; the mothers' depression began when they were both abandoned almost simultaneously by their husbands while their sons were at primary school. The fathers, both of whom were brilliant professionals, had taken up with much younger women, who were in their late thirties.

Passion can be imagined as involving very high voltages, and was experienced by Remo as extremely dangerous, so that he miniaturized it into the tiny current flows in the computer, while Lucio had done something quite similar by taking a degree in natural sciences and setting up a bonsai nursery; in his case too, intense emotions were being nursed, but once again miniaturized.

The differentiation between Remo and Lucio takes place when the former decides to embark on an analysis owing to Lucio's increasingly prolonged work-related trips to Japan. The analyst immediately realizes that Remo and Lucio are in fact like two twin brothers, or rather two masks of the same person, and finds a way of enabling them to inhabit the consulting room together as 'characters' without any hurry to decode or interpret.

Remo talks at length about himself, but at equal length about Lucio and about the hobbies of both. Discovering that his analyst's mother tongue is Argentine Spanish – and having spent all the summer holidays with his father in Buenos Aires, where he had been sent by his new company – he eventually starts addressing his analyst in both Italian and Argentine Spanish, so that his double takes on an increasingly intense life, with the two languages in the consulting room.

He then expresses disagreement with his analyst's political ideas – having discovered his signature on an international petition – criticizing him violently, accusing him and even offending him; he is actually going back over the path that he was unable to pursue to its end with a mother who was depressed and otherwise occupied.

Remo's situation changes from:

to:

$$\male \text{-----------} \rightarrow \male$$
$$\male \text{----------} \rightarrow \female$$

in which he experiences a heterosexual kind of relationship between minds.

The field is thus restructured as follows:

$$\male\male \qquad\qquad\qquad \male\male\male$$
$$\male$$

$$\female\female\female$$

This is now narrated by way of the growing emotional disturbance aroused in Remo by a female neighbour, Sabina.

For a long time, the analysis assumes the following form: Remo comes to his session full of rage, fury and jealousy because Lucio is far away. He meets with acceptance on the part of the analyst, and what had been confused finds receptivity and representation in new images and narrative plots; Remo ends the session by talking about his growing attraction to Sabina.

Then a friend of his, 'Romolo' (Romulus and Remus!), falls desperately in love with an Argentine girl. After this Remo feels very disturbed when he finds himself with Romolo, Lucio and Livia in a mixed sauna in Buenos Aires, but the experience that terrified him ultimately attracts him.

The situation now can be represented as follows:

That is to say, turbulence in the field encounters a mind that is available.

The work is still in progress, but Remo is more and more attracted by his neighbour Sabina, although he still feels affection for Lucio. Ever keener emotions are coming alive: the initial situation of 'twin' inertia has given way to more electrically charged situations involving characters and interpreters who are oddly similar to those of the legend of the foundation of Rome (Romulus and Remus): while there may not be a fratricidal struggle, we are witnessing the opening up of the space and time for more luxuriant, less miniaturized (or explosive!) passions.

Antonello between Heidi and the bison

Antonello requests analysis owing to erectile difficulties; he says that he is homosexual, but if need be also heterosexual. He claims to have no particular traumatic memories, except that he 'cut his own penis as a child'. He is now also suffering from severe hypertension and needs to have some tests carried out; he has been on beta-blockers for some time. He has a very affectionate relationship with his long-term partner, Vincenzo.

The following scenario immediately occurs to me: he has been under such severe pressure (the hypertension) that he has undergone radical therapy: 'cutting his penis' − that is, deadening the intensity of the unmanageable hypercontents $\male$ by the use of 'beta-blockers'. In other words, he has emasculated all proto-emotional aspects, to the point, however, of totally losing his potency and becoming 'impotent'.

Ultimately, β-elements are the engine of our psychic life, and if we block many, or too many, of them, we do indeed lose our potency. What Antonello has with Vincenzo appears, in terms of mental functioning, to be a female homosexual type of relationship ($\female\female$).

It is interesting to note that, from the very first session, Antonello's analyst offers a series of extremely active and, I would say, overwhelming interpretations, to which Antonello responds with two dreams.

In the first dream, 'a train gathers speed, but then it is derailed and brings down everything it crashes into on top of it', while in the second 'powerful lightning flashes and electric shocks come out of an oval'.

The analyst has taken Antonello's hypertension (the hyper-penis or hypercontent) on to himself and immediately overwhelms him with his transference interpretations, which the patient experiences as high-voltage thunderbolts.

The analyst then gives a further series of transference interpretations, to which Antonello responds with two other dreams. In the first, someone enters into him with his whole body, and in the second someone takes aim at him and bombards him with projectiles. He flees, hiding behind a wall. The analyst acts out the missing piece – Antonello's hypertension – which becomes an interpretative hypertension, whose effects are picked up in the dreams.

The field now includes a vector of high penetrativity, and, in the absence of a place to put these interpretations, it has become a male homosexual field ($\male\male$), where the analyst's interpretative penetration impinges on the patient's incapacity (the absence of a place for reception).

The next session is filled with repetitive themes and accounts of the patient's boring life with Vincenzo, with whom the highest degree of involvement takes the form of walking in the mountains to photograph beautiful scenery.

So here is a session in which the functioning is once again of the form $\female\female$. In effect, the field either can function in 'Heidi mode' (as in the children's book of that name) or it can be laden with bison (proto-emotions). The problem will be two-fold: first, to run the bison sufficiently to transform them into a herd of cows and bulls, and then to generate a 'cowboy' function for containing and managing the proto-emotional states. This will inevitably involve reduction of the 'hypertension' and the development of $\female$. It will lead to the development of the $\female\male$ (heterosexual!) relationship, not only between analyst and patient, but also between the patient and himself, in terms of his capacity to mate mentally with himself in the experiencing of containable emotions.

The excess of hypotensives (cutting his own penis) gives rise to hypotension (described as the lack of an erection). I call a hypotensive relationship $\female \equiv \female$. The field activated is generated by the introduction into it of the split-off energy represented by the symbol '$\rightarrow$' (that is, the bison). These will come to be containable with the gradual development of the container $\female\female\female$ and the presence of less 'hyperized' contents, which will be the outcome of the process of alphabetization of the field's hyper-β-elements.

From this point of view, autistic mental functioning can be seen as the maximum degree of ♀ − ♀ functioning, crushed flat into a mere line ⌐, while 'characteropathic' behaviour is the form in which hyper-β-elements are managed evacuatively if they exceed the level that can be alphabetized.

Maria and a world of the deaf

Maria comes for an initial consultation with a view to a possible analysis, and tells of her homosexual relationship with Elena:

$$♀ ≡ ♀$$

Although Maria looks very feminine, on seeing her the analyst is surprised to find himself thinking that she 'looks like a boy'. He then has a reverie that redefines the field as follows:

$$♀ ≡ ♀) ♂$$

– that is to say, he 'dreams' Maria's split-off proto-emotional aspects.

Maria now tells the analyst that her mother suffers from bronchiectasis, thus redefining the field as characterized by containers inadequate for holding excessively violent emotions:

Excess of ♂♂ ♂♂ in container ♀

The father is described as irascible, subject to fits of rage where he smashes everything in sight. So the field is once more redefined, this time being characterized by the presence of explosive mental protocontents:

♂ ♂ ♂ ♂

Maria goes on to describe how she works as an *educator* at a day centre for psychotics (unable to metabolize the proto-emotions, she can only try to 'educate' them).

Next she mentions Claudio Fragasso's film *Night Killer*, whose Italian title means *Do Not Open That Door*.

In terms of the initial drawing, the situation could now be described as:

$$♀ ≡ ♀) \ ♂♂$$
$$) \ ♂♂$$

– in other words, do not open the 'door' to the adjoining room containing the split-off proto-emotions.

She now talks about the film *Catherine and I*, starring Alberto Sordi [whose surname is the Italian word for 'deaf'], which is about a robot (Catherine) that looks like a woman: Sordi takes her in, but fails to understand the emotions that she is developing towards him. These are intense, human emotions, whose outcome, precisely because they are not received and understood, is to plunge Catherine into fits of fury in which she destroys the entire house. In other words, when a link forms, it is a source of emotions and passions, and if the Other is 'deaf' to these, they explode, need hypercontainment, or are split off. The hope is that the analyst will prove less 'deaf' [*sordo*] than the world of 'Sordi' [the deaf] that is played out in the film.

The analyst often, in effect, serves as a particle accelerator, which must also have a cooling system so that the nuclear fission of the emotions aroused by the link and its vicissitudes leads to the generation of energy and not to a psychic Chernobyl.

Between dead calm and a violent storm

After she has been in analysis for a while, Andreina – in addition to her 'female homosexual (♀♀)' relationship with Carlo, which is characterized by tenderness and affection, without any contact with strong proto-emotional states (♂) – begins to take an interest in Roberto, 'the young man who cleans the stairs'. Andreina is clearly describing two places in the analytic field, in one of which the wind has died down to a dead calm, while the other is beginning to include the possibility of sailing through turbulent emotional waters.

With Carlo, Andreina is so to speak experiencing a situation of tight vaginismus:

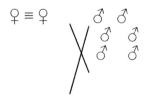

This is a relationship of fondness, which is locked and barred to prevent communication with a place of hyperturbulence made up of emotional protocontents.

128

For a long time, Andreina 'hated the blacks', whom she saw as dangerous and violent. With another friend, Mohammed, however, it is she who takes the initiative, saying: 'Why don't we see each other some time?' Mohammed is not black, but he is not white either; so it seems possible to get close to the emotional Africa, if only in stages, and perhaps for the time being only by looking at photographs.

She then announces that she might yet want to be penetrated by Mohammed, because, unlike Carlo, who is only very receptive and gentle (the blacks, then, remain completely split off), he shows signs not only of gentleness and tenderness but also of the possession of virility, which, however, he is perfectly able to control.

So there now seems to be an incipient opening in the wall that was keeping out the hypercontents:

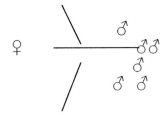

Mohammed has invited her to an ice cream parlour on the Corso San Gottardo (are her emotions being frozen?), and she feels that her 'stomach is the size of a hazelnut' (vaginismus of the stomach and the mind).

However, she adds that she has for the first time experienced unknown emotions, which gradually aroused first fear and then genuine pleasure in her. At home, she then attempts self-penetration with carrots and courgettes, and enjoys this. The analyst meanwhile tries to be like a vegetable, aseptically saying something vaguely penetrative.

Following a prolonged period of vegetable coitus tests of this kind, and having, through the receptiveness of the analyst, progressively introjected a cavity (of the mind/stomach/vagina), she finally, at the age of 35, has her first sexual intercourse with Mohammed – which is, of course, 'protected'!

Marina's keloids

Marina suffers from vaginismus, which is so bad that (sexual) 'relations' are totally out of the question. She lives with a man of whom she is very fond, but they have no sex life. However, Marina discovers that she has another symptom, the hyperproduction of keloids, so she has been to a plastic surgeon, but the outcome of the surgery is that her body is scarred all over.

As the termination of her analysis approaches, it seems fairly easy to connect a dream Marina has with her early history. She had to close herself off from any new relationship ('relations') because relating to the Other was a constant cause of narcissistic wounds: the lack of response from her primary object had marked her so badly that what remained was her wish, or need, to be intuitively understood without having to express herself.

She had had a long period of psychoanalytic psychotherapy, the effect of which had been to fill her with further keloids: 'the keloids increased after each operation, as there were more and more wounds'. Her social phobia, or vaginismus towards other people, protected her from over-intense emotions that tore her apart upon every lack of attunement with the Other – but this did not happen if, exceptionally, other people understood things without her actually having to say them. The narcissistic vulner-ability finds a solution, or at least a successful defence, in the 'vagin-ismus', in closing herself off from relating deeply to the Other. This ensures that a part of herself can function in affectionate exchanges, but only if they are unconflicted and superficial.

Marina could equally well have developed different symptoms – say, a phobia of dogs, cats or birds, in the sense of a 'phobia' of all strong emotions that bite, scratch or peck. Alternatively, she could have developed an obsessional pathology involving, for example, constant hand-washing to rid herself of intolerable emotions that could have devastated her; and so on. The chosen defence mechanism, while limiting the vital functions, allows at least some parts of the personality to function.

Luigi too has been wounded by the lack of response from the Other, and experiences disappointment and rage. He has in part effected a narcissistic withdrawal, but he could also have become a priest or developed a phobia of microbes. The same applies to Nando, who would like to be a 'marvellous Infant Jesus like the one he had in his cot when he was very small'. The room in the block where he lives may not contain the cow, the ass and the Star in the East, but is transformed into the kitchen where he took it in turns to sleep in a little bed with a baby cousin during an infancy spent in straitened circumstances: the analyst's consulting room alternates between being a cot and a cow-shed, according to the emotional specificity of the encounter.

130

Envy and homeless contents

Cristiana had begun an analysis ten years earlier owing to homosexuality of the ♀♀ kind, in which extremely primitive and violent aspects (i.e. unmanageable and unthinkable proto-emotional states) were split off. A prolonged period of analytic work not only permitted the alphabetization of 'Barbara', a partner who had appeared on the scene at a certain point and shaken up the tired affective equilibrium of Cristiana's relationship with her companion, which had prevailed since they were at school together, but also made it possible for Cristiana to name, get to know, acknowledge, contain and manage the proto-emotions and, subsequently, emotions that Barbara's arrival had unleashed: 'barbarous' rages, jealousies and disappointments.

The '*bestia*' [wild animal] which Cristiana had spoken about for a long time, referring to her father, then becomes the '*fiera*' [a double meaning in Italian: both 'wild animal' and 'the proud one'] and subsequently '*fierezza*' [pride] – his pride, of which she herself even feels proud – a pride which she feels belongs to him.

The same applies to the path on which she has embarked towards femininity, in the sense of receptive capacity. Eventually, however, the patient says that she feels an intense femininity within her, but that she must deny or hide it for fear of the envy to which it might give rise.

Rather than continuing my discussion of the various forms of mental functioning – of how the development of ♀ permitted the arrival of new emotional contents ♂ – I shall instead, unusually for me, digress into the subject of envy.

Envy does not seem to me to be one of the basic emotions with which we have to deal, as quite a few analysts have for years maintained, but in my view signals – is typical of – a moment in mental development when a certain capacity for containment has already developed, but is as yet inadequate in the face of all the contents seeking to be accommodated.

A possible metaphor is that envy corresponds to the point when boat people disembark on a beach and, although there are homes, there are not enough to accommodate them all. If one part finds a home, the part that does not is envious of the one that does. This situation thus arises out of the simultaneous presence of containers in the course of development, which have not yet developed sufficiently to accommodate a significant proportion of the contents on hand (proto-emotions and β-elements). The onset of envy indicates that

131

homeless emotions have landed where there are homes, but not enough homes. It thus indicates that the patient's split has been overcome to some extent and that he has embarked on the road to future integration.

At this point, I must ask myself an awkward question, to which I am inclined to give a paradoxical answer.

Are these 'mechanisms' that I attribute to both male and female homosexuality not too general? Could these psychic configurations not lead to other kinds of symptoms that have nothing to do with 'real sexuality'?

However, that is precisely my meaning: the same psychic configurations could perfectly well have given rise to (seemingly) totally different stories; that is after all the basis of the concept of a narrative derivative as wholly equivalent to any other narrative derivative, subject only to preservation of the unvarying structural elements involved.

5

A model of the mind and its clinical implications: how to turn back in order to move forward

A gifted therapist begins to treat a boy with an autistic syndrome characterized by repetitive body movements, echolalia and the repetition of phrases from television commercials. In his first session, the patient, Stefano, upsets the contents of his paintbox, which he gradually pours on to the big canvas boards that the therapist gives him. This scene is repeated over and over again for a long time, but eventually becomes more contained.

One day, after spilling red paint all over the board, Stefano spreads it out into a particular shape which extends from the central red area, and announces in between his stereotypic verbal evacuations: 'Look – the cook – fire.' It is hardly necessary to say how disconcerted and moved the therapist is by this first 'meaningful' communication.

The paint game continues and Stefano produces more and more outline shapes over many months of work that involves mainly the acceptance, acknowledgement and elaboration by the therapist of Stefano's emotions and sensory impressions, by which she feels invaded and sometimes overwhelmed in the sessions. Eventually, after about a year of therapy, Stefano makes two drawings, the first of which shows the shell of a kind of dugout canoe with the outline of a person inside it, and the second the rough outline of a crocodile and a lion with sharp teeth. While confining herself to describing these activities in words, on the emotional level she continues the anguished process of working through the proto-emotional and often protosensory states by which she feels 'captured'. The work of figuration is ongoing, with drawings of landscapes, houses and trees.

Stefano begins to develop significant verbal activity, using short, well-contextualized sentences to describe or comment on what he depicts in his drawings. Two drawings in particular assume meaning. The first shows houses with red roofs that seem to consist of tongues of fire; Stefano's comment in this case is 'firemen'. The second shows a forest of sharply pointed trees, about which he comments: 'Thorns . . . prick you'. This phrase is repeated over a long period, during which he makes drawings with pointed shapes.

Meanwhile, Stefano's language becomes increasingly meaningful and articulate, and one day he draws a 'pan for cooking spinach': a big saucepan can be seen in the middle flanked by two human figures – a child on one side and a woman on the other. The verbal evacuations and repetitive stereotypic movements are less and less in evidence, being increasingly replaced by play or meaningful verbal communications.

An experimental physicist might describe the development of the mind in the following terms, as Bion did, making predictions like a mathematician addressing a problem in physics. The initial trigger of the 'big bang' represented by the kindling of mental activity in our species is the child's massive evacuation of protosensory and proto-emotional states. If these evacuations (β-elements) are received, accepted and transformed by a mind that absorbs and metabolizes them (the α-function), they are gradually transformed into pictograms endowed with sense (α-elements). The mind of the person who effects this transformation not only transforms the protosensory chaos into an emotional figuration endowed with meaning, but also, through the constant repetition of this operation, conveys the 'method' of doing so (the α-function). In this way the 'spinach-cooking (or thorn-cooking) saucepan' is introjected, the thorns simply being the proto-emotional sense impressions that prick (β-elements).[1]

The constant repetition of this transformational cycle – which is tantamount to a Krebs cycle of the mind – also has other effects: the play of projection–introjection–reprojection–reintrojection permits the differentiation of a hollow space and a convex space, of a space for reception and a filled-out, 'plenum' space – in a word, of container (♀) and contained (♂).

When ♀ and ♂ first relate to each other, this is in effect the first

---

[1] Translator's note: The Italian words for spinach (*spinacie*) and thorns (*spine*) are very similar in sound.

sexual relationship between the mind and another mind, and between a mind and itself. From then on, the α-elements will arrange themselves in chains of pictograms that will confer shape and colour on everything that was previously exerting chaotic pressure and will give rise to the sequence of α-elements that comprises waking dream thought.

This dream thought, which is not directly accessible except in particular situations (Ferro 1996a), must undergo further operations, which are performed on it by the mental functions represented by the oscillations of Ps ↔ D, ♂♀ and NC ↔ SF (negative capability ↔ selected fact). Information on waking dream thought can be obtained from its narrative (or, say, graphic or play-related) derivatives. For instance, sensory/proto-emotional stimuli involving irritation, rage and finally the onset of a calmer mood could be transformed by the α-function into the following emotional pictograms:

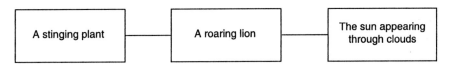

This sequence of α-elements, which are in themselves inaccessible, could give rise to an infinite number of narrative derivatives in a wide variety of literary (or graphic or play-related) genres. For instance, it could become a chain of associations that might be expressed as follows:

A childhood memory: 'When my father's friend announced at the table that he had bumped into me in the street during school hours, I was furious and would have liked to beat him up, but the unruffled expression on my father's face calmed me down.'

A scene from everyday life: 'Yesterday I saw some boys harassing an immigrant and I felt very irritated; I was about to tell them off, but then a policeman appeared and they ran away.'

A sexual scene: 'When Carla didn't want to make love, I got angry and was on the point of leaving and going back home, but then I discovered that she was having a surprise party and there were friends in the living room.'

A scene from a film: 'I remember a film sequence in which the hero takes a dim view of it when he sees his wife from behind kissing a man; he is about to attack her when he sees that she is in fact kissing their son, back from military service: my goodness, how he had grown!'

An infinite number of examples could be adduced, but I should also like to present a dream, because it is important to realize that dreams can be regarded not only as a channel affording access to the unconscious, but also as a narrative derivative of the α-sequence that belongs to the moment when it is narrated. So the scene mentioned above could also be narrated as follows: 'I dreamed that I was stung in the dark by something I thought was a scorpion; I was furious with the person who had guaranteed me a safe journey, but then discovered it was only a prickly plant.'

Of course, this conception of the mind presents us with an enormous problem in terms of analysis: what aspect of it is the most meaningful? This will of course depend on the severity of the patient's pathology, or on the level of mental functioning with which we wish – or are able – to concern ourselves.

What matters most, in my view, is to permit development of the α-function and of the capacity of ♀; this calls for an increase in the development of ♂ and in the amplitude of the Ps ↔ D and NC ↔ SF oscillations. It is only after prolonged work on these primary necessities that we find ourselves in the position of a cook with a hob and pans for 'cooking' the ingredients that reach him in raw form. For only then shall we be able to concern ourselves with historical and reconstructive aspects and allow the ongoing process of *Nachträglichkeit* to give rise to transformations of the patient's history and experience.

However, looking at our species, I am not so sure that this really does represent a once-for-all evolution. I often, in fact, wonder whether mankind is actually engaged in a process of backward evolution, or is at least passing through a phase in which it is as yet uncertain whether our minds can develop in such a way that the human species can live the best possible life, based on ethical principles, or whether the shortcomings of the human mind, in the absence of further steps towards maturation, will always give rise to terrifying destruction directed towards exorcizing everything we are unable to understand or accept, such as the transience of our existence.

However, to return to our subject, let us consider the case of a little girl who has a phobia of anything potentially suggestive of emotional explosions, such as balloons or bottles of fizzy drinks, and whose mother herself has a phobia of any kind of noise from the body. The girl draws a somewhat affected picture of a little house and a tree. In my capacity as supervisor, I develop the drawing with a reverie that adds a shark under the house, which confers meaning on the girl's statement that no one wants her: this makes the analysis more dream-like, and also gives a place to parts that are not yet thinkable.

The girl then draws a monster with long claws, thus revealing the meaning of the mother's phobias about nail-biting: if someone bites his nails, that very fact summons up the unrepresentable monster.

The intensification of the dream-like element allows the α-function to develop, while the absence of premature interpretative caesuras by the analyst, who together with the patient builds fences for wild animals (wild, potentially devouring emotions or contents ♂), makes for the development of thinkability or, in other words, the finding of wide spaces through the progressive development of ♀.

It is only later that it will be possible to link the outcome of this work both to oedipal contents and to the reconstruction of the infantile experience of a mother who is herself too 'volcano-like' to accommodate a little girl with magmatic emotions. Any assignment of historical meaning will have to be preceded by the new experience that the girl will have in sessions with an analyst capable of reverie and of reception, who will gradually transform the unapproachable emotional magma, by the use of a kind of cooling emotional syllabary, into representable and hence perceptible emotions that can be distinguished from each other. The game that will permit the development – or in some cases the very formation – of the *tools* for thinking is played out in the consulting room, between the minds of the patient and the analyst, and within a setting. After this, it will also become possible to weave the historical and often historico-transgenerational experience into a fabric and to share it.

The two advertisements reproduced here[2] illustrate a favourite metaphor of mine, of the α-function as a kind of tomato strainer:

---

[2] Kindly supplied by Jeanne Wolff Bernstein.

This is used to transform the tomatoes represented by β-elements into emotional pictograms (α-elements).

In the absence of emotional availability ('Loveless'), the β-elements remain unchanged:

Given an available mind, the tomatoes will give birth to children, or α-elements:

Laura and the pictograms

After some transference interpretations, which the analyst considers to have been cautious and appropriate, Laura feels thoroughly persecuted: 'My mother tells me I am useless'; 'It annoys me to hear your/her [the Italian word *sua* can mean either] opinion' – and then feels utterly awful. When the analyst picks up her state of mind and comments, 'Perhaps even little remarks can ruin your sense of security,' Laura pulls herself together and talks about her niece, 'who puts on some music and then dances', about herself and how she feels sometimes of one colour and sometimes another, and then about her father, who used to brush her hair for hours on end.

The process has in effect got under way again through the formation of α-elements, which transform protosensory impressions into pictograms, audiograms and kinaesthesiograms, thus giving rise to the consciousness of (affective) colour, (emotional) movement and the proximity of caring. As her capacity to think gradually becomes better organized, she says that she and her boyfriend found themselves 'kissing without her noticing it': this is a valuable technical hint, indicating that things must happen without the patient noticing it, with a spontaneous naturalness such that the patient does not undertake defensive or evasive manoeuvres.

Paola and the Other's mind

Paola dreams that she is talking to her husband about what she feels, but he is only partly listening and partly thinking of something else, and then goes away. Unlike what she would have done in the past, she follows him, continues to talk to him, does not withdraw, and then sees him talking to a girl. She in turn talks to a girl who perhaps works at a crematorium, where there are dead bodies.

I reflect that this dream in fact accurately describes my own mental state; I am listening to the patient and trying to be close to her, but cannot help thinking about some other concerns of mine involving mourning.

An interpretation along those lines would not, I believe, help the patient, and would be more in the nature of a countertransference confession. So I say that she seems to be clearly picking up the mental state of the person close to her and in particular that person's suffering. The patient is moved; she accepts this initial attempt at interpretation, supplementing it with memories of mourning and of the deaths of two little brothers that had taken place at home, and she recalls that when she was small she could feel her parents' mental state and specifically their suffering.

I continue by saying that, for her, it was and is important to have the attention and mental presence of the people she is talking to; instead of keeping quiet and withdrawing as she used to, she now seems to be saying something like: 'Doctor, I need to feel your attention and mental presence; please don't be distracted by other thoughts when you are with me, especially if they are painful ones.' She answers: 'It's so nice to hear you pronounce the words I had unsaid inside me. That's exactly what I wanted to learn to say.'

I find it quite extraordinary to see how the present situation made it possible, through my mental absence and my own mourning, to 'embody' the experience of Paola as a little girl with a depressed mother whose mental presence could not be taken for granted but had to be tested – a problem that never clearly emerged and was never put into words.

Sara and the noises from downstairs

Sara is brought along for a consultation because she has suffered from severe headaches for some years, and all tests and neurological treatments have proved negative. The onset of this condition is associated, at least in chronological terms, with the death of her grandmother from a 'highly proliferative neoplastic disease' and the birth of a little sister. She also has fits of anxiety before going to bed; she says that the less she sleeps, the more she is afraid of getting a 'headache', and that what keeps her awake is anxiety in case 'my little sister cries' or 'the old lady in the downstairs flat, just under my bedroom, might have her television on too loud' and the noise might disturb her.

The only thing that relieves her is to put on her iPod headphones and listen to music at high volume; at the same time, she says she often hears music in her head and cannot get rid of it.

Deconstructing the text of the narration already at this early stage suggests a provisional hypothesis. Of course, the result of a deconstruction, with subsequent, different reconstructions of meaning, must be confirmed by the further information that will accrue. The tentative hypothesis is that a set of 'proto-emotions' are exerting pressure in her 'head' but have no possibility of further alphabetization; so they remain in the state of 'crying', of music, or of noise coming from (or proliferating in) the room downstairs, where there is a primitive structure that she 'does not feel' and which she evacuates.

The iPod headphones seem to exorcize the music that comes from inside, or rather from down below, as with the hero of Carlo Lucarelli's thriller *Almost Blue*, who plays music over headphones at all times in order not to hear the sound of the bells that would make him kill again. The session with Sara seems to confirm these fantasies: she makes one drawing showing the face of a little girl without a mouth or ears, and another, also depicting the face of a little girl with the same characteristics, but less stylized.

She seems to be saying that there are 'silent' emotions that can be neither expressed nor listened to, and that the engorgement or proliferation of these emotions is what is then evacuated – but while this affords (emotional) relief, it also gives her a headache. The third drawing, yet again of a little girl's mouthless and earless face, also shows a beating heart, so something is apparently coming to life. Something that relieves her, she says, is the application of 'tiger balm' to her forehead; she then draws some figures that are 'pieces that do not have any place to be in'. It seems that if the rage – the tiger balm – can emerge, and if it is understood that there are pieces (of emotions) that cannot find a place for themselves, then it will be possible to take the first little steps towards the construction of a kind of emotional syllabary that may, if developed, lead to the thinkability of the proto-emotions that are proliferating unheard and in silence.

At the end of the session, Sara says that she once met a doctor who suggested that she should draw what she was feeling, and that this was to her liking. The encounter has seemingly begun to activate – in the jargon of Bion – an α-element (the emotional drawing of what is exerting pressure in the form of silent sensoriality). In another language, a pictogram could be said to have formed.

The question that of course arises here is whether the analyst's mind will be capable of acting as a mill wheel to reverse the direction of flow from downwards towards the evacuative symptom to upwards towards mentalization and thinkability.

The last drawing of the first session appears to confirm the total absence of reverie and the sense of plunging 'towards the downstairs flat' without anyone holding the patient. It shows a classroom with benches, a teacher's desk and a child in the centre; however, looking at the drawing from a different point of view, one sees a child plunging from the balcony of a skyscraper without anyone caring about or trying to 'catch' him.

Carmen and the abortions

Carmen, a young woman doing research in computer science, requests analysis because she is 'unable to stay pregnant' although nothing

141

physical seems to be wrong with her. Shortly after starting her analysis and visiting a fertility clinic, she finds herself pregnant.

Hardly has she enough time to feel 'happy' about this situation when she is assailed by uncontainable anxiety that induces her to choose to abort, all counter-arguments going unheeded. After a few months of grief, pain and incomprehension at this inexplicable choice, once again the miracle happens: she is pregnant. This time the joy lasts longer, but after a few weeks, she is again overwhelmed by uncontainable anxiety and decides to abort once more.

How is this seemingly absurd and contradictory situation to be understood?

In her analysis, Carmen reports that her mother suffered from postnatal depression, and that, when she was small, she suffered from eczema, asthma and vomiting; her mother was always far away, kept very busy by her profession as an architect, working on many sites both in Italy and abroad.

In one session she describes how she is sometimes assailed by 'terrible fantasies' and panic attacks: she was disconcerted when she went with a friend to the paediatrician and saw that 'the children never kept still for a moment'. Then she says that each time she got pregnant she felt 'invaded' by the 'child growing inside her' and that, if she were not to go mad, she had no choice but to abort; she also says that she feels that 'the child is too desperate to have a place'. These moments of anxiety alternate with periods when she sleeps, sometimes for days on end.

The problem seems to be that either her emotions are made totally quiescent – sleep and infertility ('I don't feel any emotion') – or they are activated so tumultuously as to give rise to panic and terror, as if she felt that, if an embryo of emotions was beginning to take shape inside her, she had no choice but to expel it. At this stage in Carmen's development, it is not yet a matter of a child other than herself, but of getting back in touch with herself as a child abandoned by her mother – a child who was able to express the lack of primary care only on the somatic level and who continues to use a somatic register to express its own drama. So the child taking shape inside her is still too much a fabric woven from her own pain, despair, rage and hate for it to find a place, to be listened to and to be allowed to develop.

Carmen is as yet unable to accept these primitive emotions, by which she is terrified, and must 'abort' them. Perhaps the analysis will be capable of acting as the uterus in which the split-off – or, we might say, violently expelled – proto-emotions can find a cradle and 'oven' in which they can be received and transformed. In this case the patient will no longer need to fear that she might give birth to an 'emotional monster' – as in Roman Polanski's film *Rosemary's Baby* – but will instead be able to produce a new child, liberated from the transgenerational legacy.

Stefano's 'newborn baby'

Stefano was born with a severe physical 'defect' that caused his mother to see him as a 'monster'; one is reminded of the tragic history of the hero of Thomas Harris's *Red Dragon* and its background. Stefano's mother cried for months on end and was unable to care properly for him, while he in turn constantly screamed in desperation. Stefano grew into a severely autistic child whose defence mechanisms ranged from 'evacuation' (learned from his reverie-less mother), via tics, stereotypic movements and hypermotricity, to 'sleepiness', taken from a father who always denied and thus put to sleep any problem about Stefano being different from other children.

Lengthy psychotherapeutic work enables Stefano gradually to develop linguistic competence and to become able to narrate and construct stories, thanks to his therapist's capacity for reception and reverie.

After the last summer holidays, he tells how the 'newborn baby' (one of the protagonists of his stories), after undergoing prolonged and violent ill-treatment, carries out terrorist attacks with explosives; meanwhile the Sad Man (another character) tries in turn to kill the newborn.

These initial sequences can, I believe, be seen as the narration of how the 'newborn' and still developing α-function has been overstressed by the proto-emotions activated by and in the holidays, and of how even proto-emotions of pain and sadness can suffocate an as yet 'newly born' α-function.

This is ultimately also the drama of the human species, in which an α-function that has 'just appeared on the stage' constantly runs the risk of being saturated and overwhelmed by excessive quanta of protosensoriality over and above its capacity to absorb them; this excess, in my opinion, is what we have called the death 'instinct' (or drive).

As the session proceeds, a new character appears: 'Ulk', who has no arms and cannot act as a goalkeeper: 'Perhaps he has a fever.' Displaying great intuition, the therapist asks: 'What's worrying you, Ulk?' and the child answers for Ulk: 'His mummy has died of a heart attack.' He then begins to act the part of Ulk. This time it seems possible to metabolize the mourning, even if it has to remain unexpressed in the field (on other occasions, direct relational interpretations have caused extremely violent evacuations in the form of acting-out). This shows how necessary it is, when the α-function is 'newborn', not to overtax it (not to put it excessively to the test), but instead to use tangential interpretations, which are less likely to give rise to *intense stimuli* that may destructure the 'newborn'.

The next session begins with a 'belch' from Stefano, to which the therapist promptly responds with a question: 'Who hasn't digested his food?' The session continues with an increasingly quiet game in which the feared 'attack' gives way to 'living it up in a disco' and then to the construction of two houses side by side linked by a string – in Stefano's words, a 'communications link' or, as the therapist sees it, a 'fuse so that if one explodes, the other will blow up as well'.

The presence of an available mind modulates the tensions of the field; the 'explosion/attack' begins to give way to a kind of 'violent emotional music', with the incipient development of an intricate song and countersong between projective identification and the capacity for reverie, which, while on the one hand serving the purpose of communication, on the other causes one mind to experience the mental state of another. It is now possible for something that was absent from the patient's history to happen, because now, as in a song that Stefano is later to sing, the experience is: 'There is something inside you that I can't stand' (on the record entitled *The Head That Isn't There*).

Sandra's autistic child

Sandra is a psychologist working in a child neuropsychiatry unit. In one of her own analytic sessions, she talks at length about an 'autistic child'. In a debatable interpretation – which is, of course, 'accurate' as far as the analyst is concerned – the analyst tells the patient that she is talking about 'destructured aspects' of herself. After a moment of surprise, Sandra brings – or rather *responds* to this interpretation by bringing – a dream in which her sister is pregnant with a number of children, one of whom is 'black'. Sandra adds that she has shown herself to be too willing to take on additional duties in her unit, so that her colleagues take advantage of her, and then she remembers an advertisement for 'Médecins sans Frontières'.

The patient has manifestly experienced the interpretation as something alien – something that has nevertheless occurred (the pregnancy); in particular, something alien (the black child) has occurred. The interpretation was therefore experienced as a kind of abuse of her excessive willingness and as an instance of interpretative incontinence – the 'Médecins sans Frontières' seen literally as doctors without frontiers.

She begins the next session by talking about a child with a medullary tumour, who was being treated by her *established/structured* colleagues [the Italian word *strutturate* means both established, in the sense of being on the permanent payroll, and having a firm structure]; in other words, in the next day's session there remains something tumoral and proliferative, which has to be tackled and which seems to stem from the analyst's proliferative interpretative activity.

Andrea and the tolerable voltage

In his very first session, Andrea says that he is suffering from a number of apparently psychosomatic disorders – gastric and abdominal complaints, as well as a constant heaviness in the stomach – with one particular symptom: he often compulsively plunges a finger deep into his throat as if to make himself vomit. An electrician by trade, he now tells his analyst in a matter-of-fact tone how he was struck on the arm by 'lightning' which passed through him but left him 'miraculously alive'. He continues inconsequentially by talking about the animals present on the farm where he lives: dogs, cats, rabbits and chickens.

Andrea is manifestly confronted with a kind of 'electricity' that is too intense to be managed; although he has found a psychosomatic channel for its evacuation, it seems insufficient to enable him to 'vomit up' the accumulated inchoate magma of proto-emotions inside him.

In later sessions, he mentions his passion for the world of truckers and how he too would like to obtain a licence to drive heavy goods vehicles. At the same time he mentions that he has fits of furious anger in which he smashes everything in sight.

He evidently has no choice but to evacuate, and can sometimes no longer do so into the soma, but would apparently also like to be able to 'drive' – i.e. control – his emotions.

At this point the story of his childhood emerges: it was spent with a harsh, unavailable mother, totally occupied by running the farm after being widowed shortly after her son's birth.

Eventually, Andrea's inconsequentiality diminishes and he manifestly comes along to his session 'with his head down like a bull'. He then says that the only difference between a rabbit and a cat is 'in the head', and that he has started killing the cats again, but there are always more and more of them; he goes on to describe a whole series of bloody scenes with violent and ferocious animals.

The work of analysis can, it seems, dissolve and thaw out the volcano, which can at last begin not only to erupt but also to vomit up the proto-emotional lava that probably stemmed from the tensions Andrea was unable to evacuate into his mother when he was small – tensions [the Italian word *tensioni* also means voltages] that thus came back to him in gigantic form, in addition to those that might have been evacuated into Andrea by his mother, who was not only not receptive but also full of anxiety. Owing to the absence of a functioning *projective identification/reverie* circuit, the tensions/voltages were not only not transformed but were actually increased; in particular, a 'transformer' function was not introjected.

In this connection, a particular literary example is in my view superior to any psychoanalytic theory or clinical description. This is the novel *Red Dragon*, which I have discussed elsewhere together with *Hannibal* and *The Silence of the Lambs*, a trilogy constituting in effect an admirable modern myth on the absence of primary care and its consequences. I am not concerned here with the literary quality of these books, nor am I competent to judge it, but in my opinion the author, Thomas Harris, here displays a high degree of psychological penetration.

The first book tells the story of a serial killer who, at every full moon, slays families with rituals involving humiliation of the victims, the smashing of mirrors and the positioning of the corpses in front of mirrors.

The killer had a tragic childhood: he was abandoned by his mother, and his face is so badly disfigured that he dare not look at his reflection. An attempt to return to his mother and her new family fails wretchedly, and his career of carnage begins after his grandmother's death. It goes on until he meets a 'blind' girl, who is not alienated by his facial deformity, and with whom he has an affectionate relationship in which he is fully accepted. This effectively results in split between one aspect that is irrevocably bent on revenge – the 'Red Dragon' – and another that wishes to save the girl and the tender relationship that has arisen between them.

The second book is also about a serial killer, whose victims in this case are fat women; he too has a background of abuse and violence. He kills because he wants to make himself a suit of female human skin, to serve as a 'new skin and identity'. He murders young women so as to construct, tailor-like, this new integument for himself.

A character present in both novels is Dr Lecter, a psychiatrist-and-serial-killer incarcerated in a cage in a maximum-security prison.

Officer Starling, the heroine of the second novel, sets about hunting for the killer with the aid of Dr Lecter, who forms an almost protective relationship with her. This is developed in the third novel, *Hannibal*, whose eponymous hero is Dr Lecter. *Hannibal* describes Officer Starling's attempts to 'arrest' Lecter after he escapes from prison.

However, over and above the genre of the horror-story-cum-detective-novel, what is narrated is the story of the vicissitudes of Lecter's childhood. We are told that he lost a beloved little sister at a tender age. Falling victim to cannibalistic acts, she was eaten by a gang of starving bandits who broke into the family farm and, finding nothing else on which to feed, devoured not only a scraggy deer but also the little girl.

This trauma, it seems, has to be actively repeated: as an adult, Dr Lecter in turn becomes a cannibal. He would like to reverse the flow of time and bring his little sister back to life, making time non-linear. Officer Starling could perhaps serve partly as a substitute and partly as a 'depository' for the sister, if only time could run backwards and the sister come alive again. The cannibalistic scene is repeated until the novel reaches a terrifying climax: a man Lecter sees as guilty – he himself, for not having been able to save his sister – undergoes a brain operation and, while wide awake, partakes of a meal of his own brain, which is sliced through in the frontal lobes, cooked and eaten – just as he himself gnaws at his brain out of guilt. Meanwhile, Officer Starling is kept prisoner.

I wonder whether this can be seen as an illustration of what happens in the absence of 'food for the mind' – in the absence of reverie. The tender, affectionate parts (the little sister, the capacity for ♀) are destroyed by violent parts that ultimately cannibalize the mind itself; others are then made to experience what the subject has undergone, and become victims. Had there been food – reverie – the little sister could have experienced the affects, the emotions could have found a place, and Lecter would not have been a victim and executioner devoured by guilt and at the same time an avenging angel, or rather demon.

The novels narrate the transgenerational story, the story of guilt, remorse and compulsive revenge. Officer Starling can be seen as the neurotic part of the personality, which seeks to 'arrest' the psychotic part, even if, for a time, she is fascinated and paralysed by it, conniving with it as it were by compulsion, so that she 'suckles' the psychotic part' and remains in thrall to it, at least until she hears a sound that resembles the one that hypnotized her – that of a crossbow string . . .

The criminals at the beginning of the story can be thought of as β-elements, which, in the absence of reverie and transformation (by an α-function) cannibalize the mind.

The first book's serial killer can thus be regarded as portraying the need to evacuate trauma-related emotions by acting them out: the persecutory bad objects force him to exact revenge, until he finds the loving girl, and here we observe the split between the psychotic part and the 'part capable of relating'. The unreceived and untransformed aspects give rise to madness and persecution. Similarly, the second book describes an attempt to find a psychic skin, a container, or mother, capable of 'taking inside' (a ♀ that can give birth to ♂). Finally, there emerges the most alarming character of all, who is in effect the 'director' of all these stories – namely, the mad psychiatrist, the embodiment of the archaic and cannibalistic superego, who devours everything on account of his intolerable sense of guilt, which ultimately impels him to desperate, harmful, and indeed self-harmful, action. The consequences of the absence of primary care reflected in this sequence of three books are the emergence of the killer, the attempt at self-therapy (the skin), the superego and the seduction of the healthy part of the personality.

The example of another best-selling thriller illustrates a further problem that constantly confronts us – namely, that of the analyst's mental functioning in the session. In what is perhaps a substantial interpretative drift, I should like to cite John Katzenbach's fascinating book *The Analyst*, which can be read as a thriller, as a pitiless critique of the world of psychoanalysis or in many other ways. To me, it immediately suggested the laborious process that an analyst must go through inside himself in order to become truly capable of 'treating' patients.

In brief, the novel tells the story of Dr Starks, a tired, middle-aged analyst who is bored with life and with his profession. During the last session of a fateful day, he hears the bell ring and then someone coming into the waiting room. Who is it? he wonders. A patient's relative? A patient having a crisis? Or someone else? At the end of the session he goes into the waiting room, but cannot see anyone. About to go home, he notices an anonymous letter on a chair, telling him that he must commit suicide within a month unless he finds out the

148

identity of the writer. If he fails to do so, all his relations, whose addresses are given in the note, will be killed.

In this way the suspense is built up in a plot that swings between incredulity and persecution, as *all* the analyst's certainties are undermined and then destroyed: his credit card is frozen, his bank accounts are emptied out, his homes are destroyed, and he is hounded out of his psychoanalytic society – and things constantly go from bad to worse. Eventually, however, the analyst wakes up, shakes himself, changes his mental attitude and begins to 'search' for his persecutor. He gets closer and closer to him and almost reaches him. In the end, a profoundly changed Dr Starks ceases to '*go through the motions of being an analyst*' and decides *above all to be himself* – and to care for people properly. This becomes possible after he has unmasked the person behind his persecution, who turns out to be . . . but let us not give the game away!

6

Instructions for seafarers and the shipwrecked: signals from the analytic field and emotional transformations

The focus of my interest in the last few years has been on the constant signals conveyed to us by patients to enable us to find the best way of reaching them. In my view, the interpretative formulation, the manner in which it is conveyed and its exhaustiveness should be based not on a 'marriage' of ours to a strong theory of interpretation, but instead on an increasingly well-honed capacity to receive the responses and emotional colorations contributed by the patient to the field after our interventions. Our 'listening to listening' (Faimberg 1996) must induce us to reflect not only on how the patient's mind has functioned after our interpretative 'stimulus', but equally on the way we ourselves function and are able to function on that particular day, with that particular patient, in order to facilitate as many transformations as possible.

This kind of 'flexible' interaction with the patient is, however, based on a strong theory, which is an expansion of Bion's reflections on the dream-like functioning of the mind even in the waking state. Implicit in this assertion is the choice of a theoretical field, in the sense that one and the same communication by a patient – 'When I was small, my father never took me by the hand; he only wanted me to do well at school, and if I didn't, there were unending private lessons and sometimes even blows' – can be regarded, according to the prevailing model, as a scene from infancy that helps us to reconstruct the family romance; as a persecutory unconscious fantasy about a cold and domineering internal object (which could on occasion also be 'projected' on to the analyst and interpreted as such); or as

151

an exact description, from the patient's vertex, of what is happening in the consulting room at that particular moment. From a given radically relational standpoint, it could be interpreted solely as having to do with the here and now; but this, in my view, would flatten the analytic scene, 'stretching it out' into a plane in the present and reducing it to two dimensions.

My current approach would indeed be to see this communication as having to do with the here and now, and as a derivative of the patient's waking dream at that particular relational instant, but I would also put a number of questions to myself: First, what should I say in order to bring about a transformation, in such a way as no longer to be heard as an emotionless father bent on getting results and not allowing any respite? Second, how must I change my way of interpreting, my posture, and perhaps even my internal attitude in order for this transformation to begin to be 'brought about'? Third, what is the origin of the patient's perception of me? Does it come from the patient's 'history', and can it entail the 'assumption of a role' by me? Does it stem from his projective identifications? Is it due to an enactment? Or does it result from my way of being with him or my posture towards him?

Having duly weighed these points, shall I opt for a seemingly 'reconstructive' interpretation, an interpretation of 'the unconscious fantasy', an interpretation 'of the relationship', or simply an 'enzymatic' interpretation, paying the closest possible attention to the patient's eventual 'response' to what I say?

Let us assume that I comment: 'Having such a father is surely not something that would incline you to "studying", but is more likely to put you in a constant state of agitation.' In this case, it is obvious that I am 'putting on the table' a transference interpretation: 'If that's what I am like when I am with you, that certainly does not make the work done in this *studio* any easier.' [The Italian word *studio* can mean both 'studies' and 'consulting room'.] The patient might respond: 'Yesterday I went to a photographic exhibition, but I thought all the photographs were unsharp.' I would then inevitably consider that my interpretation lacked 'incisiveness', so that I needed to bring the situation 'into sharper focus'.

However, if the patient were to say: 'Yesterday I went to visit my aunt, who always cooks a good meal, but then you are so full up that you need a whole day to digest it,' I would have to conclude that this formulation, which I had thought was already light and unsaturated enough, was still 'too heavy' for the patient.

Alternatively, at a different stage in the analysis, I might have felt it useful to give a 'strong', explicit transference interpretation, such as: 'You feel that I am not very affectionate and am more interested in the progress of your analysis than in you, and that I won't leave you in peace until you make that progress.' Here again, the patient could reply in any number of possible ways, ranging from 'But it was nice when I felt that my father understood me' to 'I saw a documentary on TV about how they make foie gras: they constantly force-feed the poor geese with a funnel until their livers become enormous'.

What I mean is that these signals, if received, allow gradual adjustments to be made, but that if they fail to be picked up, we might find ourselves all at sea.

Of course, the analyst could have given dozens of possible interpretations of the patient's very first formulation, from 'Now we understand one of the roots of your *study* inhibition [or inhibition in the *consulting room-studio*]' to 'Well, I'm sure that today you'd prefer to *study* with Maria, who never rushes you and always lets you take your time'. The number of possible routes is therefore infinite, and so is the number of 'worlds' that can open up.

However, any interpretative choice is underlain by a model of what might constitute a seed of recovery – for instance, 'removing the veil of repression', 'picking up the point of urgency of the anxiety' or 'describing the primal fantasies'. My own model involves developing the patient's capacity to think, in the sense of developing the mental equipment for producing thought processes and forming emotions from sensory stimuli of all kinds. Once again, I must resort to my Bion-inspired jargon, to say that the purpose of analysis is the development of the patient's α-function and hence his capacity to generate α-elements; development of the capacity to weave together thoughts and emotions; development of the Ps ↔ D oscillation and hence of creative originality and the ability to mourn; and development of NC ↔ SF and hence of the expectation that a meaning will come into being; and the forgoing of all possible meanings in favour of a particular choice.

Going back over the above examples, we could imagine that the patient's first formulation – 'When I was small, my father never took me by the hand; he only wanted me to do well at school, and if I didn't, there were unending private lessons and sometimes even blows' – as one of the very large number of possible *narrative derivatives*

(Ferro 2001, 2002a, 2002b) of a sequence of α-elements that could be seen as pictographed as follows:

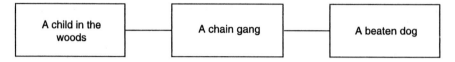

What matters is that the formation of emotional pictograms is ongoing (and constitutes waking dream thought), and that the 'narrative derivatives' can be almost infinitely diverse provided that they are compatible with the sequence of α-elements. For instance, one and the same emotional 'climate' could be conveyed by a patient who begins his session by saying: 'Yesterday I saw a film on TV about a wicked captain who ill-treated all his sailors, inflicting constant punishment on them' or 'Making love to Martina is hard work because there is no exchange of feelings: all she cares about is achieving her own pleasure, and nothing else interests her'. This has two important consequences: first, that 'free associations' are in fact 'obligatory associations', in that they stem, instant by instant, from the visual cinematic frames (or emotional pictograms) constantly generated by the α-function, thus giving rise to 'waking dream thought'; and, second, that the associations are absolutely free in terms of the 'choice of narrative genre' from a vast and unlimited sea of expressive forms (films, memories of childhood, anecdotes, an intimate diary, etc.). While the 'literary genres' are infinite in number, they must be consistent with the sequence of α-elements of the waking dream thought, whose expression they permit.

A dream narrated in an analytic session may also, almost paradoxically, appear as a 'narrative derivative' of (an obligatory free association to) the moment when it is narrated; that is to say, as something that confers the possibility of expression on the waking dream thought formed at that moment.

An analyst gives a sophisticated and complex interpretation, to which the patient replies by reporting a dream: he was at school and the teacher was writing formulae on the blackboard with extremely complicated designs like those of the murrhine vases from Murano. Unable to understand and full of rage, he wanted to smash them to pieces. This dream is precisely something that allows the patient's emotions to be expressed at the time when he brings it; in other words, it is chosen as the narrative derivative of his α-sequence. It would be just the same if the patient's communication had been along the lines of: 'Yesterday there was a TV programme in Arabic and I couldn't understand a word of it' or 'I remember that when I was small I could never understand the teacher's explanations and so I got angry'.

It is worth reflecting further on the enormous difference between a dream that is narrated spontaneously and one that is brought at the analyst's request – a not infrequent practice that is surely to be frowned on, when, at a moment of dead calm and silence, the analyst asks: 'Are there any dreams?' In the first case, the significance of the dream is two-fold, or even three-fold: first, it demonstrates an openness to a deeper level of communication; second, it illustrates how much work has been already done during sleep; and, third, it constitutes a narrative derivative of the waking dream thought of that particular moment, thus as it were permitting a 'core sample' to be drilled directly from the current emotional field.

At a certain point in the last session of the week, Rossella tells me that she received a strange telephone call during the night, from someone who claimed to be an old boyfriend asking her what size feet she had. She then brings a dream: someone's guard dog did not bark but instead slept on; this someone removed the handle of the French window and penetrated into her house, after which this 'unknown person' was 'in her bed' and she was very afraid. The dream comes at a time when Rossella, a medical student of Swiss nationality, has just begun her analysis, but face to face: she feels unable to lie down on the couch, because she needs 'to see what is happening and to remain on guard' (all interpretations of this situation have proved futile). At the end of the week, however, she finds herself disconcerted by the new emotional climate she is experiencing: unexpected telephone calls; what she fears to be a morbid interest (or is it Prince Charming?); no longer being so much on her guard (the sleeping dog); someone dismantling her defences; and finding herself close to something that terrifies her, with the idea of the couch (bed) coming nearer.

The above is a description both of the way the 'subject-matter' is elaborated and of the present state of the relational climate; the dream is also a narrative derivative of the waking dream thought.

On the following Monday, however, it proves very difficult for us to speak to each other; there are long silences, and my 'cold' attempts to interpret the long separation are not taken up by Rossella, who instead seems resolutely to resist them. At this point, in order to restart a dialogue, I ask her whether she has dreamed; it is as if I were saying: 'Do you want to re-establish communication with me or not?' Rossella answers in the affirmative and tells me the following dream: she separates from her boy-friend after a period spent together, goes home and finds her father watching television; she then goes out again with – perhaps – the intention of self-harm, and goes back because she has forgotten something, but at that moment her mother returns, goes into the kitchen with the shopping, and shows affection for her. She adds that she has no associations to the dream. I could give at least some interpretations that seem obvious to me (the separation, the desperation she felt, and the reunion), but I feel that these would be intrusive and on the level of decoding; they would consti-tute a 'cold' operation carried out on the telling of the dream and not on a spontaneous, warm dream.

I wait, and after a time Rossella, having looked all around, asks me: 'Have you painted this room? It's full of drips and smears, as if the person who painted it was in a hurry.' So *this* is the 'warm' association to the dream – an association that is in turn a narrative derivative of the waking dream thought. I enquire whether *my* asking her if she had dreamed seemed to her unprofessional, the approach of a botcher, and in particu-lar a demonstration of impatience. She answers 'yes', adding that she now remembers another dream: she met someone who had a dog, and told that person about her own Labrador and the trouble she had had in deciding to look after it: as a puppy, it had been abandoned, beaten and ill-treated, and now it did not trust anyone; it was impossible to go any-where near it. It had been a laborious process getting it to the point where she could take it home and gradually awaken its trust. This, I tell her, reminds me of the film *Dances with Wolves*, where the lieutenant in the story had to lavish so much time and attention on a wolf that had turned up near his house until it trusted him, but eventually there is a moving scene when it eats the food he puts out for it, at last without any fear or distrust.

Rossella continues: 'You don't have to tell me who is the abandoned, ill-treated puppy who is gradually learning to trust.' A few sessions later, Rossella is happy to lie down on the couch.

Whereas the first, 'extorted', dream admittedly refers to the dream work and opens the way to the resumption of communication, the second dream, which is 'spontaneous', also bears witness to the new α–elements of the waking dream thought that are in the process of formation, as well as to the continuous production of derivatives represented by my 'association-cum-interpretation' and the patient's response.

Further considerations on what happens in the analytic field arise from so-called communications of reality. This is a vexed question in psychoanalysis, which has to negotiate a path between the Scylla of attributing significance to communications of reality (but who decides what these are?) and the Charybdis of denying their existence and in some way reducing them by interpretation to the internal reality of the analysis.

In what seems to me to be a fertile period of her analysis, a patient tells me that she has just had an antenatal ultrasound examination that was very alarming because it seemed to indicate a malformation of the foetus. These indications could only be confirmed by an amnio-centesis. I of course feel, and am, close to the patient at this painful time, and I comment on, emphasize and share her emotions of uncertainty, pain and rage, as well as her mourning and sense of loss and discouragement following the miscarriage she has a few days later, which anticipates the planned therapeutic abortion.

Once the period of urgency is over, in my usual out-of-session reflections I tell myself that this time we have undeniably dealt with an incontrovertible element or fact of reality and that the analysis consisted in modulating the emotions connected with this loss and its inevitable retinue of dramatic situations, and making them thinkable and tolerable. However, I feel dissatisfied with this theory, rather like someone who has not digested something.

I frequently ponder over this 'fact' and this fertile and intense period of analysis with Rossella. Then I find myself almost involuntarily reflecting again in detail on the sessions, and seem to discover a set of signals which I admittedly interpreted, but by which I did not allow myself to be 'guided' in the timing and dosage of my interpretative activity.

It is true that I touched upon the split between 'the patient's dark skin' and her 'sister's extremely delicate skin'; it is true that I had interpreted a series of exciting activities as antidotes to a feared depression; and it is true that I had interpreted a latent homosexuality as a defence against persecutory anxieties. However, I am coming to realize that all this came from *me* – and whereas my approach was sensible and active, it lacked the element of sharing or co-construction.

Scraps of communication from recent sessions now occur to me: the computer being chock-full of data; the need to defragment the hard disk; her son's allergic reaction to a heavy meal; and an evening spent with a friend who always talked about difficult things and made her very young son listen to hermetic poetry. By putting together these fragments of communication from various sessions, I now 'realize' that my interpretative activity has been excessive, undigested and intrusive. A 'fact' or narreme from my out-of-session experience now helps me to describe something conceived in such a way that it will inevitably be lost and has no possibility of healthy development. In other words, sequences of α-elements had been generated in the patient, the narrative derivatives of which – the account of the computer, the meal and the ultrasound examination – put me in touch with the patient's psychic reality. The sequence of α-elements might have been, say:

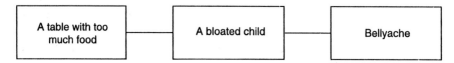

These sequences, which are usually unknowable in the waking state, gave rise to the narrative derivatives mentioned. However, they could equally well have found other narrative 'hooks' (or play-related or graphic ones in the case of a child analysis) to put me in touch with the pictographing activity of the patient's mind in the ongoing process of alphabetization.

I am not saying that my interpretative activity caused the abortion, but that the patient found a highly effective way of 'telling me' what was happening in our field. In the absence of the miscarriage, she could have told me the same story by other narrations appropriate for assigning meaning to the α-element sequences. These might, for example, have been an account of a film seen on TV in which a ship sank and could not be brought back to the surface, or the childhood memory of a friend of her father breaking a cherished toy and of the resulting pain. In other words, the 'reality' situation too becomes a narrative derivative, like any number of possible others.

This in my view fully bears out what I have often maintained (e.g. Bezoari and Ferro 1992) – namely, that what happens within the analytic situation is 'virtual', 'in between', existing in a kind of 'no man's land' between external and internal reality, provided that the analyst, patient and setting are imbued with sufficient life and vitality. If the setting were to collapse, the very existence of this virtual space, which may be likened to the concept of the transitional space or analytic field, would be impossible. Where the situation of external reality prevails, analysis ceases to be: if Osama bin Laden is no longer what a terrified patient thinks might jump out from under his bed and instead becomes the Osama bin Laden of the external world, we no longer have analysis, but instead *sauve qui peut*!

However, just as it would in my opinion be naïve to imagine that, given a functioning setting, reality communications can be distinguished from fantasy communications, so it would be cruel and inhuman to consider that seemingly reality-related communications swimming in the virtuality of the analytic field should *always* be interpreted in the transference. As in the case of the loss of the 'child', this is something from which we can learn for the future, without any need whatsoever for it to be interpreted to the patient, to whom any 'psychoanalytic' interpretation might seem tantamount to incomprehension and banalization of her 'real' drama. This is a drama which, from a different vertex, is also the 'communication' that makes it possible to confer a new and more effective *Gestalt* on the analytic field in such a way that 'children' can be born as a function of the minds of both protagonists and not as 'colonial settlements' that must be expelled.

So, if a patient says that her child must not be stimulated excessively, otherwise he will get overexcited and then irritated, what is she talking about? This will of course depend on our chosen listening vertex. However, the most useful vertex in my view would be to see this statement as a suggestion by the patient about 'technique', informing me of the approach I must use in my interpreting – a graduated and contained approach, lest I stuff her full and irritate her.

Of course, there is no reason not to follow the patient with comments and unsaturated interpretations of the manifest text, but listening to the communication as a 'narrative derivative' of the dream of the field at that instant would as it were constitute the specific psychoanalytic status of the encounter. In my language, then, I regard the patient's free associations as narrative derivatives of his waking dream thought, with differing gradients of distortion and camouflage. The same applies to the analyst's free associations and reveries in the session. By tuning into these, he can navigate back against the flow of the river to its source, which comprises the sequences of α-elements constantly constructed by the patient's (and the analyst's) α-function and – as an additional complication – perhaps also by the α-functions of the field.

Stefano's wheelchair

I arrive slightly late for Stefano's session, which as a result turns out to be very intense, enabling him to 'discover' the affects of profound tenderness and concern that he had for his father when he was small, and which he has re-experienced in the brief but significant interval between his ringing the bell and my letting him in. The session ends with a mention of Stefano's capacity to forge strong links with people even in a very short time, as is happening with me. As a final image, he mentions that a goods lift would be a helpful facility in the block where my consulting room is situated: a lift would at least be useful should anyone ever 'have a broken leg or need a wheelchair'.

In spite of the warm climate, with Stefano feeling emotions and discovering his affection for me, the image suggested to me by the wheelchair is of Anthony Perkins in *Psycho*. Of course, I must keep this to myself because I have no narrative hook for it, except for a possible disguised reference a few sessions ago to a Hitchcock review.

Before the next day's session, I wonder what to do about the forthcoming change of currency from the *lira* to the euro and whether or not to convert the amounts he pays exactly. Stefano begins by saying that he has had very little sleep because he was on duty at the hospital where he works until four in the morning. The police had brought in a young man who had killed a prostitute that day, and a judge had let him go home because there was no risk of him absconding or of the contamination of evidence: he was an ordinary citizen who had been married for two years and had a child, but who had acted in a state of 'pathological drunkenness'. Stefano dwells at length on the story of this 'patient', whom he decided to admit to the hospital, not because he might harm someone else but as a precaution in case of self-harm out of guilt feelings, or of harm to his family. This immediately provides me with a hook for my fantasy of the previous day about Anthony Perkins's wheelchair.

Meanwhile Stefano adds that the patient broke his teacher's arm when he was small and that it seemed inevitable for him to undergo an 'in-depth analysis'.

I am nonplussed; I certainly cannot say to him: 'You are talking about a part of yourself which . . .' I therefore decide to adopt a roundabout approach: what comes into my mind is Georges Perec's book *Life: A User's Manual*, in which lots of people of different kinds live in an apartment block, and a period of just two days witnesses a transition from the world of the tenderest and most intense feelings to one in which someone goes berserk and becomes a killer.

Stefano says he knows the book. I continue by commenting that what we said some time ago about the human mind being a harp with a number *n* of strings is true. 'Yes,' he answers, 'not like the one in the books that had only two or three strings; what was it called, by the way?' I reply: 'A *lira* [this is the Italian for lyre as well as the name of the former Italian currency], and its strings perhaps include the one for the affection and tenderness you felt towards me yesterday – but also the one that sounds when you say "You filthy whore, I'll kill you because of all the money you are costing me" and "With the wheelchair we can send Anthony Perkins with his anger upstairs in the goods lift".' 'I thought I knew myself,' he says after a short silence, 'but I would never have imagined I had such things in me. All the same [using a metaphor of ours], it's nice to add these roads too to our city.'

Martino: one tooth at a time

Martino is a 15-year-old boy now in his tenth year of analysis. The analysis began when he was five years old, alternating between a severe symbiotic psychosis and an autistic withdrawal in which he cut off all contact with the outside world except when he exploded in fits of rage and smashed everything in sight.

Martino decides that he wants to reduce his sessions from four to three a week because he does not have enough time to pursue other interests, but he is scared and utterly terrified by this decision. Having finally taken it, he has two dreams. In the first, some trees with very deep roots are cut down, while in the second he wanted to buy rompers with straps for his two-year-old little brother's birthday – straps like the ones used to restrain convicts – but didn't do so because they were too expensive (the price was the same as the session he will no longer be having).

The dreams show us how much pain it costs him to extirpate the Tuesday session given the deep roots represented by the ten years of analysis, but also that giving up one session has a liberating effect as compared with wearing the 'convict's' restraining straps in the forced labour of the analysis.

In the next session he says he would like to study at college, 'but it is too expensive' and he does not know if he can 'afford it'. Then he mentions something he has seen: dogs having jaw-strengthening exercises where they had to bite on a wooden stick, which was then passed over the branch of a tree leaving the dog hanging in the air clinging by its mouth. He adds that, on the previous day (the Tuesday with no session), his parents had gone out and he had been left to look after his little brother.

Although he was fond of him, he was exasperated because the brother would not let him go away from his cot, and eventually he lost his temper and smacked him, but this had made him very afraid. Finally, he brings a dream: he had to pass through a dark, black corridor, where there might also have been spiders, but then it was all right.

We comment on all these things, seeing them as a development of something we had already begun to tell each other: he wants to have his independence, but the idea of it costs him a lot; he clings to his analysis as if by his 'jaws' and is very attached to it; in the interval he had difficulty in holding the child entrusted to him, which wanted company; and his dream describes the difficult and dangerous path along the corridor from Monday to Wednesday. He now comes up with an image, like the one often seen in a Western, where teeth are drawn with forceps; he smiles, but adds that he would never have imagined that this experience of separation from me could be so painful.

Lorena and her St Anthony's fire

I shall now describe two sessions with Lorena from the third year of her 'analysis'; we have just increased the number of her sessions from three to four, but they are still being conducted face to face because she cannot yet tolerate the idea of lying down on the couch.

Prelude: Wednesday

In the previous session, Lorena had mentioned the possibility – or perhaps it was a wish – of leaving her husband and going to live by herself. Then she had wondered how it was that Silvana, one of her own daughters, had told her that cuckoos laid their eggs in the nests of other birds and that, when the chicks hatched, they were bigger and stronger than the others in the nest, which then died; cuckoos were parasites.

She wondered whether the birth of her little sister had aroused all this jealousy in Silvana. Having followed what she was saying about the jealousy problem, I was thinking of the approaching Christmas holidays, so I decided not to say that I was the cuckoo that took up her space with the holidays, and I asked her if the cuckoo's egg might also be this idea of separating from a husband who had killed off the tender feelings that seemed to me also to be there for him (the husband-as-myself). She left with tears in her eyes, although doing her best to conceal them.

162

Thursday

Lorena comes in and, as usual, moves her chair as far as possible away from the desk.

Analyst [*thinking that I shall have to say something along the lines of pointing out that she continues to keep her distance from me and from her emotions; seeing her give me a sidelong glance, I 'jokingly' catch her eye before speaking*].   Well?

Patient.   What?

Analyst.   Well, seeing that you were looking away I was trying to make contact, so as not to be like your father, who you told me always looked away from you at the table.

Patient.   I shall now tell you two dreams. In the first, there was someone who wanted to interview me and then followed me, but I ran away. I had a Cicciobello doll, but didn't know if I wanted it or not. In the second dream, there was a ship full of Albanians who arrived [she laughs] at the port of Voghera; lots and lots of Albanians landed and one of them went along to a neighbour and asked for some water. The neighbour chased him away, and I thought: 'Poor fellow, I don't know if he has enough money for the bar.'

Analyst [*thinking about the dreams: the Cicciobello doll might perhaps be a 'gift' that includes something she is afraid of. I wonder how I am to see the Albanians – maybe as aspects of herself arriving full of needs, or as the words I pronounced yesterday, which managed to come ashore, but which she does not know whether to accept or reject*].   What do these dreams suggest to you?

Patient.   Certainly not what *you* are thinking – that it is already Thursday and along come the Albanians with their hunger and thirst.

Analyst.   What about the Cicciobello doll?

Patient.   It's the little doll that cries if its comforter is taken away. That has nothing to do with me.

Analyst.   Well, the most important thing seems to me to be that in Voghera there is now a port; who knows what an effort it was to build it! What is needed now is a kind of reception structure.

Patient.   What makes you think that I might want to listen to this rubbish?

Analyst.   What about the Cicciobello doll – why don't you want it?

Patient.   I had it when I was small; my cousin had Serenella, the laughing doll, and I had Cicciobello, the one that cried.

Analyst.   So it is a burden to have the Cicciobello, or to get it back again now.

163

Patient. I'm thinking of something else, something else . . .

Analyst. I too was thinking that there are lots of restaurants in Voghera, including ones with fixed-price menus, where you can eat as much as you like and the price is always the same; I am of course talking 'with a forked tongue'! [*Our jargon for a manifestly transference-related interpretation of mine.*]

Patient. Now I understand! I was worried about my daughter Carlotta, that she might be anorexic, as she hasn't touched her food for days.

Analyst. Like 'someone' who hasn't yet been listening today. I wouldn't worry so much about the anorexia, but instead about how well the Voghera restaurants can cope with all those Albanians.

Patient. But guess what: I really did take one Albanian home with me! But he turned out to be an illegal immigrant, so I sent him away again.

Analyst. Like the neighbour in your dream – but doesn't the new immigration law allow people to legalize their situation if they get a job? [*I say this in the tone I use when I am talking about something external that implicitly applies to her.*]

Patient. No way! That was possible for a few months, but not any longer. They need a residence permit, and then they don't have to stay underground any more.

Analyst. I'm speaking with a forked tongue again. Perhaps we need to find a way of allowing these Albanians to come out from underground – in other words, to let you accept the things you *feel*, your needs.

Patient. You know, when Silvana [her elder daughter] does her homework, she absolutely refuses to hear anything from us; she says, 'I know, I already know, what on earth makes you think I don't?' Why does she do that?

Analyst. She must take after someone!

Patient. But I'm talking about Silvana – *why* is it?

Analyst [*I tell the joke about little Samuel, a boy who doesn't want to go to school because they teach him things he doesn't know!*]

Patient [*slightly disorientated, laughing*]. But I was with Silvana helping her do her homework: she had to join up the dots to reveal the 'hidden drawing' and then she wouldn't let me see what it showed.

Analyst. I think the hidden drawing is about denying the emotions and feelings that you have, in case they are excessive and too intense, so they have to stay underground, and what also has to be denied is crying about the holidays taking away the comforter. It's a bit like your moving the chair away when you come in, and saying you don't want to know about yourself and about you as the Albanians . . . but the new port of Voghera is a hopeful sign.

Monday
Patient [*after a brief silence*]. I have some things to tell you, but then you'll interpret them for me; let's see if I've got it right.
Analyst. OK.
Patient. My mother had an attack of St Anthony's fire [erysipelas] under her ears – she usually has it on one side and not both. I said to her: 'I'll go with you to A&E', but she said no; I said 'I'll go with you to the chemist's' and she said no. Then my brother said he would go with her and he took her to the Red Cross, where they prescribed injections for her. Then my cousin went, but he cut himself with the syringe; he really is an absolute wet.
Analyst. Anything else?
Patient. No, I shan't tell you the rest. You would understand too much. Well, I'll tell you something else. Silvana got angry with her teacher because when she touched up the holly she had drawn on a slate she said she had altered her drawing. And I'll tell you something else, which really comes first although I am telling you it third: why do I have an aversion to 'Carlotta' [*her youngest*]?
Analyst. Well, do you want me to give you a roundabout answer or a direct one?
Patient. As direct as you can.
Analyst. I think you are talking about someone we know, and we know who it is that cannot tolerate having needs, that wants to do everything by herself like little Samuel, and I know that the aversion for Carlotta [*who, I think to myself, stands for knowledge*] is an aversion to getting close to your emotional needs.
Patient. There you are, you're no use at all, as I had already thought of these things myself – I had understood them by myself.
Analyst. QED – *you really don't need me.* Even if I am perhaps the one who puts 'St Anthony's fire [*an allusion to my first name, Antonino*]' to your ears when I talk about the Albanians as I did yesterday, and sometimes, in uncovering your 'drawings', I spoil your plan to deny all your needs and to imagine that you can do without your analysis and can indeed give it up.
Patient. Well, I hadn't thought of St Anthony myself!
Analyst. So I am of some use after all!
Patient. You also picked up something else that I didn't say: I thought

maybe I wouldn't come any more after Christmas because it's too much trouble, but I know I won't do that. [*She leaves with a smile.*]

As stated, this session dates from the third year of Lorena's analysis, when less saturated interpretations have become possible and are sometimes required, but we are in effect still at the testing stage. For the first year we had only two sessions a week because I did not have any more free time, and then I could not give any direct interpretations. That only became possible when we moved on to three sessions, after she expressed the wish for her 'cousin to speak to her more trustingly'.

A fourth session is under consideration from next year. Lorena mentions that she expects to move soon – although she is afraid of doing so – from Voghera to Pavia, to a more comfortable house in a different position. She is afraid there might be more immigrants and yokels from the South in Pavia. In a dream, she is in the WC, but does not sit on the toilet because it is too exposed, so she pees into the bidet, which is more concealed. She also has her 'things' (her period), which make her feel ashamed. What seems to be drawing near is the time of moving towards the couch and a position that may put her needs on show and enable her to talk about her 'things'; of course, we shall also have to look at her emotions, which are like yokels from the South, and her fear of contact with me, as a yokel from the South myself.

In a recent dream, she is worried that her daughter might meet up with immigrants on the Metro and be assaulted by them, but trusts in the Security Department to ensure a safe journey. After this dream, we arrange to move on to four sessions a week on the couch after the Christmas holidays.

7

The patient's response to interpretations and events in the field

A young, gifted analyst gives a complex interpretation to a woman patient, who 'responds' to it by saying that, the night before, she had wanted to have a pizza with some friends, but they had insisted on going to an expensive restaurant, where, on top of everything else, the portions were scarily huge; then she had been bewildered when the time came to pay the bill. At another point in the same session, the analyst first sums up what the patient has said, then describes the prevailing emotion of her communication, and finally gives a transference interpretation. The patient 'responds' by saying how an uncle of hers was moved to tears on returning home after a long absence. Later in the session, she says that for her boyfriend she feels she is only really there when he sees her and phones her.

These fragments of a session are good examples of how it is only the patient – if listened to – who constantly tells us how we must address him in order to reach him. In the first case, what the patient says after the analyst's interpretation, which I quite deliberately called a 'response', indicates how the expectation of a simple meal shared with friends (the pizza) was disappointed, and how she felt the interpretation to be 'excessive' and too complex, so that she felt weighed down by it. This interpretation did not make for growth or transformation. In the second case, by contrast, the 'response' to the interpretation expresses the idea of finding oneself back at home, understood and listened to; while the third example tells us what for the present needs to be conveyed through the interpretation – namely, being seen and being reached.

In other words, every patient tells us constantly how we must be and how we must comport ourselves in order to reach him: one of the

possible ways of listening to what the patient tells us after an interpretation is to regard it as a comment on the interpretation itself – a
comment which in my opinion need not necessarily be interpreted
(that would carry the risk of a relationship 'wrapped up in itself'), but
must be used in the analytic 'kitchen' in such a way that all adjustments required can be made. With the patient in the above examples,
for instance, there must still be an initial 'concrete' level to enable her
to see that the analyst has seen; then a second level to enable her to
see that the prevailing emotion is being brought into focus; and finally
a level on which the emotion can be contextualized in the here
and now.

I have put forward my theoretical view of this contextualization
many times: it involves the patient's α-function and its capacity constantly to form a 'waking dream', whose 'narrative derivatives' then
permit a fairly close approach to the patient's emotional truth at that
moment.

At the same time, there is no communication by a patient –
whether about his history, childhood, sexuality or external life events
– that cannot, *from one point of view*, be 'listened to' as an explicit
expression of his waking dream at the relevant moment. While this
waking dream of course has its origins in the history and the internal
world, it must be borne in mind that our presence and the way in
which we do or do not comport ourselves constitute a major source
of stimuli; in other words, there is nothing the analyst does or does not
do that is not a co-determinant of the session.

This attention to the patient's mental functioning is not always of
equal importance: some patients' psychic structure is sound enough
for us to be able to work on contents, whereas with others it is
essential to begin by repairing their capacity to think. For example,
with some patients it is immediately possible to perform a symphony,
if only for four hands, while with others the piano has to be tuned first
– and with the latter the prime need is to encourage the very development of the mind and the capacity to think before trying to gain
access to content. Bion expressed this in very simple language: with
some patients, we can work immediately on 'undigested facts', whereas
with others we must first encourage the development of ♀ if not
indeed of the α-function itself. Again, whereas the first operation can
also be carried out by way of interpretations of content, the second
calls above all for repeated experiences of 'being in unison', and the
third for the experiencing of the projective identifications and reveries

168

that miscarried during the patient's early life. In other words, anxiety must be absorbed, transformed and incorporated into an image or communication that can be assimilated.

Antonello's trout

In the early stages of Antonello's analysis, I decide to abstain from explicit transference interpretation of what underlies his childhood experiences of separation: the 'mother who had forced him to separate from the dog he was very fond of', or a 'neighbour who had separated two mating dogs with such force that the bitch was badly injured and had a serious haemorrhage that blinded and then killed her'. I confine myself to emphasizing the 'cruelty' of these persons and the sense of loss he must have felt. The session continues with great intensity with a series of 'infantile memories' that describe emotions and feelings towards the mother. I follow the patient with a function that is hardly any more than 'enzymatic'.

He arrives for the next session with a dream in which the climate is very relaxed: he goes with a cousin to a little river full of trout, where they can quietly fish with a net; there are lots of fish, and although some escape, others are caught. So Antonello is describing a 'fruitful fishing expedition' in which some meanings admittedly escape, but others are generated and 'caught'. In other words, we have here an expanding emotional 'field'.

He continues his session by mentioning an affectionate aunt, on whom, however, the kids played tricks when they were small. For example, they would pretend to come home at the time laid down by the aunt, but then go out again, returning in the morning when she was having a nap (I had just agreed to the postponement of a Wednesday afternoon session to the Thursday morning). Then he talks about his unavailable mother, whom he often has to look after and who is not there in summer to fill the three little bowls for the dogs, which Antonello has to leave in town. This time an exhaustive 'interpretation' seems to me to be more useful – perhaps because I do not trust fishing with a net and want to use a harpoon instead, or perhaps owing to the activation of an interpretative superego – so I give the obvious interpretations about his fear of an 'auntlike' situation with the postponement of the session, as well as rage he feels towards me because I am not available to give him his three sessions during the summer holiday weeks.

After a moment's silence, the patient says: 'It's always frustrating being with my mother: the other day I said to her "Here are the documents you needed", and she took something out of her handbag saying that she had something for me. For a moment I imagined she had really thought of me, but it was only "bills to be paid".' That is to say, the decoding type of interpretation was not experienced as a 'thought' and a surprise or enrichment, as when the fish-meanings were swimming and could even be caught without fear of losing some of them, but instead became a further 'bill' to be paid.

It is of course never possible to know in advance what the right approach will be on a particular day, but the patient's responses are bound to guide us in seeking and constructing it in each successive session.

Stefano and his Taliban

A similar situation arises with Stefano, a patient whose narcissism I find myself confronting more and more explicitly, even drawing attention to a kind of de-escalation of his self-images and to a humanizing enlargement of his Achilles heel that makes him more vulnerable, as is happening with a number of new emotions that he is now experiencing.

In the next session he says his wife is afraid that a war might break out; she has not actually gone so far as to buy antibiotics or gas masks, but is pretty near doing so. Then he mentions religious fundamentalists. In this way, he is enabling me to see the effect of my interpretations of the previous day. This time, I decide to interpret the response to the interpretation, because I feel that his anxiety might thereby be relieved. That is indeed what happens, because when I say 'See you tomorrow', he replies with a laugh: 'If I come, that is, considering the risks I face here.'

Interpretations that 'transform': thorns and stews

Carla is a patient who has difficulty in expressing her emotions, but finds it easier to bring them by way of dreams. One Monday, after a four-day break in the analysis due to public holidays, she tells me a dream in which she went to the hairdresser's, but the girl who usually did her hair was not there; then she met a fellow she thought she did not know, but who reminded her that they had been friends in their teens, when they used to look for things together in the cellar. That is all she says. It is not difficult for me to suggest to her that the long break made her afraid of losing me, of losing the contact with someone who usually concerned himself with her, even if the idea then came into her head of meeting someone she had known long ago, with whom she used to search for hidden or forgotten things.

170

After a moment's silence, she says she has been out with her husband and three children to a place where there were beautiful chestnut trees, but the children pricked themselves with thorns; her husband wanted to leave, but she suggested that the children should stay in the car for a time while they collected some of the nice chestnuts. I tell her that there must be a subject that interests her even if it is thorny and pricks her, which on the one hand she would like to confront while on the other she would like to avoid it: could it be that through the dream she was acknowledging the importance of the bond between us? She responds by saying that one of her sons made a fuss and refused point blank to eat some stew with polenta, but once he had been left free to decide for himself he had thoroughly enjoyed it.

It seems obvious to me that in this vignette the interpretation becomes a non-persecutory element of 'transformation', in which the material stemming from the dream is gradually able to become less thorny and then positively tasty, like the stew.

A disease called 'compulsive transference interpretation'

'But that's not analysis!' is a remark often heard in the corridors of psychoanalytic centres or congresses throughout the world. Indeed, the President of the European Psychoanalytical Federation, David Tuckett, recently suggested that 'assertions' of this kind should be avoided and that more and more clinical exchanges should take place between analysts with different models. However, a long road, involving a great deal of suffering and many excommunications, had to be travelled before it became possible to accept the idea of exchanges on a basis of equality between the adherents of extremely diverse 'theories'. In my view, a sufficiently unifying theory might be one based on listening to the patient and listening to the patient's 'responses' to interpretations.

A particular shibboleth in the areas of influence of the British Kleinian school of psychoanalysis was that an intervention could only be regarded as 'psychoanalytic' if it was a 'transference interpretation'. This was deemed to be not just *one* of the instruments at the disposal of the psychoanalyst, but *the* 'instrument par excellence', in the absence of which one was at most in the realm of 'psychotherapy' or of 'support'. For a long time, saturated interpretations of transference and content were the hallmark of analysis for many analysts, although, to tell the truth, this was the case more in some parts of the world than in others (French psychoanalysis having remained virtually immune). Behind this technical option, there of course lies a strong theory and an equally strong theory of technique: the point of urgency of the anxiety in the here and now must be constantly pointed out to the patient, the idea being that 'knowing' one's unconscious fantasies and having them unveiled is in itself therapeutic.

This is not yet quite the Bionian idea of the central importance of 'transformation' as a signal of the psychoanalytic process in hand.

Transformation – whether in the form of microtransformations within the session, medium–term transformations or macrotransformations over a period of years – is triggered by various types of mental operations, including the following:

- *Listening to and sharing the manifest meaning of what the patient tells us*: What the patient tells us must pervade us and soak us through; we must 'negotiate' the road through it with him. This then becomes the first step in the process of reception: 'I have understood that you, the analyst, have understood what I am telling you.' If a patient says that, as a child, after finishing his dinner, he always used to eat a slice of toast with Nutella spread, and reflects that he saw this as a signal to his parents of his need to receive something extra from them, I transfer myself with him into his chosen scene and time, in order to assign 'value' to his communication, history and memories, as well as to the meanings that he himself is beginning to produce.
- *Abstraction and description of the prevailing emotions*: Next I take a second step, still in relation to the scenario introduced by the patient, in which I seek to abstract with 'movement, warmth and an overall approach' the emotions that belong to 'that time' (the sense of pain and of not mattering to the parents), linking them to the emotions in the present, such as, say, his suffering, or the rage at 'visiting' this scene.
- *Possible contextualization in the transference*: Only at this point could I consider whether it might be useful to give a transference interpretation, along the lines of 'Well, now we know why you always need two or three extra minutes after a session is over to finish off what we were talking about', and possibly 'Could it be that these extra minutes – the slice of toast – are telling us

172

about your need to . . . ?' In other words, the patient must feel accompanied in his thought processes, and this must take place in 'stages' that are explicitly demonstrated.

By now it will no doubt be clear that I regard interpretations of the kind that turn a patient's communication over on to a different level – decoding-type interpretations – as unhelpful.

> At the beginning of her session, a patient tells me that she is pregnant and pleased to be pregnant, but is not sure she has made the right choice of 'father for the child'. She adds that her twin sister and the other family members will surely disapprove. This patient has already had one analy-sis, which has left her with some unresolved problems. Following her 'text', I say that she seems to be pleased with her 'project' but less sure of her 'companion', while at the same time she is very much afraid of the voices that disapprove of her project.
>
> She replies: 'Yes, but why don't you interpret what I said?' I respond sincerely: 'Because I don't think that my thoughts about you are more useful than the ones we manage to construct together; the former are hypotheses, while the latter are truths for us.' 'Just interpret anyway!' 'I think you are afraid I won't be able to do so; a psychoanalytic interpret-ation might be that you are pleased with your decision to have analysis but not yet sure that your choice of me as your analyst is the right one.'
>
> The patient continues: 'Last night I had a dream: my father gave me a cheque for five million lire and I paid it into the bank, but there was another one, for 2,970,000 lire, which I couldn't pay in. What does it mean?' I reply: 'I don't know exactly: there's one transaction that you can carry out, and another that you can't, but I don't know what it is.' 'Well,' she says, 'what I thought was that the 29th of the 7th is the date when I go on holiday, and I had not yet managed to tell you how sorry I am that I shan't be seeing you for the whole length of the holidays.'

I should add that the previous sessions had centred on the subject of her son, who was nearing the end of a course of psychotherapy: the son's analyst kept saying compulsively that the child was 'suffering' because of the separation – something that was felt neither by my patient nor by the child.

Something that had been strongly denied when it came from an external/internal voice in the form of a univocal interpretation became shareable if 'played' in the session and elaborated in the form

173

of something thought up jointly (the *co-pensée* of Widlöcher [1996]), in which the idea of a strong (and mortifying) holder of the truth is relinquished in favour of that of a helmsman together with whom the patient can read the nautical charts and make his own active contribution.

Carlo's table settings

Carlo begins his session by talking about his fear – and hope – of being able to have a third child. He says that his wife's sickness might also be a sign of a hysterical pregnancy, of a 'wish denied'. He then mentions how infrequently he has sex with his wife at this time. Next he describes a scene in a restaurant where they were shown to a table for four. He adds that two children already give him a lot to think about, and sometimes also to worry about.

The analyst comments only in the form of asides, without being able to find an interpretative key. The patient goes on to say that his wife is often not very available in the evenings because she is tired, and he then spends hours by himself at the computer visiting pornographic websites.

I have not mentioned the most important thing, which is that this session is taking place in a week with only two sessions owing to a midweek public holiday, while another session is being lost because the analyst is taking an extra day off between the holiday and the weekend.

The analyst is obviously failing to pick up the significance of the numbers two, three and four and the patient's displeasure at the 'wish denied' for the third and fourth sessions, or perhaps the wish to have one of the missed sessions made up, and also fails to discern that the patient feels him to be tired, unavailable and not disposed to interact with him.

The patient spends the whole of the next session talking about quite a simple task, which he is disappointed to see that his students are incapable of mastering – a task of 'mathematical analysis': he is obviously reproaching his analyst for having failed to pick up his problem with regard to the missed sessions.

Of course, the analyst could have deployed any of a number of models, ranging from the classical interplay of 'free associations' and 'evenly suspended attention', which was Freud's brilliant intuition about the central importance of the oneiric functioning of minds, via the more

174

Kleinian notion of 'knowing' that a change of setting is bound to activate emotions, to the post-Bion model of asking the 'narrative derivatives' (narremes) of the session what sequence of α-elements they might stem from.

For the analyst, the patient seems to have chosen an excessively complex and misleading narrative genre. He would perhaps have had less difficulty if the patient had said 'I went to a restaurant, but they were in a hurry, so they gave us only the first and second courses and skipped the sweet and the fruit [the third and fourth sessions].' He might have had even less difficulty if the patient had said that he had seen a news item on television about a rail crash in which the third and fourth carriages of a train were derailed and smashed to pieces.

It is, of course, important to understand that these 'narrative derivatives' refer more or less explicitly to the sequence of α-elements that pictographed the emotions present on that day, in a way which we cannot know but which it is not hard for us to imagine as an exercise.

Amedeo's traffic lights

The first thing Amedeo's parents tell the therapist is that at the age of three months he had a proliferative tumour on his lip. This required prolonged treatment, and now Amedeo is surely out of danger. They then describe his unwillingness to go to school: he has violent fits of aggression, which are sometimes 'monstrous and uncontainable', accompanied by agonized yelling and screaming. They say that he can never take 'no' for an answer, but bangs his head against the wall until they give way to him. At the first meeting with the therapist, he says he already has a collection of over thirty weapons, including pistols, rifles and machine guns, and he begins a disorganized game involving the lion, the tiger, the rhinoceros and the gorilla, in a maelstrom of battles. Then he forms two teams of toy people, one of which is made up of policemen and the other – the therapist's – of 'blacks', illegal immigrants, tramps and thieves. The game must proceed absolutely in the way he 'dictates', otherwise he yells and screams and dashes everything to the floor.

Reflection on this clinical material and an attempt to 'deconstruct' it in terms of its reality status suggests that the 'tumour' is the proliferation of uncontrollable emotions that are also expressed by the yelling and screaming (the lip!). Amedeo's control of the adults and ordering them about – the game he plays – is in effect the therapy that he knows for the proliferation of emotions that can flare up from one moment to the next. Any 'no' then unleashes lions, gorillas and tigers, like all the other

175

emotions he is constantly splitting off and trying to keep under control by means of the police. The emotions are indeed black thieves invading his territory and taking away his peace, and he prevents them from bursting in on him by dominating and overpowering the Other and the unknown parts of himself.

The therapist, of course, joins in the game for a while, and then begins to interpret. Eventually, Amedeo comes to accept that it is the therapist who performs a 'traffic-lights' function; seemingly referring to the play constructions, he says 'Give me the reds' or 'Give me the greens', and starts playing a game in which fundamental importance attaches to the 'fire brigade' in its interaction with the 'traffic managers', these functions increasingly being delegated to the therapist.

A child for Fernanda

Fernanda is a patient who was for a long time incapable of maintaining a stable relationship; she also once broke off her analysis, but resumed it after two years. Returning from a trip to Paris with her 'sort-of' boyfriend (whom she left before the summer and then took up with again), she says that for the first time she wanted to have a stable relationship with him, without running away; she wanted to marry him, set up home and have a child. He, for his part, assumed a wait-and-see attitude, saying, 'Well, let's see how the next few months go and then we'll decide.' She felt quite good about this and understood that there were certain time constraints that had to be observed. She then brings a dream: she was in hospital and painlessly gave birth to a child; it was a very fine child, but she did not know what name to give it.

She then recalls that when she was a little girl she liked to play for hours with foam in the bath, but would have sudden fits of claustrophobia that made her rush out on to the terrace. On one occasion, unable to open the door perhaps because her hands were slippery with soap, she leapt out of the bathroom's perilously high first-floor window and ended up spending a week in hospital. There, she amused herself by hiding, so that her mother had to search for her when she came to visit.

In this sequence, Fernanda seems to be expressing the fact that a genuine transformation has taken place: the wish for a stable relationship (the name to be given to the child), which is felt to be something possible and desirable, and no longer, as in the past (when she was a little girl), something to mess about with constantly and then to feel suffocated by so that she eventually needed to run away, however risky that might be, ending up needing to be chased in a kind of eternal game of hide-and-seek or tag.

So the dream and the other communications do now indeed indicate two different forms of mental functioning, one of which is the new child of an unexpectedly painless birth (the fruit of all the years of analytic work) and can now be set up against the old, obsolete form of relating.

The truth of autobiography and the lies of psychoanalysis

The title of this section is deliberately provocative and paradoxical: it indicates that the presence of the Other – in particular, the analyst – continually subverts and transforms memory, sometimes even resulting in the extreme possibility of arousing memories that never actually happened. I was impressed by a clinical example given years ago by Horacio Etchegoyen in which a patient gradually rewrote an infantile memory as his analysis progressed. Let me try to recall the clinical situation as it were off the top of my head. The story is more or less as follows. At the beginning of his analysis, the patient described some terrible childhood experiences of being left alone by his mother in discomfort, panic and desperation. After a period of analytic work, the same memory appeared in the still traumatic form of the mother's going away, but now he was left with a servant who somehow looked after him however desperate he was. Later still, the patient again mentioned how he was left alone as a child, but always in the company of an affectionate aunt who cared for him; and finally, at the end of his analysis, he brought a story his mother had sometimes told him about the despair of a child in a nearby house when left alone – something that had in fact never happened to *him* because *his* mother always took care to ensure that he had good company when she had to go away.

This seems to me to be a good example of the 'macrotransformations' that take place when an analysis functions as it should. As the internal world is gradually restructured and previously unavailable functions and capacities are introjected, the terror of loneliness and abandonment is reduced, not only making the separation from the analyst less traumatic but also transforming the internal objects and experiences, and even memory itself.

If I can separate easily and without anxiety today, this will impart a different colour to every separation that I can remember, and might even alter memory itself.

It seems to me that this is precisely the aim of analysis, at least as regards the most badly suffering aspects of the patient. I now believe that only marginal importance attaches to removing the veil of repression, achieving insight and making unconscious or primal fantasies conscious. The ultimate goal of analysis is to enrich – or in some cases to supply for the first time – the equipment for metabolizing formerly unthinkable emotions and affective states. In other words, there is both a process of transformation in the 'here and now' of each session and – in particular – a gradual passing on of the method for performing such operations.

On the other hand, autobiography is in a way more truthful, at least in the sense of maintaining a relatively constant narrative 'skeleton', although in my view the very fact of writing (and even more so, of telling) opens the way to an increasingly extensive deconstructionist drift.

To return to my subject, however, little purpose would be served by a psychoanalysis that consisted solely in making conscious or unveiling repressed (or split-off or disavowed) events unless this was accompanied by the capacity to transform both memory and the patient's ability to think and to process all the stimuli of every kind to which he is constantly exposed.

Yet the continuous rewriting of the history and the transformations of the internal world are driven by the 'microtransformations' occurring within each session. While each session is on the one hand a microcosm in itself, on the other it is cumulatively linked to all the other sessions in an ongoing spiral of transformation.

Let us consider this proposition in detail.

The fuming of Marcello

Marcello, a senior official at the law courts, decides to embark on an analysis owing to his ill-feeling and hate for his father, whom he sees as an absolute tyrant who ruined his childhood, adolescence and young adulthood. His 'fuming' with rage and hate are so pervasive that all he can do is work, and nothing else.

He begins one session with his analyst by saying that he had to miss the previous session because he had to attend court in another town. Out of the blue, he asks whether he can be excused payment for the session he had to miss. The analyst, although competent and conscientious, and fully aware of the importance of the setting and its observance, finds herself saying 'All right, don't pay then.' Instead of engaging in a long disquisition on the behaviour of an analyst who in this way so clamorously disregards the rules laid down at the beginning as the essential framework for the conduct of the analysis, let us consider the consequences of this response of the analyst as a chain reaction in this and the next two sessions.

Immediately afterwards, the patient remarks that he has been present at an obscene and shameful *hearing*, involving incredible incompetence; that legal certainty has gone out of the window; and that nowadays everything is done by bargaining. In other words, he is harshly criticizing the analyst for not respecting the 'bargains' made and for not insisting on their being respected, fearing that she is doing so for a quiet life – so he is saying that what he 'heard' is terrible and makes him lose every vestige of trust. He then at once mentions a woman lawyer he has met, whom he likes very much, but whose views are unclear to him. So he is beginning to change his opinion of his analyst and to appreciate her, even if he does not yet understand what type of analyst she is.

He now returns to the subject of the law, which he thinks is too subjective: there are some fine laws, which are unfortunately not put into practice. This is a milder way of expressing his first thesis – namely, that the 'laws' of analysis have not been respected. The next character to appear is someone who wanted to stab his father, was placed under house arrest and supervised by a social worker [a 'social assistant' in Italian]; that is to say, his former 'fury' is being blunted by the analyst's 'assistance'. I am here omitting the analyst's comments, which are not interpretative but merely 'modulate' what the patient says.

However, that is not all. Marcello begins the next session by saying that his father has unexpectedly sent him a postcard including a sentence that may or may not be ambiguous or affectionate – he is not sure – and he doesn't know whether to calm down or to imagine that it is a trap set by his father for whatever reason. In other words, the analyst's 'reply card' has disoriented him; he was not expecting it, and, although tempted to 'make peace', suspects that there might be something concealed behind it.

In the following session, he asks if he can take off his jacket, and mentions his plan to stop smoking, adding 'I like smoking though' and commenting that he would like to find the right person for him, but is very afraid of happiness.

If he is ill, he is not worried about death, but if he feels good, then he does worry about it. He goes on to say that sometimes, in the hope of dying, he used to put a rope on his pillow, with the aim of putting it round his neck. Then he mentions his father, who left him alone too much when he was small; this time the patient is creating a more familiar climate: he takes off his jacket, would like to stop smoking/fuming [the Italian word *fumare* means both] with hate and rage and living permanently in a state of ill-feeling and accusation, but is then afraid of how his life would change and how it would assume new value; and finally he does not know whether the relationship (the rope) will kill him or make him feel less alone.

While all this takes place in the present-day relationship with his analyst, it inevitably also has the consequence of a change in his emotions and in his way of managing them, so that, for a moment, a tyrannical father whom he would like to kill becomes a father who sends postcards and whom he misses. The rewriting continues . . .

As stated, the unstable, reversible microtransformations progressively give rise to stable and irreversible macrotransformations that gradually become a new identity. In psychoanalysis, all this is of course mediated by the *relational interplay with the Other*.

There thus seems to have been a revolution in psychoanalytic models, from the original historico-reconstructive ones, via those centred on the modulation of fantasies, and finally to those in which the focus is on the 'functioning of the mind' without excessive emphasis on content. This revolution, which is perhaps simply an evolution, has also extended to the conceptualization of the unconscious.

It might also be worth while to reflect on the no man's land between autobiography – the importance of which I may not have sufficiently stressed – and psychoanalysis: namely, so-called self-analysis, which ranges from particularly naïve 'diary' forms to attempts at self-analytic introspection. My personal view is that self-analysis does have some value, but more in terms of explanation and knowledge than of transformation. I perhaps trust more in the mating of the mind's dream work with the self-analysis of dreams.

8

Terminations orthodox and unorthodox

There are perhaps some analyses that can never come to an end – or at least cannot finish with a classical termination. These are analyses of psychotic patients, with whom either analysis is conducted as it were as dialysis or, more frequently, one finds an unorthodox way of terminating. I have previously written at length on the termination (Ferro 1996a, 1999).

Tiberio's last session

Tiberio is coming to the end of a prolonged analysis that has profoundly changed him, starting as he did from a state of severe paranoid schizo-phrenia potentially involving criminal acts. He is now a person with a deep knowledge of himself and of the fact that analysis can take him only so far. I for my part have to mourn for a megalomaniacal expectation of a total recovery for Tiberio and must accept the partial cure, with all its shortcomings, that we have attained.

He takes three Buscopan tablets for the stomach ache to which the shared idea of termination has given rise. He recalls how he once killed his uncle's sick dog with blows from a shovel: this seems to foreshadow the sense that separation can only be violent, involving a tearing apart. He then has a fit of extreme anxiety like those which characterized the beginning of the analysis: his fear of having contracted AIDS shows that he is no longer immune from human feelings and emotions, which he experiences as very dangerous. Next, he announces that he wants to terminate his analysis immediately, and puts this plan into practice from one day to the next without keeping to our intention of finishing in December. He thus breaks off the analysis in October, two months before the agreed date.

A year later, Tiberio telephones for an appointment. When I open the door to him, I am greeted with a beautiful smile: 'I'm pleased to see you,' he says. Then, although I have placed a chair in front of my desk, he unexpectedly heads for the couch and lies down on it, saying: 'I prefer it here. I haven't had my last session yet.' He then tells me what has happened during the year: moments of intolerable pain, a period of intense rage towards me, accompanied by the fear of having been deceived, and, finally, awareness of the work done and of the major changes that have taken place.

He asks me about an invalidity pension to which he might be entitled, and says that any continuation of therapy would only be cruel. I agree with him that it is a mature decision to know when to stop, while being conscious of the long road behind us. We also tell each other that what we are doing is in fact having the final analytic session which was not possible last year, and that, even if the analysis is coming to an end, after so many years of work together our relationship is certainly not over. He is moved and has tears in his eyes. He asks me whether, if I had known from the beginning how difficult his analysis would be for me, I would still have accepted him, or whether it was an 'error of youth'.

I reply sincerely that with the consciousness I have today I would still take him and that I am pleased with the work we have done together, even if the cure has been limited to what it was possible to achieve. At the end of the session he leaves me with big tears in his eyes, saying that he knows that in Pavia he has someone on whom he can rely – he could say he has 'a friend'.

I forgot to mention one other thing that Tiberio told me: after he stopped coming to me, his fear of having AIDS turned into a fear of syphilis, but there was a treatment for syphilis, and so he 'prescribed' a long course of penicillin for himself (Tiberio graduated in medicine during the course of his analysis).

The skipping of the last two months in my view constituted the antibiotic therapy used to combat the catastrophic anxieties aroused by our separation. However, after this therapy, Tiberio was able to come along for his final session of analysis, his parting comment being: 'This time it really is goodbye!'

Joining up again: Luigi's long road

Luigi is very seriously ill, with dramatic symptoms, when his analysis begins. The maintenance of the setting is already a major problem: for a long time, unable to tolerate lying down or even sitting up on the couch, he ensconces himself in an armchair in the opposite corner of the room to my own, making us like two boxers in the ring. There are indeed countless 'punches' which are not only metaphorical, but never actually directed at myself, although I often feel I might be hit. Apart from that, however, anything might happen: objects might be smashed, tables knocked over and the couch overturned – and, unfortunately, once his session is over, it is not only my room but often also my mind that ends up in total disorder.

For years, ending a session is an indescribably difficult enterprise – so much so that, after Luigi's session, I always leave a buffer period before seeing the next patient. A fundamentally important factor is the help of a colleague who treats him with massive doses of medication and admits him over and over again to hospital during holidays. After immense difficulties that need not be described here, the setting eventually comes to be respected, and we can do an hour's work that no longer resembles a rodeo.

For many years we work through intense persecutory anxieties, hypochondriacal delusions, delusions of compensation and threats of 'bumping everybody off'. However, instead of describing all this and the reasons why termination becomes thinkable, I wish to focus on the impasse that arises towards the seventh year of analysis, involving questions (in which I feel confronted by the Sphinx) that give rise to catastrophic anxiety that blocks everything off. The patient himself is unable to help solve these problems, which, however, are in need of a response if we are to make progress. This response thus entails putting into words (and into thoughts) an anxiety of some kind that has accumulated unbeknown to us under the carpet. All progress unexpectedly disappears, the analysis is at a standstill, and there is only an agonizing bad feeling that makes for all-pervading paralysis.

The moments when he realizes that his bad feelings serve the purpose of renewing his 'analytic residence permit' are mere glimmers of light, because he then manages to find ways of feeling utterly terrible. He finds the most incredible reasons to torture and lacerate himself with devastating thoughts, also involving cruel forms of anal masturbation (which were already present in the first years of his analysis), sometimes accompanied by masochistic acts and actual self-harm. Every little 'fact' tends to become a source of torment; for instance, if a man follows him in his car, it must be one of the husbands whose wives he has had sex with and who wants to make him pay for it. In these orgies of self-torment, no interpretation can afford any relief whatsoever.

His dreams enable me to show him that he has to feel awful in this way because only then can he imagine that he has a guarantee that I shall continue to concern myself with him: 'Now that I've found something that is worth more to me than life itself, I can't lose it . . .' He sometimes realizes the absurdity of this idea, but nevertheless arrives for his sessions in agony. I myself despair (while understanding that my desperation corresponds to the despair which *he* is unable to experience, and to the mourning that *he* cannot yet initiate) because my interpretations are manifestly not getting through to him.

However, I wonder: 'How does he manage to feel so awful, in such a seemingly senseless way?' I am struck by an action he performs repeatedly throughout a long series of sessions: he moves his tongue strangely in a kind of buccal dyskinesia (could this be drug-induced, as in the first years of his analysis?). Eventually I ask him: 'Why do you move your tongue about like that?' He answers: 'Because I can then hurt it on a sharp tooth.' This is finally the key – the first key, as many others will still be needed before the armoured door of the termination can be opened – to how he makes himself feel so awful: in a flash, I realize that with his tongue he is going to touch on subjects and material which he knows will trigger a response on my part, which he in turn knows will make him feel bad. In other words, I realize that for a long time it was *I* – impelled by him – who gave interpretations that were correct in terms of content, but which touched areas on which scar tissue was forming, so that touching them was like turning a knife in the wound. I tell him this. He answers: 'That's absolutely right!'

After this door is unlocked, I am under the illusion that progress has been made, but he then deploys another strategy: immobilization – 'If I speak, I'll get better; if I work, I'll get better.' And indeed, in a fanlike movement from the outside world to the inside of the analysis, he stops going out and refuses to see anyone, in the end also ceasing to work and to offer meaningful communications in his sessions. At most, I am confronted with riddles: 'If the lower teeth press against the upper ones, the upper ones move and I'll lose them.' After a number of attempts, however, I realize that he is drawing my attention to the problem of loss – of his deep fear that if he really does talk (and the lower teeth touch the upper ones in both speaking and eating), he will lose something important: myself, the analysis and the sister who looks after him, and that is unthinkable.

Fortunately, however, there is a 'Telemachus' on our road (I am thinking of the episode where Ulysses feigns madness by ploughing the sand in order not to leave for the Trojan war, but stops when little Telemachus

184

is placed in front of his plough): namely, the loss of his virility. All of a sudden, boasting as he does of being a Don Juan, he becomes impotent. This impotence is partly resolved when I realize that the patient has taken my own feeling of impotence upon himself: 'My prick is not what it was; it is not as hard as it used to be.' In this way, we get in touch with the pain he feels at not being the same as he used to be, no longer so violent and cruel, but more flexible, tender and even affectionate. However, even when this has been accepted, everything is repeatedly regurgitated again. But eventually, making use of a comment of his about consulting sexologists, I suggest that the sexual aspect is a kind of secret 'dialect' whereby he can manage to indicate that, for him too, 'giving up everything and not living, so long as I don't lose the analysis' arouses terrible anxiety, and that in this way he really does risk losing his virility – in the wider sense of all his expressive potentiality – and ultimately sweeping away his most authentic identity.

Yet the Cyclopes are still stronger than we are, and with them the catastrophic and violent feelings aroused by the idea of setting a date for the termination. Ulysses comes to me in a dream (and to him in acting-out), in which I am locked in a room with armoured windows and doors and do not know how to get out, but then a trapdoor is pointed out to me as another exit. The patient in turn regularly skips the first session of the week (after eight years in which he never missed and was never late for a session); and then I have a dream in which the patient is unable to perform a figure dance. I now feel I can tell him that perhaps there is something he is acting out and wants, even if he has not yet 'figured it out' – not the unapproachable and intolerable idea of terminating, but that of reducing the number of sessions from his usual four to three per week.

He is at once happy to accept: at the end of the session he removes the bulb from my table lamp and takes it away, returning it to me with a smile and an affectionate gesture at the beginning of the next session.

Although this reduction is favourable to us, everything we have been unable to confront promptly appears again, albeit on a smaller scale: once again, jealous husbands with murder in mind because their wives have deceived them, revenge attacks and ambushes intended and feared, and so on. While it is seemingly futile to interpret the 'jealousy' about the deception of the loss of a session, we very gradually manage to metabolize all this. After about a year, fresh dreams for me and fresh acting-out for him indicate that we can cut down to two sessions. Meanwhile he seems to have rediscovered some self-esteem and a disavowed trust in me and in

185

the analysis. Yet the thought of being able to terminate the analysis makes him fear that the good and healthy forces in him are not sufficiently well equipped to hold back the violent, sick parts.

There follows a new period of difficulty, because, once again, 'my prick does not work as it used to do', but he soon realizes that it is he himself, and not me as his prick, that is not working as it used to: he now has to lean on me only twice a week, and, furthermore, the use of sexuality also changes – instead of casual, erotized relationships, he becomes aware, at the age of 32, that he has never told a girl 'I love you'.

He now clearly sees the fact of being held – considered also as the need to be held constantly by the hand – as something that emasculates and devalues him.

He has another dream: he was in Japan, working as a baker, and his brother was teaching him to cook. There was a serious little girl who 'did not give him any'. While telling me the dream, he gets up and mentions 'screwing a black woman', who was so black that you could not see her unless she put on a blouse. And she was so tall that she would not fit into his Fiat 500 even if she bent double. Rising from the couch, he conspicuously chews gum.

So that is where we are now: on the one hand, there is a good working relationship, a new world, and a serious little part, but, on the other, there is also a black part, which we are unable to see and that requires 'something contrasting' if it is to become visible – a part that is intolerant of the couch and contemptuous . . . but how are we to think of this part? As a black and bad part, or as a primitive part that wants independence? It is certainly a 'dark' part, or perhaps a project that is still obscure: the patient is preoccupied with the wish to get better and the recognition that he is no longer so attracted to the idea of being ill and looked after; he feels anxiety in the morning when he gets out of bed (and when fantasizing about the termination?).

He catches 'conjunctivitis' – the 'disease of being together'. His suntanned little nephew (the son of his brother and a black woman!) has been baptized – so a project (thinking of the termination) has been given a name, and, in particular, he is working on a mental operation that is in progress and is likely to make him feel good, involving the giving up of the fantasy of someone who will look after him in the divine form of the Son of God, born as he was on Christmas Day.

A new torment now emerges: he is concerned that a liaison in which he has got involved might give him CBS (the letters stand, in a joke, for AIDS), which is the make of tractor he used to enjoy driving, from which he

186

earned good money. There is a real reversal of perspective here, because for him it is an illness if he conceives a wish to work and get better, as that will take him far away from an idealized notion of treatment. He begins to cry, not, as in the past, by dissolving in tears and dribbling mucus all over, but with a contained weeping, endured and shy. He has an ache in a tooth in which he 'feels' things that are hot or cold, and is discovering his capacity to have feelings and to experience them: 'Yesterday I looked at myself in the mirror and saw that I had white, calm eyes. I was afraid. Can you imagine what feeling good means to me?'

I recognize the 'fear' that I feel about initiating the safe 'conflict'; I change down a gear, and hesitate to suggest a date for the termination again. I am almost grateful to him for no longer tormenting me with wearisome telephone calls: would I still be able to stand the timing he thereby forced on me? (My interpretations, at this point administered in excessive doses, must have been equally persecutory for him.) Now there appears on the scene a pornographic disco in which a porno star exhibits herself: we can imagine this as his making an exhibition of himself, of his illness and of the conspicuous anal masturbation whereby he avoids contact with feelings that have to do with time, separation and loneliness.

However, the porno star is offset by a new character who gradually takes shape: a young girl with whom he goes for gentle walks, without wanting to possess her sexually ('I respect her a lot; it's the feelings that count'). He learns to drink the sour orange drink *chinotto* and orangeade, forgoing the intoxication of whisky/hate/pornography that has been like a second skin for him. Arianna [Ariadne] is the name of this girl, who appears in one of his dreams 'giving him a thread' [the Italian phrase *fare il filo* also means 'falling for him']: she seems to be able to provide the latter-day Theseus with the thread he needs to emerge from the labyrinth of the interminability of analysis and of the non-thinkability of affects.

Having for a long time respected these characters in the form in which they are presented to me, I am now able to approach them as forms of functioning of Luigi in his sessions, as forms of perceiving and relating to me – either on a masturbatory, pornographic level, or on the level of affects that gradually become important in the parallel development of a love story with Arianna. I now suddenly realize that I too have come to accept a perversion of the analytic situation, the idea of analysis as a drug, instead of activating feelings I was afraid might still be too violent and dangerous were we to set a date for the termination. Having become fully aware of this fear, I am able to talk to the patient about this collusion and to make a shared decision with him on the termination date.

So Luigi's analysis is over, but it has left me with a bitter taste in my mouth even though in the end he has become a completely different person; while no longer the 'Raging Bull' of the beginning of the analysis, a violent, destructive, dangerous and possibly criminal or drug-addicted or suicidal or homicidal patient taking enormous doses of antipsychotic drugs, he is now an 'unhappy' man – someone who is surely in need of an analysis *now*.

Before we finally wind up the analysis, I have two dreams. In the first, I had to visit a neurologically healthy person, but when I administered the Romberg test, I found that he could not keep his balance independently and needed support; in the second, I had to go down an alleyway with Luigi, but it became impassable, or at least too difficult for us (hence the 'short cut' mentioned below?). Luigi then went off on his own road . . .

We should perhaps bear in mind Meltzer's comment about seriously ill patients who end their analysis at the point where others would begin it. I imagined that I would be relieved when Luigi's analysis came to an end, but the dreams showed me that his termination involved profound mourning for me too, including mourning for my expectations after so many years of toil. I now believe that I could have accompanied Luigi further along the road, having since made better contact inside myself with the catastrophically depressive anxieties that prevented us from having the last sessions: the analysis came to an end with a telephone call from Luigi, saying that he had not had the last sessions and could not have afforded the final month of analysis. And a period of payment 'by instalments' was indeed necessary as a 'short cut' to enable the analysis to be terminated. For a long time I was left with the sensation that we (I?) could have done more, but I had to accept that the catastrophically depressive anxieties exceeded the capacity of our 'oven', even if we had done a great deal.

One problem remains: how much can, and how much cannot, be worked through in the analysis of a thoroughly psychotic patient who has changed greatly in many respects? After all, he is no longer violent or criminal or liable to delusions and, although he is transformed from Hans Rudel, the Nazi officer in one of his dreams, into Giovanni Torta, the baker in another, he has nevertheless not made contact with the need to suffer pain in order to rid himself of the compulsion to repeat the part of Hans Castorp, who was happy to be ill so that he could stay put on Thomas Mann's Magic Mountain. However, would staying there not be tantamount to accepting the pact of timelessness, or indeed Faust's project? Would this not involve blocking off other possible routes, outside which our work has already enabled him to travel, but which have remained obstructed by the sum of our blind or pathological areas?

There is certainly something here that one analyst might interpret as the patient's 'insuperable resistance' and another as the 'phenomenon of reversal of perspective', while yet another analyst might see it as a 'bulwark' that calls for a 'third look'. However, what of the hypothesis that our minds together were able to achieve this and no more than this, and that this has been our mutual story, the result of which is specific to ourselves and to our capabilities, hopes, defences and limits? And that it is just as important not to block off other possible channels of development and of meeting for the patient? Should we not trust in the idea that we are not irreplaceable and that other stories and meetings are entitled to be narrated, with other interpreters, other journeys and other possibilities?

Two years later, Luigi phones me to say that he had been feeling well, but then had to start taking antidepressants, which are now no longer enough. In September he will be starting a new analysis (the 'sister' is pregnant and might miscarry, but it should be all right!); in the morning it was suggested that she go to A&E (the telephone call? *Pronto! Soccorso!*[1]), but he knows that what is more important is the 'new analysis', on which he has now decided to embark and which he is afraid will be very expensive, even if he has his father's survivor's pension, which is much bigger than expected, and he thinks he can afford it.

Other analyses, of course, have classical terminations – even if I am increasingly coming to consider that, as the title of the 1973 play by Eduardo de Filippo has it, *Exams Never End*, and I believe less and less in the existence of 'finished' analyses, but instead in that of journeys that come to an end and sometimes suffice, whereas in other cases there is a further path to be travelled.

Francesca's bleach
A few months after the termination of her approximately six-year analysis, which came to a somewhat abrupt end, Francesca telephones me for an appointment to discuss certain problems. She tells me that it has been

---

[1] Translator's note: A hospital's accident and emergency unit in Italian is *pronto soccorso*, but one answers the telephone by saying *pronto* ('hallo'), and *soccorso* is a cry for help.

a time of aneurysms: her father had a cerebral aneurysm, and shortly afterwards her father-in-law had an abdominal aneurysm; both had successful emergency operations, carried out by two teams of competent doctors. She goes on to say that her 12-year-old son Marco has for some months been telling her about 'fears' that assail him before falling asleep. They all concern 'dirt', and he also has a teacher who is obsessed with cleanliness. He is afraid of poisoning himself if he uses too much bleach, or, conversely, of catching an infection if something has not been cleaned properly. Francesca then mentions the rage that she often still feels towards her mother, and a time when she was about to fall in love with a young colleague because she felt neglected by her husband. She then describes various work projects, as well as her satisfaction at having found a really good babysitter for her children; finally, she adds that she has not ruled out the possibility of having another period of analysis later.

At first I share Francesca's emotions about what she is telling me, and then try to take stock [*punto*] of the situation. This meeting between us, too, is about putting a full stop [also *punto* in Italian] after her analysis. A balance sheet must be drawn up and stock must be taken. On the one hand, there is the problem of the aneurysms and that of Marco's fears, which stand for her own fears of feeling bad whether she 'bleaches' everything away or has emotions that she is afraid might be dirty, such as rage at the analyst's absence or perhaps the wish to have a period of analysis with another analyst. On the other, there is also the fear of incontinence (the bursting of the aneurysms) occasioned by the falling in love or the quarrels with her mother – but she has an operating theatre that can exorcize these bursts. And there is in addition a babysitter function that enables her to care properly for her children/emotions, and all this makes it possible for her to conceive new plans for her work and life.

I shall now present some extracts from an analysis whose particular feature was that it had a time limit and that I took on the patient without having previously met her. First, some theoretical considerations.

There are, in my view, three different loci of traumaticity in a person's mental functioning. Vicissitudes with the primal objects might have given rise to functional deficiencies on various levels.

The highest degree of traumaticity results, in childhood, from a defect in the function governing the development of the caregiver-object's capacity to transform proto-emotions and protosensoriality into images (the α-function). In this case the child's own α-function will be inhibited in its development. This is the context in which the seeds are sown of all the extremely severe pathologies involving failure to introject the instruments necessary for the basic management of psychic life and for the very development of the capacity to dream.

A second level of traumaticity is connected with inadequate, insufficient or overfragile receptivity (of an inadequate container) – again, of the caregivers and consequently of the child – that does not permit the basic introjection of a place to keep emotions and thoughts. This is the root of all pathologies in which, owing to insufficient capacity of containment, recourse is had to various defence mechanisms such as splitting or the lethargization of intolerable emotional states.

A third and less dramatic level of traumaticity is when a sound α-function and an adequate capacity for containment encounter a situation of acute or chronic stress with an excess of stimuli (β-elements) that accumulate as 'undigested facts' awaiting transformation (Bion 1962, 1963, 1965; Ferro 2002b).

All three of these configurations can often be observed to varying degrees in one and the same mind – as in the brief case history set out below, which illustrates how the fabric of the trauma sustained by the patient (whether the macrotrauma or cumulative microtraumas) must present itself anew in the consulting room, where it can be rewoven and where, in particular, the very instruments for reweaving it can be enriched.

Margot and the coat stand

I receive an e-mail from someone in Canada who tells me that she intends to come to Pavia for a year and asks if I am prepared to take her into analysis for that length of time. She adds that she is a doctor and has already had one analysis.

My curiosity is aroused, and so is my vanity. I also feel disorientated, because I wonder whether it makes sense to take a patient into analysis 'for a limited time' and 'in a closed box' or, as one might say in English, 'sight unseen'. But after a period of indecision, I accede to her request.

In September, Margot presents herself as arranged. This young woman has just arrived from French Canada with her three children, who are to attend school in Italy for a year (in Quebec they go to an Italian high school). Margot gives me hardly any other information about how she proposes to organize things and we confirm that, as agreed by e-mail, the analysis will begin on the following Monday at the appointed hour; she will have three sessions a week. On leaving, Margot hands me a large box that she had left in the waiting room, saying: 'I've brought you this from Canada.'

Again I feel disorientated: well, I say to myself, quite apart from having totally failed to consider the problem of criteria of analysability, here I am receiving a present before we even start! But the look on Margot's face now that I have reached the door – together with the thought that I did after all take on Margot in a 'closed box' – leads me to accept this big box.

Left alone, I open the box and find inside a small table clock and a fossil – a 'slice' of a tree trunk from a petrified forest. I am very struck by the fossil because it seems to represent a petrified face wearing the frozen smile of a laughing Pagliacci figure, or perhaps a clown with a desperate, suffering expression.

As I set off for home, I see the clock as a 'memento' of the period of the analysis, which of course has a time limit: one year's work. The petrified face immediately suggests petrified emotions – so perhaps what the patient hopes for from the analysis is that it will impart new life to something fossilized.

While walking home, however, I spontaneously ask myself: 'Now why such a big box for two objects that are basically not very large?' Then comes a flash of illumination: seemingly to protect the clock and the fossil, the whole box is stuffed full of gauze, of the kind used to dress wounds. A third and fundamental theme is thus kindled in my mind: bleeding and the need to staunch the flow of blood (and if possible to treat the wounds).

I feel inside myself that my reveries, fantasies or 'dreams' about these objects are important, and it is equally clear to me that I can use them as hypotheses of my own for assigning meaning to them. But I know it would not make sense to interpret them right away, as I feel I still need to 'metabolize and digest' them.

What all this seems to signify is a situation of receiving and containing Margot's urgent need to deliver something to me. My ensuing reverie enables me to transform what I have just contained into a series of images. I then need to apply a new act of containment and a new reverie to my first reverie. In other words, I can set aside the idea of a sudden unveiling of my new insight and imagine the burden it would represent for the patient. I am then able to describe my new vision of the patient in somewhat disguised terms by prolonged acceptance of the characters of our dialogue in their manifest form.

A tragic history unfolds from the very first sessions: the mother leapt to her death down a lift shaft when Margot was sixteen years old, and the father, a well-known surgeon, immediately closed down the house where they lived and moved away with the four children; no one was allowed to take anything at all from the house, not even underwear or games. A barrier of disavowal had petrified every emotion.

The first dream Margot brings me is of a vampire (who is this person behind me, and should I be afraid of him?) – but this vampire listens to her and has a lantern in his hand. The second features a mugger, but she does not resist the mugging; she does not express any feelings – perhaps she has none – nor does she cry out for help . . . (so here we have the theme of the 'petrified forest': she is always 'concerned to understand the other person and his reasons and needs').

The cost of the analysis – in all senses – is by no means inconsiderable for Margot, and she does not yet know if it will leave her impoverished or enriched.

After a few days, when Margot feels that I am managing to take her painful stories on board without immediately trying to return them to her in an interpretation that would leave her just as weighed down by them as she was before, she dreams that she receives a gift of a 'little coat stand'. In this way the coat stand at the entrance to my consulting room becomes a *character* on our analytic stage – and I do indeed often wonder if my poor little coat stand will stand up to the daily strain of being weighed down with big bagfuls of all sorts of ever heavier stuff which, oddly enough, she does not place on one of the chairs in the waiting room but 'hangs up' on the coat stand. Both I and it do somehow hold up, even if Margot often says she is worried in case the coat stand is not strong enough to support the weight of what is hung on it: shopping bags, small suitcases, packets, etc. The coat stand, for me, comes increasingly to stand for a mother whose reliability and holding capacity need to be tested (like the floor of a lift!).

During this initial period Margot dreams that she is alive on the outside and dead (petrified?) inside.

At this point, in mid-November, I suddenly fall ill and have to cancel Margot's sessions for a week. On my return she says she would like to pay me for the entire analysis up to the end of our year of work, as if to guarantee my presence throughout the agreed time (the mother who dies prematurely?). I of course do not accede to her wish to take out this insurance policy to guarantee my presence, but merely interpret her need for a guarantee that I shall be there for her until the end of her therapy.

She dreams of 'doing classical dance' as she did when she was a little girl: emotions are progressively being released and coming alive inside her, in a dance between the relationship with me (and the fear of losing me prematurely) and the history (the loss of the mother and the impossibility of working through mourning). In another dream a girl is afraid of a dog and a bear, and a woman masturbates both of them: the frightening emotions that threaten to tear her apart are tamed and calmed.

Any experience of encounters with other patients arouses jealousy, rage and frustration. I now introduce the subject of emotional bleeding resulting from emotions that are so intense that they could tear her apart, as an alternative to 'petrifying' or deep-freezing her internal world.

Margot takes up, develops and elaborates every one of my interpretative suggestions, which thus open up new and unforeseen vistas. The theme of the mother's depression comes to life, starting with a session in which my mental presence is slightly reduced after a prior session with a severely psychotic woman patient that left me feeling invaded and less available. Following this session, Margot dreams of children abandoned in a snow-filled valley who plunge into a frozen ravine while their mother is carried off by a huge black bird. Then she dreams of a lorry that runs over a family and no one lifts a finger to save the children. When I link these dreams to my reduced mental presence on the previous day, she makes a number of connections with her own experiences as a child, when her mother would stay in bed in her room in the dark for days on end, or when Margot would wait at the window for her mother to return, but she never came (my emotional congestion had rendered my participation in our dialogue less present and alive). So it is that references to the house of her childhood begin to come up in the last session of every week and, after years of silence, once again to inhabit her dreams: she experiences and feels the pain of that time as well as the present pain of separation. Already in December she broaches the subject of the 'end' of the analysis, 'because if we don't start thinking about it right away it will be an abortion instead of a birth'.

While I cannot of course describe the whole of Margot's analysis, I should like to concentrate on the new way of experiencing emotions that our work has activated in her. One day Margot remembers that in the family album there are no photographs of her in her first year of life (so here we have the year of analysis!) – a time that was characterized by a severe maternal depression, even if an affectionate 'nanny' had stood in for the mother.

A dream portrays her with lots of corpses to bury (the mourning to be done) and lots of live patients to treat (the gauze). In another dream she tells a woman friend that if she speaks and expresses what she feels, that means she is giving up the idea of the mother who is supposed to cater to her needs without her having to ask; she has indeed waited so long for a mother to come back to life. Now the idea is growing of a mother who can live and care for her again in the form of a 'coat stand/weight-supporting' function.

She goes on to tell of a visit to the Genoa aquarium (where emotions – fishes – can be 'seen', while one is at the same time protected from them), and brings a dream in which she is with Edison – yes, the inventor of the electric light bulb – making animal noises, of dogs, cats and horses (it seems that her emotions come to life again in this way if supported by someone such as the coat stand/analyst). Then she mentions a trip where she let herself go on the slide of a water toboggan and felt no fear – displaying the same intrepid bravery as in her encounters with the ever more living emotions coming up in our room.

Next she dreams she is at the hairdresser's, where she has gone to have a painful operation, and tells him: 'I don't want a general anaesthetic, I want to *feel*!' For Margot, *feeling* the pain – including the pain of the trauma of loss and of the microtraumas of her mother's reduced mental presence – and feeling joy have been one and the same thing: she asks the hairdresser to put in some 'sunny highlights' to brighten and give life to her hair.

In the final sessions she tells me that for her the analysis has been like filling up the album with photographs of her first year of life (it is, after all, the year when Margot comes back to life); she has to make good use of the traffic lights that appear in one dream and the responsible policeman featuring in another so as not to fall in love with a 'photographer' who has revealed lots of new landscapes to her – but she must return to her history, where there is also a family waiting for her in Canada.

She spends a weekend in Sicily, where 'the sun pours down' – just like Margot, who leaves full of longing but happy, having also discovered that she is entitled to an Italian passport, or rather, following enquiries, that she had a Sicilian grandfather!

This short case history illustrates some salient facts. Chief among these is a dream-like form of functioning of the analyst's mind. What guided me most in working with Margot were my reveries. These were shared with her only at the end of our work, when they were able to assume a meaning for both for us and, retrospectively (*nachträglich*), for her history. Another vital aspect was my listening to and acceptance of the manifest text of Margot's narration.

The 'characters' of the sessions found a place, and lived, in the consulting room before a meaning was discovered for them in our relationship and hence in Margot's history.

The trauma of the mother's suicide (as well as that of the dysfunctional maternal depressive mental state) called for a process of mourning that could not be worked through all at once, but was accomplished 'in small doses' – but always in the knowledge that she had beside her 'a mother with whiskers and guts' with whom she could go through the experience of absence and death.

Winnicott's famous aphorism of 1952 – 'there is no such thing as trauma, [there is, rather] a traumatizing couple' – paradoxically seems to apply to certain aspects. In other words, the focus of attention is not the actual trauma as an external event – for it is, I believe, commonly found in clinical practice that 'major' traumas have much less of an impact than 'minor' ones. Ultimately, the crucial factor is actually the presence of an external event coupled with the absence of an object capable of receiving and working through what has happened.

The word 'trauma' – from a certain vertex at least – thus assumes a less specific and more general meaning, extending to all emotional conditions which, seeking but failing to find a reverie and container function, are constantly transformed into instances of acting-out whose violence mirrors that of the primal emotions, which are either frozen or lethargized.

Whereas the effects of the trauma – its symptoms – on the one hand constitute an attack on the mind's potential for development, on the other they at the same time continue to serve the purpose of communication. They thus act as a kind of 'narrative hook', which, together with the 'history of the trauma', allows the analyst's capacity for reception and reverie to develop a new way of digesting the experience. Hence the rehistoricization of the trauma is not an experience of meticulous reconstruction of the past, but the possibility of rewriting in metaphorical form a history that was previously not fully thinkable and therefore also not fully expressible in words. The trauma now undergoes reparation no longer through the compulsion to repeat it and bring it into the present, but by expansion of the function of thought and symbolization.

The story of the trauma makes its entrance into the analytic field in this way – and it does so particularly if the analyst himself or herself acts as a microtraumatogenic object. This happens, for example, whenever the analyst becomes too rigid or mentally unavailable.

In Margot's case, the emotions were able to thaw out without haste and without the use of force, and a narration unfolded on many levels, e.g. those of our present situation, of her history and of her internal functioning. Most important of all in my view is that she was able to introject and take away with her the 'little Pavia coat stand', and rewrite a history that used to be unthinkable (the new possibility of mourning) and unknown (the new filiation of the 'Sicilian grandfather').

In more general terms, there is, I believe, a constant baseline activity of reverie (Ogden 1999), which is the way in which the analyst constantly receives, metabolizes and transforms whatever reaches him from the patient in the form of verbal, paraverbal or non-verbal stimuli. The same activity of reverie is at work in the patient in response to every interpretative or non-interpretative stimulus from the analyst. The purpose of analysis is first and foremost to develop this capacity to weave images (which remain not directly knowable). Indirect access to these images is possible through the 'narrative derivatives' of waking dream thought that stage the oneiric truth of mental functioning in various forms.

This baseline activity of reverie is the engine of our mental life, and psychic health, illness or suffering depend on its functionality or dysfunctionality.

The picture is further complicated by the invoking of the ideas of Bion and in particular of his concepts of the α-function and of waking dream thought (Bion 1962; Ferro 2002b). The patient's transference, with its burden of β-, balpha- and α-elements, collides with the analyst's mental functioning, thus immediately giving rise to a group-of-two situation, in which it is the bipersonal analytic field (Baranger & Baranger 1961–62; Baranger 1993; Ferro 2005a) itself that is constantly dreamed and redreamed. The transference in effect undergoes diffraction into a multitude of narrations and characters that are 'chimeras' not only of 'then' and 'there' but also of 'now', 'here' and the interaction of the two minds. If the field is held to assume an oneiric form of functioning immediately, there is no communication that cannot be seen as having to do with and belonging to the field itself.

197

Even facts that seemingly fall most within the province of reality – including traumas – can then be regarded as 'narrative hooks' that enable us to approach and assign meaning to dream thought. And even the most subjective elements, such as a patient's dream, belong to the field and perform the function of assigning meaning to, and signalling, the movements of the waking dream in relation to the moment when it (the dream) is narrated.

If Margot tells of a daughter who cannot tolerate being touched, a younger son who loves affection, a father who is not genuinely available, a severely depressed woman friend whose boyfriend is furious because his wife has left him, and then a film she has seen on TV in which a deceived husband tries to kill his wife, etc. etc., she is actually describing the emotions existing in the field at the present time. These could be gathered together in a transference interpretation, but that would be tantamount to serving up raw the entire week's shopping, including the deep-frozen foods.

The field makes it possible to describe, gather up and assemble these emotions, and to clarify them and bring them into sharp focus, using the characters presented by the patient (and why not, perhaps, ones introduced by the analyst too?) as 'oven gloves' for handling scalding-hot contents. Here the analyst is convinced that the patient's communication is a diffractogram of the present situation of the field, whose ingredients that await focusing, transformation and digestion have to do with the intolerability of contact (perhaps the unsuitability of containment for holding hypercontents), lumps of tender feelings in the process of development, blocked containers, fury and rage, jealousy, murder and so on.

I had to accept Margot's initial prolonged idealization of myself, which I in fact saw as a sort of crutch that defended her against too intense persecutory emotions at the beginning of her treatment. These emotions can be 'cooked' by narrative transformation with unsaturated interventions (Ferro 2002b), but the patient's response must always be 'sampled' so as to ascertain which ingredients we must supply to enrich or tone down the dish. In my view, the analyst's receptivity, together with the reverie and the affective transformations that it brings about within a stable setting are the basis of all further development of the patient's α-function. This development takes place through the silent introjection of the analyst's mental functioning and of the couple at work. The process resembles the Renaissance situation of an apprentice painter attending the Master's studio.

Let me end with the countertransference dream I had the night before Margot's last session: a patient was admitted to a trauma ward with multiple fractures; after surgery and having his bones set in plaster, he needed a long period of rehabilitative physiotherapy – but was fit to be discharged.

However, that is not in fact the end of the story. Wondering why Margot chose a time-limited analysis, for quite a while I have swung between two theories. One is that, having already had a long analysis, she merely wanted a top-up, so it was reasonable to set herself a limit and not to engage in lifelong analysis. The other is that she wanted a 'sample' before making a longer commitment. Although still unable to decide which of these ideas is correct, I can report that I recently had an e-mail from Margot asking me to make arrangements for a further period of analytic work.

9

Narcissism and frontier areas

The major problem lying upstream of narcissism is the absence, in early life, of sufficiently reliable and introjectable caregivers. The situation may be likened to that of a town in which fires that are at first of manageable proportions break out, but which lacks a fire brigade or civil defence personnel. The population therefore invents the best possible methods – which, however, are totally inadequate – for tackling these conflagrations. In other words, proto-emotions, protopassions and needs are gradually lyophilized, stripped of affect, disavowed, split off and so on, so that part of the old town is saved, albeit at the cost of sometimes very considerable impoverishment.

It is therefore quite common for trust in the object to be lacking, so that the analyst, as the new object, must earn it in the field, working for a long time like a new fire brigade or civil defence force from a neighbouring village, which is made available when necessary.

It is hardly necessary to say that narcissistic patients deny dependence; they have at any rate saved themselves – at least in part – by this denial, having as it were rolled up their sleeves and desperately tried to get by on their own.

Lots and lots of cows but no horse: an aspect of narcissism

A supervisee once worked with me on the case of a brilliant mathematician of Russian origin with a severe narcissistic pathology. In her first session the patient brought a dream in which a girl who reminded her of Shirley Temple had to look after an entire herd of desperately thirsty cows. She had only a small pail, with which she had to clamber down to a small river and then return with the water to the cows; toil as she might, it was, of course, of little avail. In the midst of the herd, there was just the head of a horse. I immediately had a reverie of a Western in which herds of cattle

interesting work

were led to a river by groups of cowboys on horseback, who contained and guided the animals, showing them the way to go.

This function was almost entirely absent, there being not a single cowboy and no horses, but only a kind of preconception of what might be necessary (which could be called, for example in the language of Bion, the α-function or the apparatus for thinking thoughts).

There would, I believe, have been no point in telling the patient that she was trying to do everything by herself, or that she was denying emotions and needs. The analyst's arrival admittedly corresponds to the appearance on the set of John Wayne and his men, but what effect will that have on a ranch full of thirsty cattle run, as it were, by a little Shirley Temple? At first, it is bound to constitute a disturbance and a further complication if these new arrivals want to eat, have their horses looked after, be recognized as important and hold Shirley Temple responsible for everything she is unable to do.

The situation is different if they from the start put themselves in the service of the patient, without adding to her work, but instead making it easier for her to manage the whole herd. It is essential not to add to the already heavy burden on Shirley Temple; on no account must the cowboys/analyst insist on naming each cow (the yellow cow is the jealousy she feels when . . . the green cow is the envy she feels when she sees that I am cleverer at . . . the black cow is the rage she feels when she thinks that instead of helping her I disturb her, so she wants to get rid of me, and so on). The analyst must instead put himself in the situation of someone who must for the time being manage the bovine emergency, by containing the cows, leading them to water, and listening to the urgent demands conveyed by Shirley Temple from the field. Only in a second, or perhaps a third, phase will it also be possible to do the work that was impossible at the beginning.

In this analysis, after the analyst's first transference interpretation, the patient dreams of 'a gunman who shoots at her' and begins a session by describing a number of very different, contrasting feelings she has had towards various people (these are surely all different ways of seeing the analyst at work). Instead of picking up and describing these emotions by bringing out the overall emotional significance of the communication in an unsaturated way – elsewhere I have compared this situation to a whole response with emotional coloration (W + C) in a Rorschach test – the analyst begins to interpret in transference terms. The patient responds by bringing a dream in which she is trying to put things in order and tidy up but her mother-in-law, who could have given her valuable help, in fact makes even more of a mess of the items she has already put away. The analyst understands this communication but thinks it inappropriate to interpret it. Fearing that it would be unanalytic to pick up the whole response with emotional coloration, he says nothing to the patient and remains silent. The patient immediately begins to talk about a cousin who was widowed just when she expected a great deal from her husband in terms of bringing up their children. The analyst fails to see this communication as a response to his silence and actively interprets the patient's displeasure at the forthcoming weekend.

The patient now gives him an extraordinary lesson in technique, saying that she cannot stand a friend who always puts on an air of superiority, whereas she greatly appreciates another friend who is able to play with children without tiring them out or frightening them, and often uses drawings made on the spur of the moment.

That is to say, the analyst is useful if he gives what I once called 'Goofy' interpretations – that is to say open, unsaturated interpretations – which are the opposite of what Florence Guignard has called *interprétations-bouchon*, these being more along intelligent, acute 'Mickey Mouse' lines (to continue with the Disney metaphor). However, such interpretations block off the sense.

The analyst ends the session with a long, complex interpretation, and the patient for her part responds by saying that, in order not to despair, she has always had to rely on no one but herself, and that she does not know if she will be able to *afford* to continue the analysis (which at this point is beyond the patient's emotional means). The analyst sees this as an attack on his analytic function rather than as an indication that he has been unable to find 'the right affective music to play with the patient'.

As I shall never tire of emphasizing, it is in my view essential to regard the patient's responses as indications he gives us so that we can reach him at ever greater depth. Bion saw the patient as our 'best colleague', and I for my part always think of Conrad's fine tale *The Secret Sharer*, in which a stowaway whom the captain has for a long time accepted on board his vessel jumps ship close to the coast and, realizing that it is about to strike a reef, flings his hat across the surface of the water as a signal of the danger, thereby enabling the captain to avoid disaster. This function of the patient, constantly throwing his hat to us as a sign of how we are proceeding, is in my opinion absolutely vital. It is basically the only way in which we can be truly in touch with the patient – and here I must stress the concept of unison – rather than with our theories, because otherwise we risk ending up in a kind of primal scene with our theories and excluding the patient. Of course, once the weight of emotions can be sufficiently borne, the time eventually comes when a more interpretative posture can be adopted.

Marcello's batteries

Marcello is a patient with a narcissistic structure, and together we have gradually arrived at a point where he is in possession of 'exceptional batteries'. With the well-known Italian advertisement in mind, we call these his Duracell batteries, which enable him to go on all by himself without ever stopping. He uses his Duracells whenever he feels he is not being 'accompanied' and thinks he can, or must, rely solely on his own resources. Let us now take a closer look at a clinical sequence with Marcello.

> It is a time when we have been working smoothly on new emotions that are flowering and which the patient is increasingly able to manage in a kind of counter-melody to a quasi-autistic form of affect-stripped functioning. In one session, my attention is distracted by a gypsy playing an accordion for all he is worth right under the window of my consulting room. I become totally incapable of listening, while the patient goes on talking uninterruptedly the whole time.
>
> Next day, I am able to tell him that by switching on his Duracells when he experiences me as mentally remote, he immediately saves himself from floundering in anxiety because these batteries make him totally self-sufficient. With a laugh, the patient exclaims: 'Message received!'

This episode thus becomes one of the most significant moments in the analysis, bridging the gap between our here-and-now and a there-and-then of his infancy. Of course, I also reflect to myself about the desperate music of the gypsy with his accordion: just when it is emerging from the lyophilized state in which it has lain for so long, the patient's split-off part projects a β-screen (Bion) that not only invades me but also constitutes the means of putting me – or us – in touch with his 'stateless' parts, or forms of functioning, which flood us with the music of their emotions. These also constitute an SOS and a signal of their existence, and their reawakening has been possible because the field was sufficiently unsaturated.

So a typical form of managing unalphabetized proto-emotions – which may achieve alphabetization if they have the good fortune to encounter a reverie function – is by way of the *narcissistic pathologies*. Some of these forms as it were resemble a lake dwelling built over an alligator-infested swamp. The resident feels fine in the upstairs rooms, even if 'cut off' from his proto-emotional roots, and contact with his emotions is of course blocked. The ego is safe upstairs, while the proto-emotion-alligators are free to swim in the swamp; contempt, the sense of superiority and even the analgesic use of intelligence are defences against being torn apart by contact with devouring (because never sufficiently metabolized) emotions.

The other face of narcissistic superiority is the sense of poverty and wretchedness, because, if one is so drastically separated from one's emotions, one is then eternally exiled from oneself, in a kind of *tramp syndrome* that must at all times be denied and cancelled out with the splendour of palaces, the alligators as far as possible being handed over to some Other for the purposes of control (Melanie Klein long ago drew attention to the way narcissistic patients cause others to experience feelings that they themselves cannot tolerate).

There is, of course, no point in trying to bring about a collapse of the narcissistic attitude before the swamp has been reclaimed. A patient had the following dream when this situation had begun to penetrate into his consciousness: 'I went to a cinema in Venice to see a film. All of a sudden, someone offered me a chance to witness something hidden and secret: there was a kind of manhole, the entrance to a basement that was the home of some men and women, who were in fact undeveloped, short, stocky dwarfs, some of them deformed, some in barrels, and others covered in shit, abandoned in wretchedness and isolation, suffocating and filthy . . . On a higher level there were masks of noblemen and swordsmen dressed in now meaningless eighteenth-century clothes. Shaken, I left the cinema and saw a kind of executioner-cum-guard with a hammer and sickle, who was about to go down below, wielding his hammer to prevent the emergence of any cry, the expression of any need or any sign of adversity . . . I left and found myself in Venice looking for my wife.'

However, let us return to our clinical sequence with Marcello, who, as stated, is a patient with a narcissistic structure who has always denied any affective dependence, having for many years adopted an autonomous, self-sufficient posture. In our routine separations, for Christmas, Easter or the summer holidays, as well as in exceptional cases when one of us has been unable to attend a session, he has progressively introduced into our field some kind of physical 'pain' that is extremely marginal and for which no shared meaning can be discerned. When he had to attend a conference, it was a 'pain in the foot'; when going away on holiday, a 'toothache'; on other occasions a 'pain in the knee'; and so on. Time has passed and Marcello has become increasingly permeable to emotions of his that had previously always been denied. I am often undecided about how to use his narrations. While not wishing to forfeit the opportunity of communicating something important, as I would if I abstained from interpreting, I frequently find that any interpretative activity that is not subliminal and allusive merely gives rise to new rigidities.

At this particular juncture, I am giving Marcello the dates of my Easter holidays and also, at his request, of my summer holidays, in quick succession. Next day he reports a severe headache, and recounts a number of episodes. He has accompanied his wife, a psychologist, on a visit to a community of psychiatric patients in Germany, and one of the boys in the group threw the food on his plate at him from behind. Another patient, who was visibly depressed, was wandering around striking his head with his fists. He then tells me that while on night duty in the emergency ward where he works, he saw a patient lose consciousness and fall to the floor. Next, he mentions a female patient with suicidal fantasies who said her mother was a 'whore', and finally he tells me about a friend of his called Nando, who is desperate because his wife is deceiving him and he cannot even slap her. I feel that the most I can do is to follow him in his text, every so often illuminating and bringing into focus the various emotions contained in his account.

He arrives for the next session with two dreams. In the first, he is photographing people on various floors of a block of flats, and then he has a rucksack full of Duracell batteries, many of which are spent. In the second, he has gone to his mother's funeral with four women (Marcello has four sessions a week), but is unable to cry; then the thought suddenly strikes him that he will never again eat the dishes from the Emilia region that his mother used to make, such as *orecchiette*, and – in the dream – he bursts into floods of tears.

I tell *myself* that the work done by the dream is bringing us close to emotions that were previously denied and unapproachable, but tell *him* that it seems to me that he has become capable of experiencing mourning, loss and the associated emotions. Proceeding from the more general description, I then also 'try' to connect the dream with the loss of myself in the summer holiday separation. Marcello remains silent but seems to me to be interested. I therefore take up the first dream, saying that he seemed to me to be interested in photographing different floors – different levels – of his emotional experience. It is as if the dream had cooked together a number of ingredients that had previously been heated up in different pans: the food thrown at Marcello, the patient hitting himself on the head (the headache!), the story of Nando, and that of the two patients. In this way he had taken a closer look at the emotions we had discussed on the previous day. Marcello again says nothing. This seems to me to be a 'digestive' silence, and I feel pleased with this interpretation, which makes it possible to express things that were previously inexpressible.

Marcello now speaks in a distant and indifferent voice, saying that, the night before, he was enjoying playing with Stefano, his four-year-old son, when the game suddenly ceased to be pleasant and turned violent: pressure on his stomach had caused Stefano to vomit up everything he had eaten; he had then coughed, remained in an irritated state and not wanted to eat anything else.

At this point I have a sense of profound disappointment and discouragement, feeling that, whoever Stefano might be in the session, everything has somehow been 'evacuated' and, I fear, also lost. Instead of interpreting this communication, I resort to receptive listening to what the patient is telling me about seemingly external 'diary' events and his lack of interest in the seminars he has attended in his specialist training.

I give up on his communication and am astonished when, in the next session, the patient reports that his 'son Luigi', just a few months old, has been crying his eyes out because his mother was away: he wanted milk and was not satisfied with what his father could give him, because he was usually breast-fed. I comment that mothers are sometimes essential to children and add, by way of a witty remark, that besides penis envy there also seems to be such a thing as breast envy. He answers that his wife does indeed have a piece of 'equipment' that he lacks. I am careful to avoid any transference interpretation, and at this point a 'double' enters the session – namely, the woman patient whom Marcello often used to meet in the street. He thinks it is the patient who came along before him, whom he sees when she goes to church. For a long time, he has been thinking 'I'm not in such a bad way as this shabby-looking girl', who often seemed to him to be sad and in pain. Then he became curious: who knows what emotions this girl is having, and whether she is suffering from separation.

I provide only 'enzymatic' interventions, taking care not to interpret the woman patient as a part of himself that is 'feeling' emotions. He goes on to say that a psychoanalyst friend of his has told him that he has strong feelings when patients finish their analyses. I comment that it seems appropriate for living emotions to pass back and forth in analyses. Marcello now amazes me by taking up (now that there is no longer any interpretative pressure) what I felt to have been irremediably evacuated – namely, the previous day's communication. He says: 'Yesterday you took an active part in talking to me about the dream, and I realized that I needed your help as a guide.' The session continues with attention again being directed towards his separation-related emotions . . . I confess that I feel deeply moved by Marcello's words, which constitute the first 'official' recognition of an important bond between us.

All this has a sequel when I happen to be mentally 'out of order' (like a lift with an 'out of order' notice) in one of Marcello's sessions a few weeks later, because I feel invaded and turned upside down by a psychotic patient who has been acting out violently in the previous session. I am indeed mentally absent in Marcello's session. In the following session, he brings two episodes. The first is about a girl who had panic attacks after her mother, who was sitting in the back seat of a car, was killed when a lorry crashed into it from behind, while the patient herself and her son, sitting in front, were unharmed; the second concerns his friend Nando, who was very disappointed on feeling that his wife was remote from him at a time when he needed her.

In the session I am indeed *denying* to myself what happened in the previous session with Marcello (my reduced mental presence) and am giving routine interpretations in which he acquiesces, having again assumed a distant and self-sufficient posture. However, it is outside the session that I am able to make contact with the emotional reality of the session itself, and to tell myself that Marcello has furnished an exact description of my not having been present in the session (because I was overwhelmed by the previous session's patient). As stated, this realization confirms to me one of the roots of Marcello's narcissism – namely, his relationship with a mother who was at times mentally absent, so that Marcello had to resort to 'Duracells' or to act as his own power source. This turns out to be the beginning of an intense, sharing process of reconstruction of his infantile history.

We thus have an emotional field involving an oscillation between splitting, disavowal and negative capability, which ultimately modulate and regulate the emotional forces that can enter the field and be metabolized. In this connection, Bion of course suggested that even dreams and waking dreams (the α-function) should be regarded as barriers or interspaces *vis-à-vis* an unattainable reality (O). It seems to me that a dialectic between defences and O (the K ↔ O oscillation) is the method of choice of the human species for approaching the truth without being burnt by it.

As we know, some patients exhibit the particular narcissistic pathology in which *success is obligatory*; for these successful people, their success is never enough to give them a sense of security, trust and self-esteem. In other situations, success is a defence against depression. Narcissism here is a kind of patch that is constantly and inappropriately placed over a kind of 'narcissistic fault' or deep wound, which in fact calls for affective reweaving or re-edging. The 'patch' represented by success is then in effect soaked through and dragged off, so that the patient suffers a fresh mental collapse, and then the whole cycle repeats. The affective reweaving is so to speak an in-depth and – hopefully – permanent repair.

Luca, a patient who cannot take pleasure in his often brilliant successes at work (as well as in the progress of his analysis) and who is always seeking new goals to attain, has a dream in which he is unable to play two pieces by Bach: he goes to the piano but not a sound is heard. Then his father, himself a brilliant professional, appears in underpants asking for help and requesting a job for 'September' (the summer holidays are imminent).

Luca seems condemned to be brilliant and ever more brilliant at all times, until this dream makes thinkable the difficulty of expressing his emotions, and in particular his needs – the need for help and for someone to listen to him. Such patients have often been used in their childhood as narcissistic prostheses by their parents, who needed additional props to avoid a feared depressive collapse. What is basically most feared and phobically avoided by these patients is contact with a situation of need and poverty – of 'Afghanistan' – which is denied through the brilliance of the Sultan's palaces.

However, for as long as it was necessary, narcissism has been a successful defence against an experience of terrible poverty and ever unsatisfied needs – an experience of rejection that would be too harsh to be endured if really felt – so that it could only be disavowed and concealed.

A not dissimilar situation is presented by the narcissism of '*self-sufficiency*', sometimes accompanied by homosexuality, in which the absence of the Other at the moment of need was experienced with such intense pain and suffering that the subject puts on a scene in which he needs no one and can do everything by himself; even sexual activity is pursued with himself, through the intermediary of a 'double'.

An entire life of success, profit and wealth is often nothing but a tungsten shield against a tragic world of internal *favelas*, which the entire state exchequer would be totally inadequate to satisfy or even relieve. Only the World Bank might have the necessary resources; that is to say, an external contribution of reception and reverie provided 'free of charge', with nothing demanded in return. In other words, the α-function itself and the 'apparatus for thinking thoughts' must be rebuilt first, and only then can they be put to work.

Another, somewhat tragic, idea is suggested to me by these reflections. Some – perhaps all – human lives stage the primal drama, which can be repeated in the form of tragedy, of farce or of comedy. In the case of 'tragedies', there are, of course, unhealable wounds that are re-exposed in the hope that something (which cannot be other than adulthood) might relieve the intensity of the pain. One of the aims of psychoanalysis might then be to enable the patient to emerge from putting on an obligatory performance made up of acting-out and, at least to some extent, to replace it by a narration.

One connection that has been made but never sufficiently emphasized (except by Meltzer) is between narcissism and autism. The only major difference between these is quantitative, both situations being attributable to a deficiency of the α-function, i.e. the subject has been unable to introject the capacity to transform sense impressions and proto-emotions into images, emotions and thoughts. Whereas in narcissism a barrier is erected against the world of the *favelas*, which remain split off and inaccessible while the false splendour of spurious wealth is celebrated, in autism the deficiency of the α-function is even more pronounced, so that the *favelas* are dehydrated and lyophilized, their very mapping being lost to such a degree that emotional mental life is absent, and replaced by a computerized substitute totally stripped of affect or, if you will, of the *favela* aspect.

A common characteristic of autistic nuclei is a domineering attitude and behaviour, which can develop in different ways. First of all, the unavailability of the parents is introjected as an unavailability that is then acted out. Unavailability is also something experienced as a domineering denial by other people of one's own needs. Above all, however, such an attitude is a way of not arousing emotions connected with anything 'unforeseen' or uncontrolled that might overwhelm a defective α-function.

Another possible connection is between narcissism, autism and characteropathy. In the latter, the *favelas* are managed by violent evacuations.

Yet another form assumed by narcissism is the *spoilt-child syndrome*, which corresponds in some respects to, while being less marked than, the 'spoilt syndrome' ably described in Italy by Franco Borgogno (1999). The children concerned did not have parents who were able to transmit to them a sufficiently well-functioning apparatus for managing and metabolizing frustration. Unlike Klein and even early Bion, I regard the capacity or incapacity to cope with frustration not as an innate quality, but as something introjected on the basis of the parents' mental functioning. A parent who always says 'yes' and never frustrates is substantially a parent who cannot stand anything other than a quiet life and who lacks an adequate apparatus for metabolizing emotions. After all, frustration arouses rage, feelings of exclusion and hate, all of which are proto-emotions that are gathered in and 'cooked'. If the parent does not have enough saucepans, the inevitable result will be avoidance tactics, which, however, will give rise to the accumulation of undigested and indigestible matter in the child.

Lastly, one could explore the connections between what one patient called his 'affability complex', symbiosis and narcissism. What seems to me to be common to these three different clinical situations is the quest for an alternative route or strategy to the experiencing and working through of one's emotions and passions; all three reflect an inability to accept, metabolize and transform high-intensity emotional states. In the first case, these are covered over, concealed and partly contained by a *thick blanket of affability* that masks and hides intolerable mental states such as jealousy, rage, vengefulness, paranoia and violence. In the second, the obligatory bond with the Other who constantly supplies fresh testimony of love becomes the antidote to the utterly split-off part of the self populated by violence, rage, hate, jealousy and envy. The subject is terrified lest these leap out violently and uncontrollably, so that an antidote must be constantly administered, as in the case of Dr Jekyll and Mr Hyde. In the third case, the subject progressively takes up a defensive position in an idealized citadel that banishes all evil, jealousy, envy and destructiveness, attributing them instead to others, or, as Melanie Klein acutely put it, making others experience them by proxy.

The relational strategies differ. In the case of 'compulsive affability', the Other must not be able to look beyond this blanket of sweetness; deception and the art of the chameleon reign supreme. The Other is outwitted, flattered and made the object of the continuous currying of favour. In the case of symbiosis, the 'love' given and demanded leads to a wish for fusion such that any difference or conflict is abolished – because differences and conflicts activate emotions of extreme violence to which the subject fears he will succumb. So-called panic attacks often represent the emergence of such proto-emotions, which may also leak out through the microfractures of symbiosis.

Narcissistic patients see themselves, and want others to see them, as good, generous, reliable and as true gentlemen, fearless and without a stain on their character; they evacuate their stains and fears into the Other, in particular exporting blows, violence and destruction, which they lack an apparatus to contain.

Whenever these three pathological defences are called into question in analysis (and sometimes also outside analysis), the result is an irruption of violent, 'raw' proto-emotions, such as one could never have imagined existing in such amiable, likeable and outgoing people; it is as if demons were emerging from the depths of Hell, the lid were being taken off a succession of Pandora's boxes, and volcanoes were spewing forth lava with unprecedented violence.

On the frontiers of these territories lies the mechanism of *paranoia*, which is based on continuous operations of *transformation in hallucinosis*, in which the alligators of the proto-emotional states fail to find a space in which to be managed and metabolized (in ♀ and, upstream, in the α-function), so that they are fired like bullets into the outside world. As a result, the outside world, or the Other, is infiltrated by these pieces of proto-emotions (rage, jealousy, curiosity, envy, etc.), by which the subject feels constantly persecuted because they basically follow the 'projector' wherever he goes, so that he deploys every possible defensive strategy in order not to be 'identified' and 'found' by these *aspects of himself* that have been violently projected outwards. The only relevant form of work with such patients is to increase the number of pans (♀) to contain these aspects and the number of burners to cook them (the α-function), so that it is no longer necessary to resort to constant 'transformation in hallucinosis' or indeed, if the projection is more violent, to 'hyperbole' (Bion 1965).

Further related considerations apply to *mental anorexia*, which no doubt arises from the primal experience of an inadequate space in the Other's mind and a need to make oneself smaller and smaller in the hope of finding a place, as brilliantly described by Grinberg. This entails the splitting off of the parts of the self that are felt to be dangerous (proto-emotions by which one fears to be devoured) by the strategy of starving the dreaded tiger – or felling it with food in the opposite case of bulimia. However, the important point is that an anorexic sees herself as fat and swollen; when standing in front of the mirror, rather than having a misperception, she 'sees' herself through eyes that have a deeper vision than ours, as swollen and full of swamping proto-emotions that she would like to split off once and for all. In other words, perceiving the reality of her inner emotional situation, she performs a kind of *transformation in hallucinosis* of her mental body image that 'covers up' the perception of the real body that ought to be reflected by the mirror; the mirror in effect returns an ultrasound image that she discerns behind the outward appearance. Plainly, therapy is possible only if the analyst's mind is not a reflecting entity or 'mirror' but instead a semi-permeable surface that can receive and transform the surplus which 'is seen because it is there'.

My reason for presenting these frontier reflections is that the frontiers of psychoanalysis have been pushed far forward. An analyst can perfectly legitimately say to himself: 'I'll stop at the Oedipus complex; that's as far as psychoanalysis goes in my book – that is, only as far as conflict or the primal scene or historical reconstruction.' However, it seems to me that equal legitimacy should be assigned to the thought and practice of an analyst for whom the frontiers of psychoanalysis are constantly moving 'forward', extending to increasingly severe pathologies such as autistic, psychotic or psychosomatic disorders. For such an analyst, other categories take precedence, such as the type and quality of mental functioning, the very capacity for symbolization and the ability to form images. In the language of Bion, what is involved is the actual quality and quantity of the α-function, of the container and of its dialectics. The locus of such an analyst's work is far upstream of that of his 'oedipal' colleague. The latter works on contents, while the former deals with the situation upstream of any contents – namely, with the capacity to generate thought and with the instruments needed for its generation.

The approach to technique is completely different. Whereas the 'oedipal' analyst sets out to 'cook' products while in the possession of

functioning pots, frying pans and kitchen, his colleague must construct the pots and frying pans before he can even begin to think of
cooking the 'products', and sometimes the kitchen itself has to be
built from scratch.

Furthermore, working on the psychotic, autistic or psychosomatic
parts of a patient calls for a completely different technique. With these
highly 'deprived' patients, there are two main problems. One is the
weight of their experiential history, which prevents the acquisition
of any trust and must therefore undergo prolonged metabolization;
while the other, which is even more serious, is the absence of receptors for positive experiences, these having been destroyed or put out
of action, so that it is extremely difficult to find where and how to
'hook up new positive experiences'. The excess of β is so great that
there is virtually no alphabetization that can withstand it, and in addition there is nowhere to deposit α-sequences. Something similar was
described, albeit in different language, by André Green in *The Work of
the Negative* (1993) in connection with certain extreme forms of the
negative therapeutic reaction.

Continuing our discussion of work at the frontiers of psychoanalysis, I wish to draw attention to one of the major technical difficulties with which we are sometimes confronted – namely, that of
the 'non-speaking patient', in whom inhibition often represents the
opposite, claustral, extreme to that of evacuation. This is the subject of
the fine book by Dina Vallino Macciò (1998), whose title translates as
'Tell me a story'. Here she shows how it is frequently possible to find a
tangential method of 'opening up' some level of communication with
children by the construction of a story composed jointly with them
while avoiding interpretative caesuras or over-explicit approaches.
The 'story' develops in what the author calls the 'imaginary place' – a
kind of transitional space outside the territory of the here-and-now.

The situation is not very different with an adult patient. As in many
other thorny problems that confront us, here too a conflict arises
between orthodoxy and creativity, and the stronger the analyst's
superego and also his ego ideal, the more intense this conflict will as
a rule be. In such a case, I would have no difficulty in inclining
towards creativity. In other words, the analyst must be capable of
'inventiveness' – of 'narrative inventiveness' – although of course
without losing sight of 'psychoanalytic relevance'.

A frequent issue with such patients is that of a severe superego
that suggests that the things they say will be deemed 'stupid' or

'uninteresting'. Another problem is 'shame' and 'the other person's indifference'. All this is indicative of a primal insufficiency of parental reverie.

Yet another problem in these cases is the patient's fear of the uncontainability of his emotions or needs, sometimes because the patient is afraid that they might be 'criticized', 'disapproved of' or seen as 'contemptible' by an analyst who is incapable of accepting, containing and working on them. *Silence on the analyst's part in such cases is at least as traumatic as was the primal silence of the object, which failed to respond with solicitude and 'passion'.* It is, of course, impossible to lay down a hard-and-fast rule in such situations, but the only way forward is to proceed by 'inspiration', 'trial and error' and 'invention'. It is important in the first place to strip the element of guilt from the patient's silence, and for this purpose it is useful to introduce metaphors whereby the superego structures can be depicted in images – for instance: 'We are, of course, not at a *police station*, where you are compelled to speak.' At the same time, we must make it clear that there is no hurry: 'We're here to solve this problem, for as long as it takes.' As Roberto Speziale-Bagliacca (1997) tells us with respect to guilt, it is always helpful to give the superego the status of an image (a court, a police station or the Inquisition), as well as to make tactful attempts to make explicit the fear of a 'negative judgement' or disapproval.

Another strategy is to tolerate – and, where necessary, to encourage – tangentiality in the analytic discourse or, in other words, for long periods to tolerate the 'dislocation' into characters of emotions that the patient cannot yet own.

A further difficulty with some patients, which again raises the problem of the frontiers of psychoanalysis, is the excessive asymmetry resulting from the *use of the couch*. Is there anything that might argue against a face-to-face setting, possibly even for long periods? Yes: the analyst's superego structures.

References

Anzieu, D. (1974) 'Le moi peau', *Nouvelle Revue de Psichanalyse*, 9: 195–208.

Barale, F. and Ferro, A. (1992) 'Negative therapeutic reactions and microfractures in analytic communication', in *Shared Experience: the Psychoanalytic Dialogue*, L. Nissim Momigliano and A Robutti (eds), London: Karnac.

Baranger, M. (1993) 'The mind of the analyst: from listening to interpretation', *International Journal of Psychoanalysis*, 74: 15–24.

Baranger, M. and Baranger, W. (1961–62) 'La situación analítica como campo dinámico', *Revista Uruguaya de Psicoanálisis*, 4: 3–54.

Baruzzi, A., and Nebbiosi, G. (1995) 'Presentazione a *Inedita di F. Corrao*', in *Koinos. Gruppo e Funzione Analitica*, 16: 6–21.

Bezoari, M. and Ferro, A. (1989) 'Ascolto, interpretazioni e funzioni trasformative nel dialogo analitico', *Rivista di Psicoanalisi*, 35: 1015–1051.

—— (1992) 'From a play between "parts" to transformations in the couple. Psychoanalysis in a bipersonal field', in *Shared Experience: The Psychoanalytic Dialogue*, L. Nissim Momigliano and A. Robutti (eds), London: Karnac.

Bick, E. (1968) 'The experience of the skin in early object-relations', *International Journal of Psychoanalysis*, 49: 484–486.

Bion, W.R. (1962) *Learning from Experience*, London: Heinemann.

—— (1963) *Elements of Psycho-Analysis*, London: Heinemann.

—— (1965) *Transformations*, London: Heinemann.

Bleger, J. (1967) *Simbiosis y ambigüedad; estudio psicoanalítico*, Buenos Aires: Editorial Paidós.

Borgogno, F. (1999) *La psicoanalisi come percorso*, Turin: Bollati Boringhieri.

Botella, C. and Botella, S. (2001) *The Work of Psychic Figurability*, trans. A. Weller, Hove, UK: Brunner-Routledge, 2005.

Brenman, E. and Pick, I. (1985) 'Working-through in the counter-transference', *International Journal of Psychoanalysis*, 66: 157–166.

Chiozza, L.A. (1986) *¿Por qué enfermamos? La historia que se oculta en el cuerpo*, Buenos Aires: Alianza Editorial.

Corrao, F. (1981) 'Struttura poliadica e funzione gamma', *Gruppo e funzione analitica*, 2: 25–32.

—— (1991) 'Trasformazioni narrative', in *Orme*, Vol. 1, Milan: Raffaello Cortina, 1998.

Faimberg, H. (1996) 'Listening to listening', *International Journal of Psychoanalysis,* 77: 667–677.

Ferro, A. (1992) *The Bi-Personal Field: Experiences in Child Analysis*, London: Routledge, 1999.

—— (1993) 'From hallucination to dream: from evacuation to the tolerability of pain in the analysis of a preadolescent', *Psychoanalytic Review*, 80: 389–404.

—— (1996a) *In the Analyst's Consulting Room*, trans. P. Slotkin, Hove: Brunner-Routledge, 2002.

—— (1996b) 'Carla's panic attacks: insight and transformations: what comes out of the cracks: monster or nascent thoughts?', *International Journal of Psychoanalysis*, 77: 997–1011.

—— (1996c) 'Los personajes del cuarto de análisis: ¿Qué realidad?, *Revista de Psicoanálisis de Madrid*, 23: 133–142.

—— (1999) *Psychoanalysis as Therapy and Storytelling*, trans. P. Slotkin, Hove: Brunner-Routledge, 2006.

—— (2000a) 'Temps de la rêverie, temps d'évacuation', *Enfance Psy*, 13: 129–136.

—— (2000b) *Antes Ali Quem*, São Paulo: Hirondel Editora, 2005.

—— (2000c) 'L'après-coup et la cigogne: champ analytique et pensée onirique', lecture to the Paris Psychoanalytical Society (May).

—— (2001) 'Rêve de la veille et narration', *Revue Française de Psychanalyse*, 65: 285–297.

—— (2002a) *Seeds of Illness, Seeds of Recovery: The Genesis of Suffering and the Role of Psychoanalysis*, trans. P. Slotkin, Hove: Brunner-Routledge, 2005.

—— (2002b) 'Some implications of Bion's thought: the waking dream and narrative derivatives', *International Journal of Psychoanalysis*, 83: 597–607.

—— (2002c) 'Superego transformations through the analyst's capacity for reverie', *Psychoanalytic Quarterly*, 71: 477–501.

—— (2003a) 'Marcella: the transition from explosive sensoriality to the ability to think', *Psychoanalytic Quarterly*, 72: 183–200.

—— (2003b) *Pensamento clínico de Antonino Ferro*, São Paulo: Casa do Psicólogo.

—— (2005a) 'Commentary' on *Field Theory* by Madeleine Baranger and on *The Confrontation Between Generations as a Dynamic Field* by Luis Kancyper, in: *Truth, Reality and the Psychoanalyst: Latin American Contributions to Psychoanalysis*, ed. S. Lewkowicz and S. Flechner, London: International Psychoanalytical Association.

—— (2005b) 'The analyst at work: four sessions with Lisa', *International Journal of Psychoanalysis*, 86: 1247–1264.

—— (2006) 'Clinical implications of Bion's thought', *International Journal of Psychoanalysis*, 87: 989–1003.

Green, A. (1993) *The Work of the Negative*, trans. A. Weller, London: Free Association Books, 1999.

Guignard, F. (1996) *Au vif de l'infantile*, Lausanne: Delachaux et Niestlé.

—— (1998) 'The interpretation of oedipal configurations in child analysis', *Psychoanalysis in Europe*, 50: 33–41.

Kernberg, O. (1998) 'Thirty methods to destroy the creativity of psychoanalytic candidates', *International Journal of Psychoanalysis*, 77: 1031–1040.

Klein, S. (1980) 'Autistic phenomena in neurotic patients', *International Journal of Psychoanalysis*, 61: 395–402.

Mancia, M. (2006) *Psychoanalysis and Neuroscience*, New York: Springer.

Meltzer, D. (1976) 'Temperature and distance as technical dimensions of interpretation', in: *Sincerity and Other Works: Collected Papers of Donald Meltzer*, London: Karnac, 1994.

Ogden, T.H. (1989) 'On the concept of an autistic contiguous position', *International Journal of Psychoanalysis*, 70: 127–140.

—— (1997) 'Reverie and interpretation', *Psychoanalytic Quarterly*, 66: 567–595.

—— (1999) *Reverie and Interpretation: Sensing Something Human*, London: Karnac.

Renik, O. (1993) 'Analytic interaction: conceptualizing technique in the light of the analyst's irreducible subjectivity', *Psychoanalytic Quarterly*, 62: 553–571.

Rocha Barros, E.M. (2000) 'Affect and pictographic image: the construction of meaning in mental life', *International Journal of Psychoanalysis*, 81: 1087–1099.

Speziale-Bagliacca, R. (1998) *Guilt: Revenge, Remorse and Responsibility after Freud*, trans. I. Harvey, New York: Brunner-Routledge, 2004.

Tuckett, D. (2000) 'Dream interpretation in contemporary psychoanalytic technique', English-Speaking Conference of the British Psychoanalytical Society (October).

Tustin, F. (1981) *Autistic States in Children*, London: Routledge & Kegan Paul.

—— (1990) *The Protective Shell in Children and Adults*, London: Karnac.

Vallino Macciò, D. (1998) *Raccontami una storia*, Rome: Borla.

Widlöcher, D. (1996) *Les nouvelles cartes de la psychanalyse*, Paris: Odile Jacob.

Index

abandonment 10, 11, 17, 56, 177
abortion 80–1, 82, 142, 157, 158
abuse 2, 93, 94
acting-out 19, 51, 91, 94, 143, 196, 210
'affability complex' 30, 211, 212
affective tone 15
'agglutinated nucleus' 90–1
allergies 79, 105, 106
Almost Blue 141
a-elements 25, 54, 100–2, 141, 153, 159; narrative derivatives 74, 76–7, 78, 80, 97, 158, 175; pictograms 42–4, 83, 85–6, 134–5, 138–9, 154; waking dream thought 156
a-function 18, 21, 100–1, 122, 134; analytic field 159; contextualization of emotion 168; defects in caregiver's capacity 190–1; development of 37, 121, 136, 137, 153, 198; group 8; homosexuality 120; hypertrophic 115; lack of 24; narcissism 210–11; 'newborn' 143–4; pictograms 44, 135, 154; quality and quantity of 213; tomato strainer metaphor 137–8
alphabetization 14, 115, 131, 140, 158, 205; hyper-β-elements 126–7; psychosomatic illness 86, 88, 89, 92, 97, 98
The Analyst 148–9
analysts: baseline activity of reverie 1; communication with patients 14–24;

epistemic arrogance 48–9; failure to listen 6–7; interpretation 53–4; mental functioning 148, 151, 197, 198; metaphorization 77; narrative web 14; relational listening 45–6; self-analytic function 44–5; subjectivity 6, 36
analytic field 39, 40–1, 48, 128, 157, 159, 196, 197–8
analytic relationship 35–6, 40–1
'analytic third' 67
anorexia 12, 21, 75, 89, 213
anxiety 6, 25, 83, 140, 142; catastrophic 182, 183, 188; homosexuality 107–8; separation 91, 182
Anzieu, D. 92
asthma 78, 93, 94
autism 2, 59, 133, 143–4, 213, 214; autistic nucleus 77, 91, 92, 210; communication with patients 14–16; narcissism link 210–11; withdrawal 57
'autistic' scar 94, 95
autobiography 178, 180

'balpha' elements 85–6, 94, 97
Baranger, Willy and Madeleine 39
bed-wetting (enuresis) 19, 20, 89
β-elements 25, 36, 54, 73, 148; alphabetization of 86, 97, 126–7; blocking of 125; child's projection of

β-elements – *Contd.*
119; 'hyperbole' 94; pictograms 85–6,
134, 138; psychosomatic illness 78,
81, 99–101; 'undigested facts' 191
Bezoari, Michele 39
Bick, Esther 108
Bion, Wilfred 1, 6, 49, 134, 203;
a-function 18, 24, 42, 44, 213;
β-elements 25, 100; dreams 209;
explosion of the container 91;
'hyperbole' 94; intestinal model
of the mind 88; K 29; lies 113;
mental functioning 151; negative
capability 102; 'undigested facts'
168
bipolar disorder 16
Bleger, J. 90
boredom 26, 27, 30–1
Borgogno, Franco 211
bulimia 8, 112, 213

castration 116
Catherine and I 128
chameleon strategy 3, 5
children: autistic traits 15–16;
communication with 214
Chiozza, L.A. 78
co-pensée 67, 174
colitis 75, 88–9
communication 14–24, 27, 31, 54–5, 73;
analytic relationship 41; with children
214; excessive 86; failure to listen 6–7;
interpretation 151–2, 157–8;
meaningful verbal 133, 134; of
reality 157, 159; spontaneous
narration of dreams 155; transference
53, 111
Conrad, Joseph 203
constipation 88–9
containment 23, 24, 57, 134, 192;
β-elements 25; insufficient capacity
for 131, 191; psychic skin 92
Corrao, Francesco 39, 47–8
countertransference 23, 26, 71, 96,
198–9
creativity 5, 6, 214
Crohn's disease 75, 78–9, 106

defences 2, 34, 191; homosexuality 109;
narcissistic patients 212
depression 10, 17, 122–3
destructiveness 81, 82, 211–12
diarrhoea 88–9, 100
'digestive apparatus' 25, 26, 122
dirt phobia 16, 79–80, 190
disavowal 2, 193, 208
dreams 9–10, 11, 13, 96, 139, 197–8;
analyst's 44–5, 96, 185, 188, 198–9;
Bion 209; capacity to dream 191;
Filippo's case 69–70; homosexuality
114, 125, 126; interpretation 47, 49,
50–1, 170–1, 173; Lisa's case 56, 57,
61, 62–3, 64–5, 66, 67; Lorena's case
163, 166; Luigi's case 186, 187, 188;
Marcella's case 26, 30, 34–5; Margot's
case 193–5; narcissistic patients
201–3, 205, 206–7, 209; as narrative
derivatives 136; self-analysis 180;
spontaneous narration of 155, 156–7;
see also waking dreams
Dumas, Alexandre 10

emotions 3, 14, 71, 128, 215; abstraction
of 172; alimentary metaphor 36;
analytic relationship 40; biological
sex 119; containment of 57;
contextualization of 168; denial of
164; envy 131–2; evacuation of 8, 19,
21, 27, 74, 98, 148; explosion of 117,
122; female homosexuality 116; Lisa's
case 57, 63, 64, 65–6, 67; Marcella's
case 24–5, 27, 30, 33, 34, 37; Margot's
case 194, 195, 197, 198; narcissistic
patients 202, 205, 206, 207, 208, 212;
pregnancy 142; proliferation of
175–6; psychosomatic illness 80, 90,
100; 'silent' 141; transformation 196;
visual pictograms 83, 84; *see also*
proto-emotions
enuresis (bed-wetting) 19, 20, 89
envy 131–2, 211–12
epilepsy 76, 77, 87, 88, 90, 91
erectile difficulties 125
Etchegoyen, Horacio 177
ethical considerations 5–6, 76

evacuation 8, 19, 21, 74, 143, 148; integration of split-off aspects 94; proto-emotions 14, 27, 77, 92, 134, 145–6; psychosomatic illness 78, 86, 88–91, 97, 98, 99–100, 145

fantasies 111–12, 113, 142, 172
fathers 9–10, 12–13, 151, 152, 178, 179–80
fear 83, 106
Ferrandino, Giuseppe 5
free associations 154, 159, 174
Freud, Sigmund 174
Freudian model 18
frustration 211

ghosts 31–2, 33, 37
Green, André 53, 214
group supervision 8
Guignard, Florence 203
guilt 12, 49, 107–8, 147, 148

haemophilia 76–7
hallucinations 32, 37, 56
hallucinosis, transformation in 212, 213
Hannibal 146, 147–8
Harris, Thomas 143, 146
headaches 140–1
heterosexuality 117, 118
home 70
homosexuality 100, 101, 107–32, 157, 209; biological 118; female 115, 116, 125, 128; male 114, 115, 117, 126; types of 107–8
hope 83
'hyperbole' 94, 212
hypercontainment 23, 92–3, 128
hypercontents 107, 108, 111, 114, 118, 129
hypercontrol 23, 88, 89
hypertension 125, 126
hypochondria 81

impotence 185
incontinence 8, 19, 190
'internal narrator' 14

interpretation 14, 24, 39–71, 73, 151–3, 157–8; analyst's interpretative style 36; communication of reality 159; decoding 55, 156, 170, 173; homosexuality 125–6; intrusive 111; persecution 29, 35, 69; response to 19, 56, 167–71, 197, 203–4; 'saturated' 50, 67, 69, 76, 166, 171–2; transference 35, 45–7, 69, 126, 152–3, 171–3, 198, 202; 'unsaturated' 27, 67, 159, 203; violent 109, 110–11
introjection 10, 99, 134, 191, 198, 210

jealousy 12, 17, 86, 162; explosion of 116, 122; metabolization of 120; narcissistic patients 211–12

K 29
Katzenbach, John 148
keloids 129–30
Kernberg, Otto 6
Klein, Melanie 6, 205, 212

leucopenia 80
listening 46, 151, 159, 167–8, 207
loneliness 67, 112, 114, 177

Macciò, Dina Vallino 214
masochism 183, 184
medication 56, 57, 59, 60
Meltzer, Donald 188, 210
memories: infantile 28, 80, 82, 83, 169; narrative derivatives 135; subversion of 177; transformations 178, 180
mental anorexia 213
metaphorization 77
mind: analyst's 44–5; as 'digestive apparatus' 25; intestinal model 88; mental functioning of analyst 148, 151, 197, 198
mothers 9, 17, 22, 58–9, 122–3; absent 208; Margot's case 192–3, 194, 195
mourning 9, 10, 139, 153, 188; after miscarriage 157; blocked 103; Margot's case 196, 197
myth 47–8

Nachträglichkeit 71, 81, 136
narcissism 2, 130, 170, 201–12
narration 14
narrative derivatives 80, 132; a-elements
  97, 136, 158, 175; pictograms 42,
  43–4, 83–4, 135, 153–4;
  psychosomatic illness 73–4, 76–7, 78,
  90; sexuality 118; waking dreams 1,
  155, 156–7, 159, 168, 197
narrative transformation 47–8
narremes 47–8, 75, 77, 78, 158
negative capability 102, 208
Night Killer 127
nightmares 19, 20, 62–3

O 209
Ogden, Thomas 67, 91
Other 117, 128, 130, 209–10; mental
  anorexia 213; mental mating with the
  118; narcissistic patients 211, 212;
  relational interplay with the 180;
  subversion of memory 177; types of
  homosexuality 107, 108

paedophilia 110, 113
pain 104–5, 112, 206, 210
panic attacks 6, 7, 56, 57, 62, 63–4, 142,
  212
Panic Room 92
paralysis 104–5
paranoia 212
parents 2, 211
Pasolini, Pier Paolo 110
Perec, Georges 160
persecution 29, 35, 36, 47, 69, 149
perversions 113
phobias 16, 21, 89, 130, 136–7
pictograms 42, 76–7, 82–6, 134–5,
  138–9, 141, 154
pregnancy 80–1, 82, 141–3, 157, 173
projection 134
projective identification 25, 27, 95, 144,
  168–9; a-function 85; baseline 1; β-
  elements 99; 'hyperbole' 94
prostitutes 10–11, 55
proto-emotions 24–5, 37, 140; a-
  function 143, 190–1; alphabetization

of 97, 98, 205; evacuation of 14, 27,
  77, 92, 134, 145–6; frustration 211;
  heterosexuality 117; homosexuality
  108, 120–1, 122, 123, 125, 126, 131;
  mental anorexia 213; narcissistic
  patients 205, 212; pictograms 42;
  psychosomatic illness 77, 81, 82, 91,
  92–3; split-off 142; transformation
  into a-elements 85
Psycho 160
psychoanalysis 6, 45, 54, 79, 180; aims of
  210; frontiers of 213, 214, 215;
  homosexuality 117; Kleinian 171;
  psychosomatic illness 78
psychosis 110, 148, 160, 181, 213, 214
psychosomatic illness 2, 73–106, 75,
  145, 213, 214

Quasimodo, Salvatore 67

rage 6, 7, 17, 122, 127, 161; against
  mother 69; interpretation 47, 50, 54;
  metabolization of 120; narcissistic
  patients 211, 212
Red Dragon 143, 146, 148
reformulation 39
relational listening 46
revenge 17, 122, 146, 148
reverie 5, 34, 96, 168–9, 192; absence of
  141, 147, 148; a-elements 85–6;
  baseline activity of 1; baseline activity
  of 197; capacity for 144, 196; parental
  215; projective identification 94, 95;
  'reversed' 99
rumination 110

sadomasochism 120
self-analysis 44–5, 180
self-harm 183
self-penetration 129
self-sufficiency 209–10
sensory overload 2
separation 9, 10, 17, 51, 177–8;
  catastrophic anxieties 182; narcissistic
  patients 205–7; psychosomatic illness
  91
sexual abuse 2

sexuality 118, 186; *see also*
  homosexuality
shame 215
signals 151, 157
silence 215
The Silence of the Lambs 146–7, 148
social phobia 91, 130
Speziale-Bagliacca, Roberto 215
splitting 2, 191, 208, 213
spoilt-child syndrome 211
subjectivity 6, 36
suffering 18–19, 44–5, 210
suicide 2, 86, 110, 192–3, 196
superego 214–15
supervision 7–8, 20
sweating 22–3
symbiosis 9, 57, 58, 59, 211, 212
symbolization 25, 86, 90, 97, 103, 196,
  213
symptoms 79, 88, 89, 97

technique 5, 6, 53, 159, 172, 213–14
termination of therapy 59, 66, 181–99
terror 83
thinkability 77, 81, 86, 90, 137, 141
tranquillity 115
tranquillization 107, 114, 120

transference 18, 53, 197
transference interpretation 35, 45–7, 69,
  126, 152–3, 171–3, 198, 202
transformation 79, 134, 152, 176,
  177–80; in hallucinosis 212, 213;
  interpretation 55, 56, 171, 172–3;
  narrative 47–8
transsexualism 108
transvestism 113, 114
trauma 40, 52, 190–1, 196
Tuckett, David 171
Tustin, F. 91

'undigested facts' 191

vaginismus 128, 129, 130
violence 22, 94, 110, 111, 113, 120
visual pictograms *see* pictograms
voice 15

waking dreams 44, 83, 101–2, 135, 152,
  154; Bion 209; narrative derivatives 1,
  155, 156–7, 159, 168, 197
Widlöcher, Daniel 67, 174
Winnicott, Donald 53, 56, 196

Zelig 3

Chris Mawson — Book on Bion's Theory